*Music
as Cultural
Practice,
1800–1900*

California Studies in 19th Century Music
Joseph Kerman, General Editor

MUSIC
AS CULTURAL
PRACTICE,
1800–1900

LAWRENCE KRAMER

University of California Press

BERKELEY   LOS ANGELES   LONDON

University of California Press
Berkeley and Los Angeles, California
University of California Press, Ltd.
London, England

© 1990 by
The Regents of the University of California

First Paperback Printing 1993

Library of Congress Cataloging-in-Publication Data

Kramer, Lawrence, 1946–
   Music as cultural practice, 1800–1900 / by Lawrence Kramer.
      p. cm. — (California studies in 19th century music ; 8)
   Includes bibliographical references.
   ISBN 0-520-08443-8
   1. Music—19th century—Philosophy and aesthetics.   I. Se-
ries.
ML3880.K7   1990
780'.9'034–dc20   89-20445
                                                     CIP
                                                     MN

Printed in the United States of America
1   2   3   4   5   6   7   8   9

Contents

Figures

Musical Examples

x

Musical Examples

Preface

The subject of this book is the much-disputed idea that music means something, or better yet, something we can talk about. This idea has been gaining ground in recent years, though it can still elicit strong resistance, both from those who understand music mainly as a quasi-autonomous unfolding of structure and from those who feel that instrumental music, at least, is somehow compromised or contaminated when meaning is ascribed to it. I will not be arguing with the holders of these positions in what follows, but I do hope to talk some of them around.

Even those who are not averse to the idea of musical meaning often assume that music is too imprecise to support critical interpretations of any complexity. Mendelssohn, coming at the problem from the other direction, once said that the meaning of music is altogether too precise for language to represent. My efforts to challenge these positions began in an earlier study, *Music and Poetry: The Nineteenth Century and After* (1984). That book, however, is primarily concerned with the possibility of finding constructive parallels between poetic texts and musical works; it does not confront the general problem of musical meaning. In the present book, I will be testing the idea that the semantic precision or imprecision of music simply does not matter. Music, among other things, is a form of activity: a practice. If we take it in these terms, we should be able to understand it less as an attempt to *say* something than as an attempt to *do* something. As a practice, music should be subject to the same kinds of rigorous interpretations that we customarily apply to other cultural practices, be they social, artistic, technical, discursive, ritual, or sexual.

To this end I will be drawing on various techniques of understanding that have not yet had much — not yet had enough — impact on the study of music, including speech act theory, psychoanalysis, feminism, deconstruction, and the theory of practice. I should add at once that no one need fear strong-arm tactics from these theoretical orientations. They are used eclectically, only as needed, with as little jargon as possible, and always to serve the end of understanding the music under discussion.

This eclecticism notwithstanding, some account of my critical perspective may prove helpful. Like many of my colleagues in cultural history, philosophy, anthropology, and literary criticism, I am essentially interdisciplinary and contemporary in my methods. Broadly defined, my aim is to unite two widely consequential intellectual trends: poststructuralism and what might be called a critical or nonidealizing historicism. Both trends affirm that the meaning of a text, representation, or cultural practice is multiply determined and exceeds what such things declare themselves to mean. Poststructuralism (or deconstruction) proposes that texts find it difficult to restrict what they mean and that their very effort to restrict meaning often propagates it further. Critical historicism, avoiding all notions of progress or development, proposes that texts are produced within a network of social, intellectual, and material conditions that strongly, though often implicitly, affect meaning. My position is that the proliferations of meaning traced by deconstruction are not arbitrary but rather arise from and in turn modify the "horizon of expectations" imposed by history. The present book applies this position to the cultural embeddedness of music, in an effort to move from contemporary critical theory to a contemporary musical criticism.

The music studied here is drawn from the period 1798–1888, and is mostly instrumental. The principal pieces addressed are Beethoven's two-movement piano sonatas, Opp. 54, 78, 90, and 111;

Chopin's Prelude in A Minor; Liszt's *Faust* Symphony; Wagner's *Tristan und Isolde*; Wolf's "Ganymed"; Beethoven's "La malinconia" (the finale of the String Quartet Op. 18, no. 6); and a segment of Schumann's *Carnaval*. In keeping with the premises of the book, my discussion of these works will often require close attention to non-musical texts and practices. Unlike *Music and Poetry*, however, *Music as Cultural Practice* is not primarily concerned with parallel or comparative analysis. Its aim is to show how musical forms and processes appropriate, reinterpret, and contribute to the complex dynamics of culture.

Acknowledgments

It is a pleasure to acknowledge the various silent hands at work in the making of this book. My special thanks go to colleagues who read all or part of the manuscript in various stages of its development and responded with invaluable suggestions: Joseph Kerman, Ruth Solie, Richard Swift, Walter Frisch, Steven Paul Scher, and Marshall Brown. Earlier versions of several chapters have benefited from the suggestions of colleagues who encountered them at lectures and conferences at Columbia University, the Royal Musical Association, the Modern Language Association, Bard College, the University of Pennsylvania, Temple University, Stanford University, and the University of California at Berkeley. Some of my more explicit debts are acknowledged in footnotes. As always, I owe a general, and generally incalculable, debt to Nancy Leonard. Claire Kramer Leonard helped me in ways unique to herself. Franz Eder, Lorenz Eitner, and Eva Maria Stadler gave timely help with the illustrations. My thanks also go to my editors at the University of California Press, Anne Canright and Jane-Ellen Long. And special thanks to Doris Kretschmer, Humanities Editor of the Press, whose editorial guidance has been both patient and creative.

An earlier, abbreviated version of Chapter 2 appeared in *Studies in Romanticism*; about half of Chapter 3 appeared, again in an earlier version, in *19th-Century Music*. I am grateful to the editors of these journals for permission to reprint this material.

TROPES AND WINDOWS:

An Outline of Musical Hermeneutics

The aim of this book is to give practical confirmation to four closely related claims:

1. that works of music have discursive meanings;

2. that these meanings are definite enough to support critical interpretations comparable in depth, exactness, and density of connection to interpretations of literary texts and cultural practices;

3. that these meanings are not "extramusical," but on the contrary are inextricably bound up with the formal processes and stylistic articulations of musical works;

4. that these meanings are produced as a part of the general circulation of regulated practices and valuations—part, in other words, of the continuous production and reproduction of culture.

I am well aware that these claims exceed (and then some) the customary ambitions of what has come to be called musical hermeneutics.[1] Problematical though my claims may be, they are by no

1. Critical surveys of the recent literature, as well as important statements of position, appear in Monroe C. Beardsley, "Understanding Music," in *On Criticizing*

means merely polemical. Meaning is an irrepressibly volatile and abundant thing; you really can't have just some of it. My purpose here is to appropriate this strength of meaning on behalf of music—and most especially on behalf of textless instrumental music. For if my claims are tenable where music is furthest from language, they will a fortiori be tenable where music and language meet.

One obvious qualification needs to be entered at this point. For present purposes, *music* refers to European art music composed between 1798 and 1888. This restriction is not meant to be exclusionary, however. The following chapters on nineteenth-century topics are to be understood as case studies. The techniques of interpretation that I apply here to nineteenth-century art music are meant to be equally applicable—in hands more competent than mine—to the music of other periods and to music of other sorts.

As to the present chapter, its concerns are with the need to give my claims a *practical* confirmation. All of the claims stand or fall on the possibility of making certain kinds of interpretation. And though interpretive practices benefit enormously from hermeneutic theorizing, a hermeneutic theory is only as good as the interpretations that it underwrites. Freud, whose name will come up more than once in this book, repeatedly insisted that psychoanalysis was unconvincing as a body of theory. Only by *doing* analysis, by engaging in the work of interpretation whether as analyst or analysand, could one be persuaded that Freudian claims are credible—or, as Freud forgot to add, of the reverse. The same is true of musical hermeneutics, which, like psychoanalysis, seeks meaning in places where meaning is often said not to be found. I will, to be sure, theorize a little in what follows, both about music and about interpretation. The value of the theory, though, must rest with the interpretive practices that it empowers.

The essential hermeneutic problem about music is usually put by saying that music is all syntax and no semantics, or that music lacks denotative or referential power, or, to revert to Hanslick's much-quoted aphorism, that "sounding forms in motion are the one and

---

Music, ed. Kingsley Price (Baltimore, 1981), 55–73; and Anthony Newcomb, "Sound and Feeling," *Critical Inquiry* 10 (1984): 614–43. See also the discussion of "expressive potential" in Edward T. Cone, *The Composer's Voice* (Berkeley and Los Angeles, 1974), 158–75.

only content of music."[2] This view—the formalist view that has since Hanslick and even since Kant set the terms for serious thinking about music—rests on an implicit comparison of music with verbal utterance or written discourse. Not surprisingly, music emerges from this contest with language in thoroughly poor shape, conceptually indefinite and semantically impoverished. As Kant puts it,

> Although [Music] indeed speaks by means of pure sensations without concepts, and so does not, like poetry, leave something over for reflection [*etwas zum Nachdenken übrig bleiben lässt*], yet it moves the mind more variously and, though fleetingly, with more fervor; but it is certainly more enjoyment [*Genuß*] than culture (the neighboring thought-play excited by its means [*das Gedankenspiel, welches nebenbei dadurch erregt wird*] is merely the effect of a sort of mechanical [*mechanisch*] association).[3]

Kant's phrase "leave something over for reflection," however, quietly points up the weakness in the formalist attitude. Where does this incitement to reflection come from when language is in question? Where, for example, does it come from in Kant's own statement? Most obviously, it comes from Kant's truth claims: the assertions that music communicates by means of pure sensations, that poetry communicates by means of concepts, that culture entails a hierarchy of concepts over sensations, and so on. Each of these claims can be elaborated or contested: hence they leave something over for reflection. Yet there is another way to reflect on this text, a hermeneutic way that bypasses truth claims to consider the dynamic elements in the act of writing itself, to treat the text precisely as a *Gedankenspiel*, though not at all a mechanical one.

Kant's labyrinthine series of qualifiers (*ob, zwar, doch, obgleich bloß, doch, aber freilich, bloß*) suggests a struggle to control some very equivocal materials. The suggestion is borne out by the submerged and perhaps inadvertent metaphor of neighboring thought-play that is called on to crown the case against music. Kant sets out to ratify the inferiority of music to poetry as a simple consequence of the supposed inferiority of sensation to reflection. Yet he cannot stabilize

2. Eduard Hanslick, *Vom Musikalisch-Schönen* (Leipzig, 1854), 32.

3. Immanuel Kant, *Kritik der Urteilschaft*, sec. 53; from *Sämtliche Werke*, ed. G. Hartenstein (Leipzig, 1867), 5:339.

his terms. In particular, he cannot both take music as his instance of pure sensation and still maintain the difference between sensation and reflection. For music, too, provokes the mind to reflect; it excites a neighboring thought-play. As Kant's terms make explicit, the primary features of this form of reflection are intimacy (*nebenbei*) and unruliness (*[ein]-spiel . . . erregt*). The *Gedankenspiel* transfers what is palpable and impulsive in musical sensation to the detached realm of reason, culture, meaning; it intrudes bodily pleasure into the space reserved for thought. Kant later ascribes an explicit bodiliness to the "free play" (*das freie Spiel*) of both tones (*Tonspiel*) and thoughts (*Gedankenspiel*). In music, he adds, "this play goes from bodily sensations to aesthetic ideas . . . and from these back again, but with united force, to the body."[4]

But music and its *Gedankenspiel* inhibit reflection proper, the "true" reflection that for Kant is the bearer of culture. The blockage seems to derive from too much immediacy; the subject of reflection, the Kantian subject of culture, requires a space of detachment in which to operate. In order to safeguard this space, Kant peremptorily severs pleasure from meaning, pronouncing ex cathedra that the *Gedankenspiel* is only the effect of "a sort of mechanical association." This statement shifts the metaphorical ground from the coalescence of mind and body to impersonal mechanism. Kant thus demotes the sensitive body to mere extension in space and pleasurable impulse to simple physical movement. With the same stratagem, he also detaches the quasi-autonomous subject of reflection from the anarchic, pleasure-seeking, decentered subjectivity of *Gedankenspiel*.

In preferring poetry to music, therefore, Kant is striving, indeed rather desperately striving, to shield a group of higher values— culture, reflection, subjective autonomy—from encroachments and appropriations by a group of lower values—enjoyment, sensation, subjective contingency. Music is the loose cannon in this process. Kant treats it as a principle of pleasurable intrusion, so much so that he later compares it to the unwelcome scent of a perfume. In denying meaning to music, Kant not only theorizes but also legislates; he responds less to an absence of thought than to the presence of danger.

4. Ibid., 342–43.

Where does our reflection on Kant's text leave us, as would-be interpreters, with regard to music? As far as truth claims go, it leaves us nowhere at all. A certain formalism to the contrary, music does have referential power, even if we are not prepared to be very precise about it. To affirm, for example, that nineteenth-century overtures named for Coriolanus, Manfred, and Hamlet fail to represent those characters seems foolish if not perverse. Yet truth claims are quite another matter. Music—and this is precisely the truth claim of Kant's text—cannot make them. Music may seduce us, but it never makes propositions. And here we must acknowledge the kernel of truth in the formalist position. If meaning begins with (forms around, clings to) a truth claim (implicit or explicit, real or fictive), then music has no meaning in the ordinary sense. One may wish to reinterpret this admission in order to endow music with a higher than ordinary "meaning"; E. T. A. Hoffmann does just that when he claims that instrumental music conveys the sense of the infinite and is therefore the quintessentially Romantic art. Even Hanslick, and later Schenker, make similar moves.[5] The fact remains, however, that on this view music may be spoken of rigorously only in formal terms. Anything else is—at best—inspired impressionism.

Yet to argue that meaning begins with a truth claim is merely to give a restrictive definition of meaning. The hermeneutic approach that we took to Kant's text begins, on principle, somewhere else: on this occasion, with the resonance of a metaphor. In taking up the hermeneutic attitude, we approached the text by assuming that it resists fully disclosing itself, that in certain important respects it is mute, and that we ourselves understand it at first in terms we must work to articulate. To put this another way, we approached the text very much as we would be compelled to approach a piece of "abso-

---

5. E. T. A. Hoffmann, "Beethoven's Instrumental Music," in *Source Readings in Music History: The Romantic Era*, ed. Oliver Strunk (New York, 1965), 35–41. On Hanslick's concept of form as spirit or *energeia*, see Carl Dahlhaus, *Esthetics of Music*, trans. William Austin (Cambridge, 1982), 52–54. Schenker's invocation of Nature as a transcendental category is well known. The kernel of his "higher" hermeneutic is succinctly formulated in the preface to his early *Harmony* (ed. Oswald Jonas, trans. Elizabeth Mann Borgese [Chicago, 1954], xxv): "I should like to stress in particular the biological factor in the life of tones. We should get used to the idea that tones have lives of their own, more independent of the artist's pen in their vitality than one would dare to believe."

lute" music. The hermeneutic attitude, which begins to assume its modern form at just about the time that instrumental music begins its cultural ascendancy,[6] works by assigning to discourse the nondiscursive opacity that is supposed to belong to music. We enable the interpretation of a text by depreciating what is overtly legible and regarding the text as potentially secretive, or at least as a provocation to understanding that we may not know how to answer. The text, in this frame of reference, does not give itself to understanding; it must be made to yield to understanding. A hermeneutic window must be opened on it through which the discourse of our understanding can pass.

Once that window opens, the text appears, or at least may appear, not as a grid of assertions in which other modes of meaning are embedded but as a field of humanly significant actions. In the example from Kant, the window opened by the metaphor of neighboring thought-play revealed an intricate spectacle of intrusion and protection in which philosophical judgment, ambivalence about bodily pleasures, and the work of building culture all play a part.

Where, then, to repeat my earlier question, does our reflection on Kant's text leave us with regard to music? As far as interpretation goes, the answer may well be: here, there, and everywhere. Under the hermeneutic attitude, there is and can be no fundamental difference between interpreting a written text and interpreting a work of music—or any other product or practice of culture. This is not, of course, to say that it has suddenly become obvious how to interpret music; what is obvious is that we still lack the techniques for that. But we should now know how to develop the techniques we need; analyzing the hermeneutic attitude at work has given us our clue. In order to practice a musical hermeneutics we must learn, first, how to open hermeneutic windows on the music we seek to interpret and, second, how to treat works of music as fields of humanly significant action.

It will prove convenient to take up these projects in reverse order. Much of my discussion so far has been guided implicitly by a critical adaptation of J. L. Austin's theory of speech acts—a theory in which

6. On this topic see Tilottama Rajan, "The Supplement of Reading," *New Literary History* 17 (1985–86): 573–94.

language as action takes precedence over language as assertion. In his book *How to Do Things with Words*, Austin begins by distinguishing between two types of utterance, which he calls constative and performative.[7] Constative utterances make truth claims, and are accordingly evaluated as true or false. Performatives attempt to achieve something, and are accordingly evaluated as successful or unsuccessful. "The path is steep" is a constative; "Be careful: the path is steep" is a performative—namely, a warning. In developing this distinction, Austin deliberately works up to an impasse: he shows that we cannot find a reliable criterion by which to separate constatives from performatives. In particular, any constative utterance can also serve as a performative: in the right setting, "The path is steep" can also be a warning. The constative and the performative thus become dimensions of utterance rather than types of utterance, and to underline this change Austin changes his terminology.[8] The constative dimension is now said to manifest itself in *locutionary meaning*, the claims or assertions that a speech act puts into play. The performative dimension manifests itself in *illocutionary force*, the pressure or power that a speech act exerts on a situation.[9]

Illocutionary force quickly proves to be a very unruly thing. Its relationship to locutionary effects (not meaning, *pace* Austin) is loose at best and highly variable; a speech act may say things that are widely at odds with what it does. Speech acts, moreover, are constantly in danger of going awry, "misfiring," as Austin puts it:

QUEEN
    Do not for ever with thy vailèd lids
    Seek for thy noble father in the dust.
    Thou know'st tis common. All that lives must die,
    Passing through nature to eternity.

7. J. L. Austin, *How to Do Things with Words*, ed. J. O. Urmson and Marina Sbisa (Cambridge, Mass., 1962).

8. Ibid., 94–108.

9. Austin also distinguishes between illocutionary and what he calls perlocutionary forces, the former referring to what one does *in* saying something, the latter to the results one achieves *by* saying something. The distinction complicates matters with no very clear gain; I use the term *illocutionary force* to cover both meanings.

HAMLET
>Ay, madam, it is common.

>   (*Hamlet*, 1.2.70–74)

This famous exchange exemplifies both types of unruliness. Gertrude in all likelihood wants to help Hamlet, but her help shades too easily into manipulation. She tries to control his grief—and his rage—by getting him to consent to some platitudes about mortality. Hamlet pretends to comply, but his withering multiple pun on *common* not only refuses the manipulation but also attacks the manipulator.

Austin is ambivalent about this sort of discursive skittishness; he alternately unleashes and tries to limit the instability of illocution. For present purposes, the most important fact about his proposed limitations is that none of them works. The reason why becomes apparent in a decisive critique of speech act theory put forth by Jacques Derrida.[10] Derrida points out that all acts of communication presuppose the possibility of their repetition in new contexts. In order to function at all, a speech act, like a piece of writing or a visual image, must be *iterable*, that is, capable of functioning in situations other than the occasion of its production, among persons other than those who immediately produce and receive it. In their iterability, speech acts necessarily presuppose the possibility of difference, and hence also the possibility of their being redirected, reinterpreted. The prospect of what Austin thinks of as "misfire," an "infelicitous" deviation from the norm, is actually the norm itself. Even though certain speech acts may, and do, recur in typical settings with typical illocutions, we are not spared by that fact from understanding them anew with each recurrence. Speech acts are radically implicated in the situations that they address; they come to life as a kind of improvisation.

10. Derrida's essay, "Signature Event Context" originally appeared in the short-lived periodical *Glyph*, where it provoked a now famous exchange with the speech act theorist John Searle; the essay is reprinted in Derrida, *Margins of Philosophy*, trans. Alan Bass (Chicago, 1982): 307–30. For a fuller account, see Stanley Fish, "With the Compliments of the Author: Reflections on Austin and Derrida," *Critical Inquiry* 8 (1982): 693–722. For more on the instability of the performative dimension, and on Austin's treatment of it, see Shoshana Felman, *The Literary Speech Act: Don Juan with J. L. Austin, or Seduction in Two Languages*, trans. Catherine Porter (Ithaca, N.Y., 1983).

Taken together with Derrida's critique, Austin's theory of speech acts holds great promise for musical hermeneutics. Although Austin privileges what he calls the "speech situation,"[11] speech act theory generalizes easily to cover writing, which also has a busy performative dimension. And although locutionary effects are confined to the sphere of language, illocutionary force need not be. Any act of expression or representation can exert illocutionary force provided, first, that the act is iterable and, second, that in being produced the act seeks to affect a flow of events, a developing situation. In their illocutionary dimension, therefore, speech acts exemplify a larger category of expressive acts through which illocutionary forces pass into general circulation. Musical processes clearly count as expressive acts according to the terms just given. If we can learn to recognize them as such, to concretize the illocutionary forces of music as we concretize its harmonic, rhythmic, linear, and formal strategies, we can then go on to interpret musical meaning.

What techniques can we use to this purpose? An expressive act can be recognized as such only within the situation that it traverses, and here again speech acts enjoy certain advantages. Either their situation is explicit, as in the example from *Hamlet*, or they imply a situation while apparently concentrating on locutionary business, as in Kant's metaphor of thought-play. Unfortunately for the interpreter, these situational signals have no exact parallels in music. They do, however, have inexact parallels—sometimes oblique ones, elliptical, latent rather than manifest, but still and all sufficient to work with.

In recognizing and reflecting on an expressive act, we empower the interpretive process; we open what I earlier called a hermeneutic window through which our interpretation can pass. When it comes to music, at least three types of hermeneutic window are available to us, either as the expressive act to be recognized or as a signpost to such recognition.

   1. Textual inclusions. This type includes texts set to music, titles, epigrams, programs, notes to the score, and sometimes even expression markings. In dealing with these materials, it is critical to remember—especially with the texts of

11. Austin, *How to Do Things with Words*, 139.

vocal pieces—that they do not establish (authorize, fix) a meaning that the music somehow reiterates, but only invite the interpreter to find meaning in the interplay of expressive acts. The same caution applies to the other two types.

2. Citational inclusions. This type is a less explicit version of the first, with which it partly overlaps. It includes titles that link a work of music with a literary work, visual image, place, or historical moment; musical allusions to other compositions; allusions to texts through the quotation of associated music; allusions to the styles of other composers or of earlier periods; and the inclusion (or parody) of other characteristic styles not predominant in the work at hand.[12]

3. Structural tropes. These are the most implicit and ultimately the most powerful of hermeneutic windows. By *structural trope* I mean a structural procedure, capable of various practical realizations, that also functions as a typical expressive act within a certain cultural/historical framework. Since they are defined in terms of their illocutionary force, as units of doing rather than units of saying, structural tropes cut across traditional distinctions between form and content. They can evolve from any aspect of communicative exchange: style, rhetoric, representation, and so on.

The loose network of structural tropes operative at any given moment forms a kind of illocutionary environment in which expressive activities of all kinds go forth. Such a network forms an extension, in the expressive/hermeneutic sphere, of what Pierre Bourdieu calls the habitus of the social sphere: "systems of durable, transposable *dispositions*, structured structures predisposed to act as structuring structures, that is, as principles of the generation and structuring of practices and representations which can be objectively 'regulated' and 'regular' without in any way being the product of obedience to rules." The habitus, Bourdieu continues, enables us to form the strategies

12. For a discussion of this last type of citational inclusion, see Peter Rabinowitz, "Fictional Music: Toward a Theory of Listening," *Bucknell Review* 26 (1981): 193–208.

by means of which we cope with "unforeseen and ever-changing situations."[13]

For a simple example of a structural trope, consider the citation of one's own earlier work, which in nineteenth-century expressive practice often marks an important moment of reorientation. At the close of *Adonais* (1821), his elegy for Keats, Shelley tries to disentangle himself from "the web of being" and to fasten his desires on death. His success, if "success" is the word, turns on an allusion to his own "Ode to the West Wind":

I.

O wild West Wind, thou breath of Autumn's being,
Thou, from whose unseen presence the leaves dead
Are driven . . .

V.

Be thou, Spirit fierce,

My spirit! Be thou me, impetuous one!
Drive my dead thoughts over the universe
Like withered leaves to quicken a new birth!

("West Wind," 1–3, 61–64)

The breath whose might I have invoked in song
Descends on me; my spirit's bark is driven
Far from the shore, far from the trembling throng
Whose sails were never to the tempest given;
The massy earth and sphered skies are riven!
I am borne darkly, fearfully afar.

(*Adonais*, 487–92)

Condensed in the key words *breath*, *driven*, and *spirit*, the ode's language of rebirth returns as the elegy's language of death. Shelley's self-citation is almost penitential; it recants the text of what has come to seem false hope.

In his String Quartet in A Minor, D. 804 (1824), Schubert makes a similar, if less drastic, recantation. After an unsettled Allegro, the Andante seeks an idealized Biedermeier repose with the help of a

13. Pierre Bourdieu, *Outline of a Theory of Practice*, trans. Richard Nice (Cambridge, 1977), 72, 78.

melody borrowed from the incidental music to *Rosamunde*. The third movement then introduces a problematical counterquotation from Schubert's setting of Schiller's poem "Der Götter Griechenlands"—namely, the accompaniment to the line "Schöne Welt, wo bist du?" The force of this new quotation is both to acknowledge the unhappy destiny of all Biedermeier innocence and to withdraw, perhaps self-accusingly, from the illusion of a "schöne Welt" housed in the Andante. Schubert, however, is not quite ready to be borne darkly, fearfully afar. He qualifies his negative gesture with a dialectical irony by making the third movement a minuet—itself a relic of a "schöne Welt" gone by.[14]

Structural tropes operate freely across the entire cultural field. They act independently of received ideas about resemblances among various practices, discourses, and representations, and may even override obvious dissimilarities in style, scope, and context on behalf of shared ways of proceding, of valuing, of presenting. They may or may not derive from the explicit vocabulary that a historical period uses about itself. Their structuring effect ranges from the local and fragmentary pinpointing of a structural perspective to the large-scale unfolding of a structural rhythm.[15] In their malleability and semantic openness, structural tropes implant the hermeneutic attitude within the object of interpretation itself. As latent hermeneutic windows with a diversity of cultural affiliations, they form something like the body language of an interpretive community.

Recognizing structural tropes is an empirical, even a catch-as-catch-can, matter: no formal discovery procedure is available for them. We can, however, formulate a few rules of thumb. Hermeneutic windows tend to be located where the object of interpretation appears—or can be made to appear—explicitly problematical. Interpretation takes flight from breaking points, which usually means from points of under- or overdetermination: on the one hand, a gap, a lack, a missing connection; on the other, a surplus of pattern, an extra repetition, an excessive connection. In some cases, our effort

14. The quotation in the minuet is identified by J. A. Westrup, "The Chamber Music," in *Music of Schubert*, ed. Gerald Abraham (1947; rpt. Fort Washington, N.Y., 1969), 93.

15. On structural rhythms, see my *Music and Poetry: The Nineteenth Century and After* (Berkeley and Los Angeles, 1984), 4–24, 229–30.

to turn these breaking points into sources of understanding may involve no more than reflection on the explicit expressive acts that are particular to the object. Structural tropes tend to appear, to be called on by the interpreter under one name or another, when we widen the scope of reflection: when, guided by the problem posed by the breaking point, we begin to play with analogies and recategorizations, seeking to throw light on one object by seeking out its multiple affiliations with others. The goal of this process, at least its ideal goal, resembles what the anthropologist Clifford Geertz calls a "thick description": an account of "a multiplicity of complex conceptual [read: expressive] structures, many of them superimposed upon or knotted into one another, which are at once strange, irregular, and inexplicit, and which [we] must contrive somehow first to grasp and then to render."[16] Structural tropes, actualized practically and experimentally during the interpretive process, emerge both as means and as ends in our approach to this mode of understanding.

A strategic map for musical hermeneutics might thus read more or less as follows:

1. Locate the hermeneutic windows of the work, starting with the most explicit (textual inclusions) and working up to the least explicit (structural tropes).

2. Identify the expressive acts found among or by means of these materials. Interpret the interplay of their illocutionary forces.

3. Ask whether the formal processes and stylistic articulations of the music can be said, either literally or figuratively, to exemplify the same or associated expressive acts. Interpret the interplay of illocutionary forces as a correlate—loose or tight, whatever seems practicable—of the interplay of musical forces. Where the music is linked to a text, treat the interplay of musical meaning as an appropriation and reinterpretation of the (already interpreted) textual meaning.

16. Clifford Geertz, *The Interpretation of Cultures* (New York, 1973), 10. Geertz takes the term *thick description* from Gilbert Ryle, "Thinking and Reflection" and "The Thinking of Thoughts," in *Collected Papers* (New York, 1971), 2:465–79 and 480–96, respectively.

4. Connect the results to similar interplays elsewhere in the cultural field, freely allowing the activity of musical and nonmusical materials to comment on, criticize, or reinterpret each other as well as to repeat each other.

5. Perform these steps in any order and as often as you like, omitting any that you do not need. Avoid burdening the interpretive process itself with labels like "hermeneutic window" and "illocutionary force" except when there is little other choice. In fact, throw away this map before you use it.

The last step is not a joke, but a sober recognition of the character of interpretation. As I acknowledged earlier, hermeneutic theories can be very useful. Many flexible and powerful ones are available, from the Freudian system of condensations and displacements to the textual codes of Roland Barthes's *S/Z.* The usefulness of all such theories, however, including the one I have outlined in this chapter, depends on our according each particular theory only a provisional, implicit, occasional authority. To do otherwise leads merely to the conventionalized recycling of theoretical terms in concrete instances, and not to anything we can properly call interpretation. Real interpretation belongs decisively to the sphere of what has been called practical consciousness. However guided it may be by precept, it is learned only by example and performed only by applying tacit, unformalized knowledge to individual cases. The knowledge of how to interpret is social in its structure and origin, the product of a habitus. And such social knowledge, as Norman Bryson puts it, "cannot be abstracted from the situations in which it is revealed *in profiles,* that is, immanently within its contextual embodiment."[17]

Interpretation, accordingly, cannot be regimented, disciplined, or legislated—at least not successfully. As a practice, it is opportunistic, unruly, and contestatory, inescapably committed to both preserving and appropriating whatever it addresses. As nineteenth-century critical thought insisted, especially through the unholy trinity of Nietz-

17. Norman Bryson, *Vision and Painting: The Logic of the Gaze* (New Haven, 1983), 70. Bryson borrows the term *practical consciousness* from Raymond Williams, *Marxism and Literature* (Oxford, 1977), 35–42; *in profiles* is from Bourdieu, *Outline,* 18.

sche, Marx, and Freud, interpretation is intimately bound up with questions of power and desire. "Whatever exists," Nietzsche argues,

> having somehow come into being, is again and again reinterpreted to new ends, taken over, transformed and redirected by some power superior to it. . . . The entire history of a "thing," an organ, a custom can in this way be a continuous sign-chain of ever new interpretations . . . a succession of more or less profound, more or less mutually independent processes of subduing, plus the resistances they encounter, the attempts at transformation for the purposes of defense and reaction, and the results of successful counteractions. The form is fluid, but the "meaning" is even more so.[18]

An interpretation unhesitatingly seizes on any association, substitution, analogy, construction, or leap of inference that it requires to do its work. If it is guided by rules, then it partly makes up the rules as it goes along. Not for an idle reason does the term *hermeneutics* invoke the name of Hermes, the wing-shod messenger of Olympus and god of invention, cunning, and theft.

The inherently problematical character of interpretation is perhaps most evident in the paradox that while bad interpretations may be manifestly false, good interpretations can never be manifestly true. Unlike a true account of something, an interpretation can never exclude rival, incompatible accounts. For any given interpretation, an alternative always exists; as we have seen from Derrida's critique of Austin, the availability of alternatives is the very condition that makes interpretation possible. Lacking the power of exclusion, interpretations must convince by other means. My claim in this book is that they convince by their power to sustain a detailed scrutiny of a text that also reaches deep into the cultural context.

Again, unlike a true account, an interpretation cannot stabilize its key concepts—or if you prefer, cannot afford the illusion that concepts are stable in the first place. On the contrary: interpretation can only proceed by intensifying conceptual mobility, by tautening the associative threads between ideas to suggest relationships, by expanding the relationships between ideas to suggest equivalences, by prizing

18. Nietzsche, *On the Genealogy of Morals*, essay 2, sec. 12; from *"On the Genealogy of Morals" and "Ecce Homo,"* trans. Walter Kaufmann (New York, 1969), 77–78.

apart equivalences to locate differences. In the terms provided by Kant's theory of music, we can state the case by saying that interpretation is the art of putting the concepts that Kant cherished into the *Gedankenspiel* that he mistrusted. And if Kant's description of musical *Gedankenspiel* has any credibility, we can even suggest that interpretation is an art modeled on the experience of music.[19]

None of which is to say—emphatically not—that interpretation must forgo all claims to be credible, scrupulous, and rational. What it does say is that these terms are susceptible to continual redefinition, continual transposition to unexpected planes of discourse. In order to present itself as knowledge amid so much volatility, interpretation must meet certain demands—demands for explanatory power, interconnectedness, telling detail, and honesty. Nor is that enough. Responsible interpretation also involves a principled refusal to monumentalize its own efforts, while at the same time sparing no efforts; a willingness to allow the object of interpretation its measure of resistance; a readiness to admit that interpretation, too, is an expressive act, urging truth claims—which is not the same as exhibiting the truth—while also exerting power or pressure on behalf of the interpreter's values.

This interpretive ethic is particularly important when we try to connect the object of interpretation to its cultural/historical situation; no enterprise is more vulnerable to the lure of monumentalization, the illusion that the wavering movement of meaning has been arrested at last. The danger here is to place too much restraint on the language and conceptual reach of the interpreter, as if doing so represents an allegiance to "objectivity" rather than the exercise of illocutionary coercion. A plausible alternative position might be built around Hans-Georg Gadamer's claim that all interpretation necessarily arises through a "fusion" of past and present "horizons" of meanings and presuppositions—though we might see this claim, too, as overidealizing, a rewriting of Nietzsche without Nietzsche's radicalism and risk-taking.[20]

19. The role of music, as heard, in providing a model for interpretation was not lost on Kant's contemporaries. For a discussion, see Kevin Barry, *Language, Music, and the Sign* (Cambridge, 1987).

20. Hans-Georg Gadamer, *Truth and Method*, ed. Garrett Barden and John Cumming, from the second German edition (1965) (New York, 1975). For a tren-

My own position was anticipated when, in point 4 of my hermeneutic roadmap, I urged the interpreter to allow musical and nonmusical materials to comment on, criticize, or reinterpret each other as well as to repeat each other. The implication is that we will quickly run aground if we treat the object of interpretation, in this case the music, merely as an instance of anterior claims or forces—merely, that is, as the reflection of some context, however thickly described. In order to release the energies of interpretation, the relationship between the object—call it the music—and its situation must be understood as dynamic. The music, as a cultural activity, must be acknowledged to help produce the discourses and representations of which it is also the product.

This principle is one of the cornerstones of what literary critics have taken to calling "the new historicism," an approach to literary and cultural history that conjoins elements of historicism, cultural materialism, and poststructuralism.[21] That is a large wad of isms, but for present purposes we can set them aside to focus on enabling principles—two in particular. First, the cultural field has no stable or privileged sites of meaning. Meaning is produced everywhere, and, like air or money, it circulates everywhere. Second, the works, practices, and activities—for us, the music—that we address as interpreters are not only the products but also the *agencies* of culture, not only members of the habitus but also makers of it. In recent years, important projects have been outlined for understanding music in its cultural/historical situation, notably by Joseph Kerman, Gary Tomlinson, and Leo Treitler.[22] My purpose in adding my voice to theirs

chant, if brief, critique of Gadamer's hermeneutics, see Terry Eagleton, *Literary Theory: An Introduction* (Minneapolis, 1983), 71–74.

21. The best overviews of the new historicism emerge from the field of Renaissance studies, where the new-historicist viewpoint is especially strong. See Louis Adrian Montrose, "Renaissance Literary Studies and the Subject of History," *English Literary Renaissance* 16 (1986): 5–12; Jean Howard, "The New Historicism in Renaissance Studies," *English Literary Renaissance* 16 (1986): 13–43; Jonathan Goldberg, "The Politics of Renaissance Literature: A Review Essay," *ELH* (*English Literary History*) 49 (1982): 514–42; and Edward Pechter, "The New Historicism and its Discontents: Politicizing Renaissance Drama," *PMLA* 102 (1987): 292–303.

22. Joseph Kerman, *Contemplating Music: Challenges to Musicology* (Cambridge, Mass., 1985); Gary Tomlinson, "The Web of Culture: A Context for Musicology," *Nineteenth Century Music* 7 (1984): 350–62; and Leo Treitler, *Music and the Historical Imagination* (Cambridge, Mass., 1989).

is to urge that this understanding can proceed only if it proceeds in two directions.

"Grau . . . ist alle Theorie / Und grün des Lebens goldner Baum"— said Mephistopheles. This chapter has not paid much attention to particular works of music. The chapters that follow will make good the omission, but I would still like to conclude with one example, a kind of microcosm of musical hermeneutics in action. The example is a particularly suggestive one, in part because it represents a collaborative effort and in part because it focuses on a formal question that *must* receive a hermeneutic answer.

In his *Grande messe des morts*, Berlioz recapitulates the opening section of the Sanctus with a remarkable addition. Shortly after the recapitulation begins, soft strokes on the bass drum and cymbals, the latter allowed to vibrate, begin to set up polyrhythmic patterns and continue to do so until the end. The series of polyrhythms forms an independent, well-organized whole, as if an independent movement for percussion were being superimposed on the Sanctus, a portent of things to come in Elliott Carter. At first, the repetition of a single rhythmic pattern by the percussion articulates 5/2 against the basic 4/4 (mm. 3^3–23^2); next, the polyrhythms become irregular while the rhythmic pattern breaks down (mm. 23^3–33^3); finally, the repetition of a new rhythmic pattern articulates 3/2 against the basic 4/4 (mm. 33^3–47). The overall design is a lucid ABA: metrical regularity–metrical irregularity–metrical regularity reinterpreted.

What are we to make of all this? When I posed the same question to the members of a 1988 colloquium on music and narrative, some compelling answers came to the fore.[23] Reinhold Brinkmann heard the drum-and-cymbal music as a kind of *Klangfarbenmelodie*, something in keeping with Berlioz's exploitation of acoustic space in the Requiem. Anthony Newcomb seized on the fact that the bass drum and cymbals are military instruments, and suggested that the Sanctus incorporates military music in estranged or defamiliarized form, as if to subsume martial strife to religious peace. Christopher Reynolds recalled Beethoven's use of drums and cymbals in the finale of the

23. The conference, organized by Karol Berger and Anthony Newcomb, was held at Stanford University and the University of California at Berkeley in May 1988.

Ninth Symphony. Beethoven, like Berlioz, employs a solo tenor at this point, and does so to set a portion of Schiller's text that is remarkably pertinent:

> Froh, wie seine Sonnen fliegen
>> Durch des Himmels pracht'gen Plan,
>> Laufet, Brüder, eure Bahn.
> Freudig wie ein Held zum Siegen.[24]

The allusion reinforces both the spatial and the military resonance of Berlioz's percussion.

Once we put interpretive materials like this into play, we can also put them together, both with one another and with their formal environment. Take the environment first. The ABA pattern of the percussion "movement" suggests a process of gradual stabilization. The series of polyrhythms first lapses from and then recovers a state of metrical regularity. Moreover, the third part replaces a complex or irregular meter (5/2) with a simple meter (3/2)—a simple meter that can even be taken as an element of the complex one (5/2 = 2/2 + 3/2 in mm. $6–8^2$, $16–18^2$). And not to stop there, the 3/2 meter is articulated, as Edward T. Cone has observed, by twice-five repetitions of a basic group of three.[25] The five-beat grouping is stabilized by transposition to a higher structural level.

In the presence of so much dynamism, the spatial and military dimensions of this music demand to be understood as a process. The defamiliarization that Newcomb speaks of can be taken to increase as the drum-and-cymbal polyrhythms evolve from an immediate expressive effect to a superimposed "movement" with an autonomous structure. At the far end of this process lies Brinkmann's *Klangfarbenmelodie*: the subtilization of the sound of a military band into sound pure and simple. This sound, especially the swooshing vibration of the

24. Glad as His suns fly / Through the glorious order of Heaven, / Run your course, brothers, / Joyfully as a hero to victory.

25. Edward T. Cone, "Berlioz's Divine Comedy: The *Grande Messe des Morts*," *19th-Century Music* 4 (1980): 13–14. Cone understands the percussion "movement" as an instance of a disposition toward reinterpretation, toward the creation of multiple perspectives, that rules both the Mass and Berlioz's music as a whole. This reading is amply congruent with the others developed here. My thanks to Walter Frisch for drawing Cone's essay to my attention.

cymbals, resonates through the huge performance space demanded by the Requiem—in the case of the premiere, the Church of St. Louis des Invalides in Paris, with its great amplitude and high dome. Thus employed, the performance space becomes an embodiment of the cosmic space invoked by Beethoven's Ninth. The order of the heavens is remapped in the architecture of the church, which on this occasion is also the order of public space and of state authority. (The Requiem was commissioned to commemorate the dead of the 1830 revolution but premiered instead as a memorial for a French general killed in Algeria.) Within the multiple valences of this space, the strife of the world is nullified and one is free to praise God in peace.

It now remains to bring the claims of this chapter to life in more detail, and more than once. I will pause only to risk a personal—or perhaps I mean a political—conjecture. It is scarcely a secret that the extraordinary value ascribed to music, and to the arts in general, during the nineteenth century has lost much of its credibility; not much survives except a certain quantity of impoverished rhetoric. Professional students of all the arts have been increasingly confronted with a sense of cultural marginalization, an unhappy awareness that their work is tolerated rather than encouraged by the academy and by society at large. One response to this state of affairs has been a retreat into ever more arcane languages of inquiry and ever more exclusionary specialities, a result that Nietzsche foresaw as early as the third essay of *On the Genealogy of Morals*. Yet there has also been a more affirmative response, particularly among literary critics. This has taken the form of developing communicative languages of inquiry that empower and even demand the breaking of disciplinary barriers, and of using those languages to (re)open—to discover, construct, provoke—a dynamic, dialogical relationship between cultural processes and cultural products. The growing interest in musical hermeneutics, without which this book could scarcely have been written, is a sign of this same affirmative development struggling to be born in humanistic studies. My purpose here is simply to assist in the birth.

BEETHOVEN'S TWO-MOVEMENT PIANO SONATAS AND THE UTOPIA OF ROMANTIC ESTHETICS

Beethoven's Piano Sonata in C Minor, Op. 111, puzzled Anton Schindler, who once asked the composer why the sonata has only two movements. Beethoven replied that there had been no time to compose a finale, so he simply made the slow movement a little longer.[1] Which is to say: a stupid question deserves a stupid answer. Nonetheless, it makes perfect sense to ask why Op. 111 has only two movements, as long as one isn't deluded into thinking it ought to have three. The same question might also be asked of the other two-movement piano sonatas—Op. 54 in F, Op. 78 in F♯, and Op. 90 in E Minor—that Beethoven composed at significant moments in his career.[2] Although they are not usually thought of together, these sonatas form a coherent group. Their twofold design can be understood as a means of working through some of the central preoccupations of Romantic esthetic theory and practice. That working through is my subject in this chapter.

1. Anton Schindler, *Beethoven as I Knew Him*, ed. Donald W. MacArdle, trans. Constance S. Jolly (Chapel Hill, N.C., 1966), 232.
2. The pair of two-movement works published as Op. 49 is negligible in the present context. These works are really sonatinas and lie outside Beethoven's serious concern with the piano sonata.

I

During the late eighteenth century a structural trope that we can call *expressive doubling* came into wide circulation. Expressive doubling is a form of repetition in which alternative versions of the same pattern define a cardinal difference in perspective. This rather schematic definition will grow fuller as we proceed; meanwhile, a series of examples can concretize and to some degree historicize it.

William Blake's sequence of illustrated poems *Songs of Innocence and Experience* (1794) shows "The Two Contrary States of the Human Soul" by matching most of its innocent numbers with a disturbed counterpart. Blake's *The Marriage of Heaven and Hell* (1793) applies the same principle to contrary modes of seeing the world. At one point, an angel who sees with the eye of orthodox Reason shows the poet a cavern where "a void boundless as a nether sky appeard beneath us, & we held by the roots of trees and hung over this immensity." The sight of the abyss—a combination of Newtonian physics and brimstone theology—terrifies the angel, who flees. Left alone, the poet discovers that his own eye, which is guided by rebellious Energy, sees rather differently: "I remain'd alone, & then this appearance was no more, but I found myself sitting on a pleasant bank beside a river by moon light, hearing a harper who sung to the harp."

A second example: E. T. A. Hoffmann's novella *The Golden Pot* (1813) is based on the conjunction and opposition of two ideal worlds. One is a bourgeois paradise identified with Biedermeier Dresden; the other is an ideal realm of poetry and erotic bliss that Hoffmann calls Atlantis, though it seems to come straight out of *The Magic Flute*. Dresden and Atlantis double each other through an extensive network of parallel elements; the parallels are constantly reconfigured as characters and images assume different identities under the sway of one or the other world. In Dresden, for example, the heroine Serpentina appears as a little gold-green snake that sparkles as it moves; in Atlantis she is a woman whose loose gown shimmers prismatically. (I simplify here; the details of the parallel become quite intricate.) Serpentina also has an appealing human counterpart named Veronica and a less appealing serpentine form, "white, diaphanous, [and] enormous."

J. M. W. Turner's paired paintings *Shade and Darkness—The*

Evening of the Deluge and *Light and Colour (Goethe's Theory)—The Morning After the Deluge—Moses Writing the Book of Genesis* (1843) take expressive doubling to its apocalyptic extreme. Both paintings center on huge circles of light. In *Shade and Darkness*, dark masses extend from the right side of the canvas and sweep across the top; they outline a downward-circling vortex that seems to be swallowing the light. In *Light and Colour*, rich red-orange masses extend from the left side of the canvas and sweep across the bottom; they outline an upward-circling vortex from which the light pours forth. Again, I omit details, but one that must not be omitted concerns Goethe's theory. In his *Theory of Colors*, Goethe divides the spectrum into a "Mystic Hexagon": the "plus" colors—reds, yellows, and greens—which are associated with warmth and happiness, and the "minus" colors—blues, blue-greens, and purples—which are associated with restlessness and anxiety. Turner painted *Shade and Darkness* in Goethe's minus colors, *Light and Colour* in the plus ones.[3]

Expressive doubling in music can be exemplified by Beethoven's famous use of a modified da capo structure in the third movement of the Fifth Symphony. This highly innovative movement returns in whispers to music first presented with loud insistence; it nullifies the contour of earlier changes in dynamics as well as the absolute dynamic level. The da capo in this form, which deletes the overt rhetoric of harshness and urgency but keeps their motivic and harmonic substance, sounds like a musical image for a haunting memory. What was violence in the present tense becomes anxiety—perhaps distanced, half-mastered anxiety—in the musical equivalent of the past.

A secondary expressive doubling also plays between this movement from the Fifth and the scherzo of the later "Harp" Quartet, which also features a whispery da capo. Like its symphonic precursor, the quartet movement is based on the signature rhythm of the Fifth, is in the key of C minor, and ends with a lengthy transition to the finale. The quartet movement, though, accents the fading rather than the persistence of anxiety; it suggests the possibility of mastery without struggle, something unthinkable in the Fifth. There is no

3. Jack Lindsay notes this complementarity in his *J. M. W. Turner: A Critical Biography* (New York, 1966), 211–12.

danger that an uncanny fragment of the da capo will return to trouble the quartet finale in the celebrated manner of the symphony.

As these examples suggest, expressive doubling is a process that submits a well-defined *Gestalt* to reinterpretation and revaluation. More particularly, it exemplifies what Jacques Derrida calls the logic of the supplement, that is, the completion of something that at first seems complete in itself.[4] The initial term of an expressive doubling is always presented as a totality: in our examples, as a scene, a fictional world, a musical section, a musical movement. The supplemental term of an expressive doubling is an extra, a discontinuity, that displaces—but does not nullify—the original term. When the two terms are considered together, the effect is compelling, hermeneutically provocative; each term energizes the other as if a spark had leapt between them.[5]

Beethoven's reading would certainly have offered him models of expressive doubling. Goethe's *Wilhelm Meister's Apprenticeship*, which Beethoven had in his library, makes extensive use of this trope, especially in connection with Wilhelm's protégé, Mignon.[6] Mignon's thrice-famous song, "Kennst du das Land, wo die Zitronen blühn," is a striking case in point, the more so because Beethoven composed a setting for it (Op. 75, no. 1). The song unfolds by doubling its first stanza, in which Mignon describes an earthly paradise and urges her beloved to take her there. Each subsequent stanza recasts the paradisal scene in a disrupted form and displaces the term *beloved* accordingly. Stanza 2 intrudes a note of suffering ("Was hat man dir, du armes Kind, getan?") and addresses the beloved as a protector; stanza 3 adds anxiety, even dread ("In Höhlen wohnt der Drachen

4. On the supplement, see Jacques Derrida, *Of Grammatology*, trans. Gayatri Chakravorty Spivak (Baltimore, 1976), 141–64.

5. The logic of doubling requires one further comment at this point. As our examples have shown, expressive doubling is transacted between wholes, but only by means of structural parallels between the parts that compose the wholes. These parallels may be based on any sort of relationship, and merely *as* parallels they may not be considered "doublings" in any meaningful sense. Individual parallels count as doublings only as constituents of the larger doubling (reinterpretation and revaluation) of one whole by another. To avoid circumlocution in what follows, I will speak of doubling in relation to both parts and wholes, but only on the terms set by this note.

6. For the text and a translation of the poem, see the Appendix.

alte Brut") and addresses the protector as Mignon's father. (Mignon is the child of brother-sister incest; her father appears in the novel as a wandering harper.)

Mignon's stanzaic doublings are so haunting to Wilhelm that he is compelled to repeat them at the level of narrative. After hearing her sing beyond his closed door (and mistaking her for the harper!), Wilhelm has Mignon repeat her song in his presence. He proceeds to write down the text, and even to translate it "into his native language," only to find that his actions imitate those of the text itself. Like the paradise of the first stanza, the pleasure of Wilhelm's first hearing is progressively disrupted with each act of doubling. Something similar but far less obtrusive occurs in Beethoven's setting. Although it is strophic in form, the setting uses variations in tempo and pianistic texture to echo the doublings within the poem. In performance, the variations should prompt telling changes in vocal inflection—changes of the sort that Goethe, as it happens, ascribes to Mignon's own performance.

Goethe aside, Beethoven found something like expressive doubling simply "in the air" around him. A brief look at his intellectual climate is therefore in order; it should show us how his use of expressive doubling is linked to his general culture and to his musical preoccupations. Afterward, I will amplify my account of this structural trope, pursue it further in an important text by Wordsworth, and finally bring it to bear on the two-movement sonatas.

II

In 1809, Beethoven wrote to one of his publishers: "I have not the slightest pretension to what is properly called erudition. Yet from my childhood on I have striven to understand *what the better and wiser people* of every age were driving at in their works." As Maynard Solomon points out in his biography of the composer, this statement is perfectly trustworthy.[7] Beethoven's intellectual curiosity was voracious, driven by the same kind of demanding idealism that led him to slave tirelessly over his composition sketchbooks and repeatedly to redefine the major genres in which he composed. From the heady mix of Enlightenment and Romantic concepts that made up his intellec-

7. Quoted by Maynard Solomon, *Beethoven* (New York, 1977), 37.

tual milieu, three seem to have had an especially forceful impact on his work as a composer. The first, and best documented, is the conflict between political liberty and tyrannical authority, which decisively influences a series of landmark works from the *Eroica* through *Fidelio* to the Ninth Symphony.[8] The second is the assumption of a strong subject-object polarity, with emphasis on the sometimes intractable forcefulness of the subject. As M. H. Abrams puts it, this cardinal principle of Romantic culture rests on the "split in the mind's unity with itself that converts unself-consciousness to self-consciousness—the awareness of the self as a subject distinct from the object it perceives, and the intervention of reflection and choice between instinct and action.[9] Romantic literature and philosophy represent the interplay of subject and object in agonistic terms that also give the measure of vitality. As Goethe put it, "where object and subject touch each other, there is life."[10]

In 1820, Beethoven wrote out a paraphrase of Kant that may have served him as a touchstone on this matter: "The moral law [with]in us, and the starry sky above us—Kant!!!"[11] What is most revealing about this jotting is its presumably unconscious editing. Beethoven picked up Kant's famous sentence from a newspaper article;[12] his alterations suggest a classical Freudian slip of the pen. The original reads: "Two things fill the mind with ever new and increasing wonder and reverence the oftener [and more steadily] the mind dwells on them—the starry sky above me and the moral law within me."[13] Positioning the starry sky and moral law as sources of wonder and reverence, Kant follows a religious hierarchy from height to depth.

---

8. On this subject see Solomon, *Beethoven*, 131–41, 197–200, 260–61, 309–16.

9. M. H. Abrams, *Natural Supernaturalism: Tradition and Revolution in Romantic Literature* (New York, 1971), 213–14. For a fuller discussion, see Thomas McFarland, *Romanticism and the Forms of Ruin: Wordsworth, Coleridge, and Modalities of Fragmentation* (Princeton, 1981), 289–341.

10. Quoted by McFarland, *Romanticism*, 311.

11. Quoted by Solomon, *Beethoven*, 37.

12. A point noted by William Kinderman, "Beethoven's Symbol for the Deity in the *Missa Solemnis* and the Ninth Symphony," *Nineteenth Century Music* 9 (1985): 102n. Kinderman's analysis of the mass persuasively suggests Beethoven's "affinities" with the Kant of the famous dictum.

13. Text as quoted by Solomon, *Beethoven*, 37. Kant's statement is from the conclusion to the *Critique of Practical Reason*.

The sky above precedes the law within, in a rhetorical sequence that cannot plausibly be reversed. Beethoven's paraphrase sweeps the two terms into an absolute, unqualified polarity between inner and outer, self and nature, in which the subjective term (democratically expanded to "us") gets pride of place.

It is no doubt simplistic to remark that this reversal of hierarchies spells the difference between Enlightenment and Romanticism, but the temptation to say so is too great to resist. In any case, Beethoven's commitment to the Romantic subject/object polarity forms a basic subtext to the conflict in his music between the impulse to revise, violate, or transfigure the high Classical style and the impulse to preserve it. This linkage finds something like a manifesto in the finale of the String Quartet in B♭, Op. 18, no. 6 (music we will focus on in Chapter 6). The movement unfolds as an explicit dialectical clash between a "subjective" Adagio entitled "La malinconia" and an "objective" Allegro: the one harmonically problematical, the other straightforward; the one combining block chordal writing with fugato, the other dancelike; the one fragmented, the other continuous.[14] The association of the subjective term with a heterogeneous, somewhat anarchic play of intensities—what Wordsworth called "trances of thought and mountings of the mind" (*Prelude* [1805], 1.20)—is very much in line with literary practice.

The third of what might be called Beethoven's masterplots rests on the principle that art, and in particular Romantic (i.e., "present-day") art, is essentially utopian. As Schiller puts it, the Romantic artist must

> set himself the task of an idyll . . . that will lead humanity, for whom the path back to Arcadia is forever closed, onward towards Elysium. . . . It is of infinite importance for the man who follows the path of civilization to see confirmed in a sensuous mode the belief that this [utopian] idea can be realized in the world of sense.[15]

14. This finale is the culminating point of the impulse towards disruption that Joseph Kerman identifies in the last three of the Op. 18 quartets to be composed; see his *The Beethoven Quartets* (New York, 1966), 54–86.

15. Schiller, "Über naive und sentimentalische Dichtung," in *Sämtliche Werke*, ed. Otto Güntter and Georg Witkowski (Leipzig, n.d.), 17:542.

Beethoven could have taken versions of this idea from Schiller himself, or from Friedrich Schlegel, Novalis, or Hoffmann, or simply from the intellectual vernacular of the day.[16] A diary entry that probably dates from 1815 shows him working out a typical formulation:

> All things flowed clear and pure from God. If afterwards I became darkened through passion for evil, I returned, after manifold repentance and purification, to the elevated and pure source, to the Godhead. —And, to your art.[17]

Early and late, Beethoven's career is driven by the effort to give utopian esthetics a practical realization—an effort that culminates in the communal ritual of the Ninth Symphony and in the "vocal impulse" that Joseph Kerman finds in the late quartets, where "[instrumental] evocations of the human voice . . . mean to sing or to speak instantly to the heart, like the songs imagined by Beethoven's poet at the climax of *An die Ferne Geliebte.*"[18]

Beethoven's comments on this subject regularly resort to the rhetoric of striving and apotheosis evident in the 1815 diary entry. The idiom (which is also Schiller's) is consonant with his habit of relentless self-criticism and with his belief, half a rationalization of suffering, half compulsive self-punishment, that art demands sacrifice from the artist—and further that the only reward for such sacrifice is art itself. ("Only in my divine art," he writes, "do I find the support which enables me to sacrifice the best part of my life to the heavenly

16. On Beethoven and Schiller, see Maynard Solomon, *Beethoven Essays* (Cambridge, Mass., 1988), 205–15. Beethoven may have been familiar with one important claim that his music "wakens just that longing for the infinite which is the essence of Romanticism," namely Hoffmann's. In a letter to Hoffmann, he says that a friend "showed me in his album some lines of yours about me" (March 23, 1820). We do not know which lines, but Hoffmann's essay repeatedly reasserts its idealizing argument. Both the essay and the letter are reprinted in *Source Readings in Music History: The Romantic Era*, ed. Oliver Strunk (New York, 1965), 35–41.

17. Beethoven's diary of 1812–18, entry 67a; the whole diary is reprinted in Solomon, *Beethoven Essays*, 246–95.

18. For a full discussion of the "vocal impulse," see Kerman, *Quartets*, 192–221. On the Ninth Symphony in this context, see Solomon, "The Ninth Symphony: A Search for Order," in *Beethoven Essays*, 3–34.

muses.")[19] Two expressions of Beethoven's esthetic idealism are particularly revealing. The first has a special authority because it was addressed to a ten-year-old girl, Emilie M., who had given the composer a pocketbook. The gift moved him to a spontaneous outburst of goodwill that also reflected his wishful identification with the innocence of the giver. Beethoven's remarks are offered as universally intelligible, almost proverbial advice:

> Persevere, do not only practise your art, but endeavour also to fathom its inner meaning; it deserves this effort, for only art and science can raise men to the level of gods. . . . The true artist has no pride. He sees unfortunately that art has no limits; he has a vague awareness of how far he is from reaching his goal.[20]

In a similar vein, he writes five years later to Xaver Schneider, an aspiring composer: "Continue to raise yourself higher and higher into the divine realm of art. For there is no more undisturbed, more unalloyed or purer pleasure than that which comes from such an experience."[21]

The esthetic quest outlined in these statements appears as a subtext in much of Beethoven's music, especially after 1801. Repeatedly the music projects an almost hermetic formal discipline as the means to resolve conflict and ascend toward a vision of human happiness— what Schiller called "an effigy of the ideal."[22] Repeatedly the vision acknowledges, but without dread, the possibility of its own disruption. This last element is critical. For Beethoven, the utopian joy achieved through art is as free as possible, but never entirely free, from suffering and doubt. This limitation springs in part from personal sources—Beethoven's emotional balance was precarious at the best of times—but it is also a basic tenet of Romantic esthetics after Schiller. The Romantic artist, Schiller argued, must always deal "with two conflicting ideas and feelings, with the actual as a limit and

19. Letter to Georg Nägeli, September 9, 1824; in *Letters of Beethoven*, coll., trans., and ed. Emily Anderson, 3 vols. (New York, 1961), no. 1306.

20. Letter of July 17, 1812; in ibid., no. 376.

21. Letter of August 19, 1817; in ibid., no. 803.

22. Cited by Solomon, *Beethoven Essays*, 214.

with his idea as the infinite."[23] The actual may even be allowed to dominate the content of a work of art while the utopian idea retreats to the play of pure form. In giving his advice to Emilie M., Beethoven neatly pirouettes on the problem of the actual: he first proposes an apotheosis, then quickly sets it at an infinite distance.

III

The practice of expressive doubling is closely bound up with the utopian esthetics and subject/object polarity of early Romantic culture. As illocution, doubling gives the utopian project of art a concrete lyric or dramatic shape. It inscribes the sought-for historical progress from the actual to the ideal within a definite temporal frame: the unfolding rhythm of the individual work or the developmental interval between two works.

It follows that the terms of an expressive doubling form a hierarchy; one term represents a freer, happier, or more enlightened condition than the other. Or, to be more exact, one term represents the transposition of the other to a higher or deeper plane, a more brilliant or profound register. Adrift in London, Wordsworth transforms a bewildering crowd of strangers into a "second-sight procession" until

> . . . all the ballast of familiar life—
> The present, and the past, hope, fear, all stays,
> All laws of acting, thinking, speaking man—
> Went from me, neither knowing me, nor known.

(Prelude [1805], 7.604–7)

Shelley, recalling a calm afternoon on which images cast in forest pools seemed to form microcosms, values the reflections as "more perfect both in shape and hue" than their originals ("To Jane: The Recollection," 63). The images are "Elysian," as if their serenity, unlike that of the actual landscape, were imperishable.

Romantic esthetic theories typically posit a human creative faculty based on organic metaphors: a "blending, fusing power," as Coleridge

23. Schiller, *Sämtliche Werke*, 17:509; trans. M. H. Abrams in *Natural Supernaturalism*, 214. For discussion of this problematic duality in Schiller and Romantic esthetics generally, see Tilottama Rajan, *Dark Interpreter: The Discourse of Romanticism* (Ithaca, N.Y., 1980).

described it, that animates the parts of a whole as life animates a body, so that the whole and the parts are vitally interdependent.[24] Expressive doubling marks the blind spot in this organic model. Far from blending or fusing, it concentrates, repeats, reinterprets. One result—the most radical result—is that whatever conflicts or instabilities appear in the lower term of the doubling tend to be carried over into the higher term. This imported or transferred ambivalence acts to problematize the higher term, which must somehow overcome it, somehow answer this intrusion of the actual as a limit.

Transferred ambivalence goes to the very core of early Romantic esthetics. It forces the recognition that resistance to the ideal is a part of the effort to idealize: aspiration carries resistance on its back. Furthermore, it is by no means always possible to meet the psychological demands imposed by that resistance. Wordsworth eventually found a radical estrangement from familiar life too isolating or disorienting to affirm, at least for anyone past early childhood; he cut the "second-sight" lines I quoted earlier when he revised the 1805 *Prelude*.[25] Shelley ends "To Jane: The Recollection" by recalling how the Elysian imagery was erased from the pools by an "envious breeze," a negative breath of inspiration that corresponds to anxiety rather than rapture. The last lines ruefully acknowledge that the whole poem may have been wishfully overidealized:

> Though thou art ever fair and kind
> And forests ever green,
> Less oft is peace in S[helley's] mind
> Than calm in waters seen.

(85–89)

Beethoven's String Quartet in E Minor, Op. 59, no. 2, sets a highly demanding moment of transferred ambivalence at the climax of its slow movement. The movement opens with a tranquil chorale theme that subsequently recurs four times with variations in harmony and, in each case but the last, with increasingly elaborate counter-

24. On this subject, see M. H. Abrams, *The Mirror and the Lamp: Romantic Theory and the Critical Tradition* (New York, 1958), 167–77.

25. *The Prelude*, Wordsworth's poetic autobiography, exists in three versions, conventionally referred to by date: *1799*, in two books; *1805*, in thirteen books; and *1850*, in fourteen books. None of these is now considered "definitive."

EXAMPLE 1.   Beethoven, String Quartet in E Minor, Op. 59, no. 2. (A) Theme. (B) Climax.

point. The last recurrence can be experienced as an expressive dou-bling rather than as a variation. After Beethoven has seemingly finished with it, the chorale intrudes on the coda; framed by six-four chords, it stands alone like a kind of sublimated cadenza.[26] Tran-quillity gives way to extreme intensity: the chorale–quasi-cadenza begins fortissimo and continues at that dynamic through closely spaced sforzandi. The theme sounds an octave higher than before against block chords rather than countermelodies; the harmonies are strongly dissonant and slow to resolve. The communal aspiration of the chorale has been reconfigured into an individual moment of vision: and at that moment, it becomes impossible to tell rapture apart from anguish.

Crucial to the effect of this passage is the fact that its dissonances have been implicit in the chorale from the outset. As Example 1 shows, the climactic sonority is ruled by a pair of diminished-seventh chords: one a dominant-oriented chord (x) that enters on the initial sforzando, the other (y) a chromatic auxiliary of the first. Chord x, with the same bass note, also occurs on the downbeat of measure 3 of the original theme. As to chord y, it progresses in the climax

26. Cadenzalike; see Kerman, *Quartets*, 129.

through the ambiguous diminished triad z (derived from x) before resolving to a dominant; the progression anticipates the third of the dominant chord by means of a D–D♯ step on the viola. The same step appears in retrograde, again in an inner voice, at m. 4^{3-4} of the theme, where the D♮ secedes from a dominant chord to hint plaintively at the dominant minor. Restrained as elements of the theme, these dissonances assume a peculiarly timeless quality when they are unloosed at the climax. This effect derives in part from the pacing of the climax and its framing by six-four chords, but more from its thrusting of the fundamental action of the theme—prolongation of the dominant—into the foreground. Joseph Kerman has called attention to the timeless quality of the movement as a whole; perhaps this passage is Beethoven's way of concretizing, from the ambivalent perspective of human time, an idea he later set down in his diary: "For God, time absolutely does not exist."[27]

Some further insight into expressive doubling and its deferred ambivalence can be gleaned from an autobiographical fragment by Wordsworth, which I propose to examine rather closely. The passage, one of those visionary episodes that Wordsworth called "spots of time," was originally intended for *The Prelude*; it wound up, in pieces and rather the worse for wear, in the didactic epic *The Excursion* (1814). Here is the original version:

> Whether the whistling kite wheeled in the storm
> Maze intricate above me or below,
> As if in mockery or in proud display
> Of his own gifts compared with feeble man;
> Or facing some huge breast of rock I heard,
> As I have sometimes done, a solemn bleat
> Sent forth as if it were the mountain's voice,
> As if the visible [mountain made the cry]
> And hark, again [that solemn bleat, there is]
> No other, and the region all about
> Is silent, empty of all shape of life—
> It is a lamb left somewhere to itself,
> The plaintive spirit of the solitude.
> In those same careless rambles of my youth,
> Once coming to a bridge that overlooked

27. Ibid., 128; Solomon, *Beethoven Essays*, 276 (entry 94d).

> A mountain torrent where it was becalmed
> By a flat meadow, at a glance I saw
> A twofold image; on the grassy bank
> A snow-white ram and in the peaceful flood
> Another and the same. Most beautiful
> The breathing creature was, as beautiful
> Beneath him was his shadowy counterpart;
> Each had his glowing mountains, each his sky,
> And each seemed centre of his own fair world.
> A stray temptation seized me to dissolve
> The vision, but I could not, and the stone
> Snatched up for that intent dropped from my hand.
>
>   (Unutilized draft of 1804)

The episodes of the lamb and the ram are set down and juxtaposed without interpretive commentary. The same rhetorical practice dominates Wordsworth's orginal attempt at poetic autobiography, the *Two-Part Prelude* of 1799. The memories of formative experiences are taken as primary; they are compelling in excess of any explanations that might be devised for them—explanations they will invariably evade in later versions of the poem. In this case, however, the mere juxtaposition of memories is revelatory. Wordsworth's impulse to shatter the image of the ram, and the happy failure of that impulse, represent a reversal of his attitudes toward the invisible lamb. One expressive doubling (ram and image) clarifies Wordsworth's deep-seated need to preserve another (ram and lamb).

In the lamb episode, Wordsworth twice represents the free-floating solemn bleat as the mountain's voice, then abruptly undoes this personification by explaining the sound rationally. In so doing, he also disenchants an apparently privileged spot of its presiding genius: the "plaintive spirit of the solitude" is just a lonely lamb. The motives for this rhetorical reversal are deliberately left obscure, but the plaintiveness of the cry, the blankness of the rock, and the lifelessness of the scene all carry hints of a pain that cannot be assuaged, an isolation that cannot be broken. The "huge breast of rock" is indifferent rather than maternal—or worse, indifferent *and* maternal: the cry is like that of an abandoned child. Faced with this subtext, Wordsworth understandably prefers an abandoned lamb. The lamb, a mere natural fact, displaces the fantasy of maternal abandonment.

It may even allow Wordsworth to form a screen memory for the loss of his mother, who died when he was eight.[28]

In the ram, Wordsworth finds a counterimage of self-sufficient maturity. The ram is in possession of a grassy meadow and a torrent wrought to calm, the oxymoronic "peaceful flood." His silence and stillness suggest a secure bliss at odds with the lamb's desolation, and his solitude is a measure of his commanding place at the center of "his own fair world." In this context the calming of the waters seems to emanate from the ram's sovereign presence. Wordsworth's impulse to "dissolve" the vision that doubles the ram may correspond to a wish to preserve the singleness, the self-sufficiency, of the creature that symbolically undoes the dependency of the lamb. Or Wordsworth may not want to be reminded by the vision that the natural ram is finally just a "breathing creature," no less subject than the lamb to natural sorrows. Being "shadowy," the ram's counterpart is exempt from that fate. It is both an Elysian shade and a "shadow" (early-nineteenth-century usage for an image) that lies as much in the mind's eye as in the mountain pool. To dissolve the vision would protect the ram, transfer the harm.

Nonetheless, the stone drops from Wordsworth's hand. His defensive preference for the natural creature cannot withstand the transfixing appeal of the perfected vision. Touched by anxiety though it may be, the shadowy ram survives as an image of desire, the desire for a peace and beauty beyond vicissitude. Read in these terms, the image triumphs by reconfiguring the very forces that oppose it.

When Wordsworth came to rework this material for *The Excursion*, he faltered, as he would later do with the "second-sight" passage, over his original affirmation of ambivalence. Cutting the episode of the lamb, he hastens to control its erstwhile double by means of allegory. The ram and its image become

> Antipodes unconscious of each other,

28. The concept of screen memories derives from psychoanalysis. Such memories are constructions in which problematical early experiences are both revived and disguised. On the role of Wordsworth's mother in *The Prelude*, see Richard Onorato, *The Character of the Poet: Wordsworth in the Prelude* (Princeton, 1971).

> Yet, in partition with their several spheres,
> Blended in perfect stillness, to our sight!

(9.449–51)

The stilted phrasing is an index of Wordsworth's effort to preserve his idealization of the image from strain or disruption. The lofty diction is a means of securing poetic authority at a discount. Similar motives might explain a demotion of the ram's "mountain torrent" to a more tractable "hasty rivulet" and an emphasis, missing earlier, on the "manliness" of the ram, with his "imperious front / Shaggy and bold, and wreathed horns superb" (443–44). Even more telling is what happens here to Wordsworth's earlier impulse to dissolve the vision. A companion, "not without awe," speaks up:

> "Ah! what a pity were it to disperse,
> Or to disturb, so fair a spectacle,
> And yet a breath can do it!"

(452–54)

The impulse returns as the one thing that always returns—the repressed: denied by displacement onto someone else, stripped of aggressiveness by the deletion of the stone, and rationalized by turning its failure into a moralizing cliché. It would be hard to imagine a better means of dissolving the image than such an overzealous effort to protect it.

IV

Wordsworth's lamb/ram fragment and the Adagio from Beethoven's E-minor quartet strongly rely on two aspects of expressive doubling that I have so far left implicit. First, expressive doubling is in some sense never mandatory; it is the trope of the possible, the extra, the unforeseen. A basic way to schematize the repetitions that structure works of art is to arrange them on a continuum that runs from the periodic to the uncanny or obsessive, from the measured to the fixated.[29] Expressive doublings seem to fall outside this scheme, at

---

29. On obsessive repetition in Romantic works, see my *Music and Poetry*, 25–56; on uncanny repetition as a principle of narrative, see Peter Brooks, *Reading for the Plot: Design and Intention in Narrative* (New York, 1984), 3–37, 90–113.

least initially; they are presented as opportunities seized, as primary, not secondary or derived, gestures. This nonpareil quality, however, is put into question by means of deferred ambivalence, which often presses precisely in the direction of the uncanny. Hence Wordsworth's play with the meanings of "shadowy," Beethoven's sforzando attacks on his climactic diminished-seventh chords.

Second, expressive doublings typically proceed from low to high in the sphere of value; that is, they fulfill the masterplot of utopian esthetics. (The vertical order of value can be read suspiciously as a trace left by social and metaphysical hierarchies that are at odds with the utopian program, but that story is beyond the scope of this chapter.) "Low" and "high" are far from absolute terms, though; the low term may be strongly affirmative in its own right. Furthermore, some expressive doublings go in the other direction. This inverted form of the trope typically implies that the higher term has failed to master a transferred ambivalence and offers the lower term as an unorthodox alternative.

Beethoven's two-movement sonatas, which we are now ready to confront, pursue expressive doubling in both its utopian and inverted forms, and this in a consistent way. In the earlier pieces, Opp. 54 and 78, there is a descent from high to low: the second movement travesties the first. The contrary pattern informs the later two sonatas, Opp. 90 and 111, where the second movement transfigures the first. The sonatas of travesty keep to the same key and mode in each of their two movements, and in both cases the harmony of the second movement is unstable and even capricious in relation to the harmony of the first. The sonatas of transfiguration travel from a minor key in the first movement to the parallel major in the second, which is to say from harmonic tension to its resolution. And here the harmony of the first movements is restless, disquieting, while the harmony of the second movements is virtually static.

The conventional wisdom about these four works is that they constitute studies in contrast. Thus Op. 78 begins in lyric suspension and ends with fantastic wit, while Op. 111 begins with heroic struggle and ends in a meditative rapture. Like most conventional wisdom, this characterization is true up to a point — and it is beyond that point that things really get interesting. The second movement of each of these sonatas forms or incorporates an expressive doubling of something in the first movement. In the sonatas of travesty, the effect of the doubling is to break down a blindness or obstruction that appears, in retrospect, to set the first movements awry. The mood of the second movements is close to carnivalesque, in Mikhail Bakhtin's sense of the term.[30] This is music that disrupts hierarchies, celebrates change, and thrusts the physical energy of performance to the fore.

In the sonatas of transfiguration, the doublings patiently undo the underlying terms of a violence that fills the first movements with angular textures and brutal dissonances. The result resembles a process of healing, something akin to the "manifold repentance and purification" that Beethoven speaks of in the diary entry we considered earlier. The slow, transfiguring second movements seek a radical simplicity that can stand as the musical counterpart to inner peace, the acceptance of passing time, and inviolable joy.

Writing of Op. 54, Donald Tovey observes that its two movements "speak naively in their own characters" and that "Beethoven does not intrude with any indication that he could write a different kind of music with his fuller knowledge."[31] The first movement follows a simple ABA'B'A" design. The A sections elaborate on a placid little tune that Beethoven marks "In Tempo d'un Menuetto"; the tune's placidity corresponds to a marked harmonic inertia. The B sections shift the texture from melody and accompaniment to rigid, if not rigorous, imitative counterpoint. The first of them (mm. 25–57), after four bars on the dominant, is also quite volatile in harmony. These sections are outbursts of bearish, surly aggressiveness in feeling. In form, they are blatant send-ups of a two-part invention—in the shape of a *perpetuum mobile*.

As the movement proceeds, the A sections adorn their melody with increasingly lavish ornamentation; the coda rounds off this melodic enrichment by adding some enrichment in harmonic color. Meanwhile, the B section falls to pieces. Its second appearance (mm. 94–103) is so abbreviated that the earlier aggressiveness dwindles to

30. Mikhail Bakhtin, *Rabelais and His World*, trans. Helene Iswolsky (Bloomington, Ind., 1984). Solomon (*Beethoven*, 212–13) also sees a Bakhtinian element in Beethoven, here in connection with the festive character of the Seventh and Eighth Symphonies.

31. Donald Francis Tovey, *A Companion to Beethoven's Pianoforte Sonatas* (London, 1931), 161.

mere bluster. Furthermore, the harmonic volatility heard earlier fails to rematerialize; after its dominant opening, the second B section merely jumps on the tonic and runs through an overlong, overinsistent half cadence. As a whole, then, the music subdues its rawboned aggressiveness by continuously enfranchising an opposing lyrical impulse.

Or does it? The movement sounds considerably patchier than its design should allow; its sections are as much jumbled together as dynamically opposed. The naiveté that Tovey speaks of is openly problematical. The expressive polarities of this music are conceived too crudely, contrasted too starkly. Something is wrong.

The second movement quickly suggests that the problem is an unwillingness to throw caution to the winds. Here again we find a *perpetuum mobile* — and this one really tries to live up to its name: it just cannot seem to stop. The movement is a virtual anthology of excess. Its binary form is grossly misproportioned, the second half being lengthened to accommodate a harmonic process that equals the melodic figuration in sprawling repetitiousness. Starting from the dominant of D minor, the harmony rotates (with some backing and filling) around an entire circle of fifths, continuing the rotation until it reaches the tonic (mm. 21–115).[32] The texture of the movement is just as single-minded: it consists of virtually nothing but two-part counterpoint. To put all these features together, the second movement constitutes an expansion of the first B section of the first movement — an expansion *and* a liberation. The mood is no longer aggressive but energetic and uninhibited, and this in decidedly physical terms. The contrapuntal texture is shot through with syncopated accents and with cross-rhythms hammered out on single pitches. (The cross-rhythms, I should add, hark back to the first movement, where the B sections use sforzandi to form cross-rhythmic passages.) From the perspective of this antinomian tour de force, the first movement appears in retrospect as genteel, almost priggish. The minuet theme seems to aim, not at curbing superfluous anger, but at preventing the outbreak of raw, untrammeled impulse, of carnivalesque noodling, key pounding, and nose thumbing.

32. Ibid., 165–67.

Op. 54 is plainly an offhanded exercise, but its offhandedness is partly camouflage. To write music like the finale of the Seventh Symphony, which imports the carnivalesque into a great public genre, Beethoven imposes rigorous formal demands on himself. An offhanded little sonata, however, is something else again: a perfect excuse for turning from clumsy restraint to utterly unprincipled rowdiness.

The Sonata in F♯, Op. 78, is far more civilized. The piece is immediately striking for its odd dimensions: the first movement is nearly three times as long as the second. Beethoven effects this disproportion by writing both movements in sonata form, with a critical difference between them. The first movement is expansive: it repeats both halves of the form. The second movement is terse: it omits a development section and withholds the second group of the exposition until the (written-out) repeat.[33] Where one movement dilates musical time, the other compresses it.

The expressive force of this temporal difference depends on a parallel difference in texture. The first movement is a study in pure continuity, but a continuity that derives from the seamless weaving together of melodic fragments that are disjunct among themselves. Tovey suggests that this *discordia concors* "belong[s] to those things which we 'can understand perfectly so long as you don't explain.' "[34]

---

33. Not everyone will hear this movement as a sonata form; on the account I am about to give, it might even be called a quasi-strophic hybrid. Nevertheless, its essential action conforms to the sonata principle: the recapitulation at the tonic of an extended passage first heard as a structural dissonance. I would outline the movement as follows; parts of the structure will concern us later on:

Exposition of first group only, ending on dominant (mm. 1–31).
Full exposition (mm. 32–88):
    first group with slight variation (mm. 32–50); overlapping with
    second group at VI and vi, beginning on V/VI (mm. 51–73);
    closing passage on Aug 6/IV (mm. 74–88).
Recapitulation (mm. 89–149):
    first group of full exposition at IV, ending on V (mm. 89–109);
    second group at tonic, beginning on dominant (mm. 110–32);
    closing passage on Aug 6/I (mm. 133–49).
Deferred recapitulation of part of first group at tonic (mm. 150–61), extended and merging into **coda** (to end).

34. Tovey, *A Companion*, 178.

Beethoven's secret, however, is to let different strands of continuity overlap throughout the movement. Prominent among these are running sixteenth-note figuration, the rhythmic figure ♪♩♩, and the inversionally related three-note motives marked *a* and *b* in Example 2. The sixteenth-note figuration arises melodically in the first half of the exposition; it is almost continuous as an accompaniment throughout the second half, and again throughout the development. The exposition closes by combining the sixteenth notes with the head of the first theme; the recapitulation leads into the final cadence of the movement by expanding this process sequentially. The primary rhythmic figure recurs throughout the exposition and fills in the main action of the development. This figure is often associated with motives *a* and *b*, which together rule most of the exposition.

Beethoven uses these sources of continuity to weave a kind of web. The sixteenth notes act as a principle of large-scale association, while the primary rhythmic figure establishes a series of tiny, immediately perceptible points of connection. As Example 2 suggests, the motives *a* and *b* act in both these ways on different structural levels. The result, thanks to a relaxed pace and a lack of dramatic incident, is a glittering, dreamy texture, a condition of lyric suspension. Even the development yields to the spell: short and quiet, it is little more than a group of sequences aimed at the dominant.

All in all, this music has the sound and movement of an idyll—the very idyll that Schiller had demanded from the Romantic artist. As Mikhail Bakhtin has suggested, the idyll as a narrative form became increasingly important after the mid-eighteenth century, when Rousseau and others found that its elements could "provide material for constituting an isolated individual consciousness, and from the point of view of such a consciousness . . . act as forces that can heal, purify, and reassure it."[35] According to Bakhtin, idyllic narrative is marked by a specific spatial-temporal profile (or "chronotope"). Among its major temporal features are continuity, cyclical movement, and the absence of rigid boundaries: precisely the major features of the movement before us.

---

35. Mikhail Bakhtin, *The Dialogic Imagination*, trans. Caryl Emerson and Michael Holquist (Austin, Tex., 1981), 231.

EXAMPLE 2.   Beethoven, Piano Sonata in F♯ Major, Op. 78. Opening.
Motives *a* and *b* invert each other both directionally and in-
tervalically. Simple directional inversions, used transitionally,
are marked *a'* and *b'*.

EXAMPLE 2 *(continued)*

The movement also reproduces a further feature of the idyllic chronotope, the figure of growth or germination. Beethoven begins Op. 78 with a brief cantabile introduction. As Example 2 shows, this apparently fragmentary passage adumbrates both the primary rhythmic figure and the primary interval set. These elements, however, are not yet singled out, not yet differentiated within the musical texture. The introduction "contains" the whole movement, but contains it in embryo. The movement proper begins with the first gesture of differentiation: the coalescence of the rhythmic figure and motive *a*.

EXAMPLE 3.   Beethoven, Piano Sonata in F♯ Major, Op. 78. Opening of finale.

The introduction, however, also adds a certain quality of longing to the music, as if to suggest that the idyll is finally no more than a beautiful fiction. This effect derives partly from the tonic pedal deep in the bass, which forms gentle dissonances on the downbeats of mm. 2–4, but there is also a more explicit resonance. As Erich Leinsdorf observes, the introduction unobtrusively alludes to Beethoven's nearly contemporary setting of Mignon's "Kennst du das Land?" from *Wilhelm Meister*, with its own idyllic, indeed paradisal, longings.[36]

The second movement turns abruptly away from idyllic time to a mode full of energy and foreshortening. The music is again dominated by melodic fragments, but now the fragments fail to interlock—they repeal continuity at every turn. Or better: they celebrate the mercurial, slightly malicious pleasures of discontinuity. The first theme is unabashedly a jumble: three parallel but disjointed statements of a melodic fragment disjointed in itself (Example 3). For

36. Erich Leinsdorf, *The Composer's Advocate: A Radical Orthodoxy for Musicians* (New Haven, 1981), 10.

our purposes, the most telling effect of this material is to parody the devices that hold the first movement together. The rhythmic substance of the theme derives from the primary figure ♪♪♩, the note values of which are both repeated and augmented in the new tempo. As to motivic substance, the first thematic statement begins with a three-note motive, *c*, which reappears in inversion (*c'*) to begin the third statement; the second statement revives the earlier motive *b* in ascending form.

Fragmentation continues as the theme breaks down into a scurrying, spiky figuration that will prove to dominate the movement. Pairs of rising or falling sixteenth notes run up and down the keyboard, saw-toothed versions of the running sixteenth notes of the first movement. As in Op. 54, a decidedly physical, performative energy impels this music. Five times the spiky episode takes flight unaccompanied; in each case the episode begins with alternating right- and left-hand attacks on a series of identical two-note figures, so that the separation between the figures becomes an extension of the separation between the hands. Two of the passages also go on to demand some rapid-fire hand-crossing once the alternating attacks proceed between different figures. If the first movement glitters, this one spurts.

And as with melody, so here with structure. The exposition (see note 33) begins with an augmented sixth and proceeds to cadences on V and IV before reaching a cadence on I. This nonchalant treatment of the tonic is later elaborated on a larger scale with cheerfully vertiginous results. The close of the exposition (mm. 74–88) harps on the augmented sixth of IV; the recapitulation, which follows directly, takes this chord as a pretext to repeat the whole first group in the subdominant. Only at the end of the movement does the first group—and then only a piece of it—return in the tonic.

The sum of all these centrifugal forces is an essay in anarchic charm. Beethoven uses the second movement of Op. 78 to withdraw from the imaginary satisfactions, the implicitly unavailing longings, of the first. Not that the second devalues the first, as it does in Op. 54. Instead, the music exchanges an idyllic ideal for a less rarefied alternative: the haven of Romantic irony, in which the artist can savor the dissolution of a beautiful daydream no less than the daydream itself. This finale is a foray into that "poetical character" which, according to Keats, "has no character—it enjoys light and shade; it lives in gusto, be it foul or fair, high or low."[37] On this reading, we might expect the sonata to end exactly as it does: at the furthest possible remove from its evocative opening, with an unexpected frolic of the spiky figuration.

The Sonata in E Minor, Op. 90, reverses the temporal pattern of Op. 78, so that the idyll of its expansive finale transfigures the compressed drama that precedes it. The first movement opens with a strong internal conflict as its first theme splits into a rough declamation (mm. 1–8, itself divided into a forte/piano dialogue) and a flowing response in lyrical counterpoint (mm. 8–16). Classical sonata form usually reserves a cantabile answer to a more vigorous opening theme until the second theme initiates a swing to the dominant. By encapsulating the melodic drama of the form in its opening gesture, Beethoven suggests that the formal drama derives from something more primary, more subjective, and more difficult to control. Not surprisingly, the movement as a whole continually echoes its troubled opening; it proliferates into a wide variety of abruptly juxtaposed textures amid considerable agitation. The harmony is restless throughout, its free-floating tensions crowned by the use of the dominant minor for the decidedly noncantabile second theme. The movement does end quietly, dying away in a series of echo effects, but in terms haunted by latent unease. The closing passage is a repetition of the last eight measures of the first theme: music that leads in the exposition and recapitulation to a painfully bright outburst that thrusts the harmony from the tonic to the submediant. The prolonged rest that ends the movement thus tingles with an unsettled air of anticipation. The remembered sound of the submediant seems to loom faintly beyond the finality of the cadence.

The E-major finale is as serene a movement as Beethoven ever wrote, a rondo that traces idyllic circles by luxuriating in a double statement of its songful main theme, not just the first time the theme is heard, but every time. The instabilities and textural collisions of the first movement all but disappear in the enraptured suavity of this music. A rippling accompaniment runs through nearly every mea-

37. Letter to Richard Woodhouse, October 27, 1818; in *The Letters of John Keats*, ed. Maurice B. Forman, 4th ed. (Oxford, 1952).

sure, creating an aura of continuity even more palpable than its counterpart in Op. 78. Disruptive forces are admitted only once, in the central episode, where the unsettled accents of the first movement are revived and smoothed away. The episode begins by darkening unexpectedly. E major reverts to the earlier E minor (m. 103), which turns with a crescendo to the dominant of C, that is, V/VI. Then a broadly flowing theme, heard earlier during the first episode, returns four times in every possible form of E-major/minor submediant harmony (C, c, c♯, C♯; mm. 109–29). At once remote and rueful, these sonorities seem to bear out the uneasy submediant expectancy that hovers over the close of the first movement. Once realized, however, the troubling sonorities can also be resolved—and Beethoven resolves them without fuss, traveling easily down the circle of fifths to the home dominant (m. 129).

The second movement is now free to fulfill, by expressive doubling, the thwarted lyrical aspirations of the first. Just before the final statement of the rondo theme, Beethoven returns to the dominant of C and proceeds to the home dominant through ten measures of lyrical counterpoint (mm. 212–21). The same texture recurs just before the coda in a more crystalline version (mm. 266–75). The affinity between these passages—call them A and B—and mm. 8–16 of the first movement is striking enough in general terms, but it is not merely general. All three passages make use of common tones to link symmetrical phrase units in the upper voice (Example 4; passage A partly substitutes linking octaves to give B a more consummatory role). Heard in retrospect against passages A and B, the lyrical counterpoint of the first movement becomes a premonitory venture into the heart of idyllic time. A and B are the only extended episodes in the finale to suspend the rippling accompaniment. The result, however, is not a break in continuity but an enrichment of it; the counterpoint takes its impetus from a portion of the rondo theme and moves at the same pace as the theme. Stripped of embellishment, this melodic motion seems to embody the movement of idyllic time in its pristine form. The effect is particularly strong in passage B, which answers the movement to the dominant traced by both the counterpoint of the first movement and passage A. When B closes on a full cadence to the tonic, the E major that emerges is untouched by the tensions that fringe the earlier E minor. As the cadence sounds, the first phrase of

EXAMPLE 4.   Beethoven, Piano Sonata in E Minor, Op. 90. (A) First movement, lyrical counterpoint. (B) Second movement, first lyrical
counterpoint (Passage A). (C) Second movement, second lyrical counterpoint (Passage B).

the rondo theme returns, lingers, then yields to a lyrical codetta that brings the sonata to an end in undisturbed possession of its happiness.

And Op. 111? We can continue to speak of drama and idyll in this work, but only if we greatly enlarge the force of the terms. Commenting on the "incisive reworking of idyllic time and idyllic matrices" in Rousseau and his followers, Bakhtin observes that "the basic elements of the ancient complex—nature, love, the family and childbearing, death—are isolated and undergo sublimation at a higher philosophical level, where they are treated more or less as forms of the great, eternal, wise force of earthly life."[38] Bakhtin's remarks transfer remarkably well to Op. 111, with the qualification that Beethoven's sublimation is religious or quasi-religious as well as secular.

To review the well-known contour of the work: Beethoven begins by writing the fullest heroic movement of his late period, comparable in its turbulent intensity only to the finale of the Quartet in C♯ Minor, Op. 131, and the first movement of the Ninth Symphony. This Allegro con brio ed appassionato can be taken as an effort to sublimate, whether philosophically or psychologically, the negative and destructive aspects of music, its corybantic fury as opposed to its Orphean sweetness. Beethoven had taken up similar tasks before, but always over the full span of multimovement works like the Fifth Symphony, the *Appassionata* Sonata, the *Serioso* Quartet. Here the effort is compressed—contorted?—into a single terse all-or-nothing framework. What follows is a vast, serene Adagio: a set of variations on a theme that, writes Martin Cooper, "[in its] simplicity and static quality . . . suggests a spirit completely at rest, at peace with itself, not so much resigned to suffering as willingly accepting and transfiguring it into something that is indistinguishable from joy."[39]

The expressive doubling between these two movements is all but subliminal. It does not depend on the recurrence of musical textures like its counterparts in the three earlier sonatas, but on underlying affinities between textures as different as Beethoven can make them. These affinities have many sources, but the one about which the

38. Bakhtin, *Dialogic Imagination*, 230.
39. Martin Cooper, *Beethoven: The Last Decade* (London, 1970), 200.

others ultimately revolve is a referential sonority built from the strongest dissonance known to Classical harmony: the diminished-seventh chord.

In Op. 111, Beethoven takes the unprecedented step of giving primary structural value not just to a dissonance, but to a chromatically saturated aggregate consisting of all possible forms of the dissonance. In this case, of course, that means three forms, which I will arbitrarily designate as Dm7-1, -2, and -3. As Charles Rosen has shown, the Maestoso introduction to the sonata can be reduced to a series of three resolutions: Dm7-1 to the dominant, Dm7-2 to the tonic major, and Dm7-3 to the subdominant (minor).[40] The introduction closes with hints of a cyclical pattern, returning to the Dm7-1/V nexus before closing into the main Allegro. (The hint is dropped until the movement is nearly over—as we shall see.) Rosen describes the significance of what happens next:

> The main theme of the Allegro that follows is derived from these diminished-sevenths and their resolutions . . . [which also] provide a basis for [the] development, [where] the order of the chords is . . . always that of the introduction. The expressive significance of these chords needs no comment; they color most of the piece, occur with extreme violence at every important climax, and supply the dynamic impulse for most of the harmonic transformations.[41]

By building on so radically dissonant a foundation, Beethoven tests the limits of Classical sonata form. At the heart of the form is the resolution of structural dissonance. The effect of the diminished-seventh aggregate in the first movement of Op. 111 is to extend structural dissonance across a hierarchy of structural levels.[42] To resolve this extended dissonance is to venture the claim that no dissonance, musical or otherwise, is too extreme to be mastered. In this instance, the fulcrum of mastery is order: the fixed order of the diminished-seventh aggregate and its resolutions, an order always

40. Charles Rosen, *The Classical Style: Haydn, Mozart, Beethoven* (New York, 1972), 442–43. Robert K. Wallace (*Emily Brontë and Beethoven* [Athens, Ga., 1986], 109–15) also follows Rosen in emphasizing the role of diminished-seventh sonority in this movement.

41. Rosen, *Classical Style*, 444.

42. My thanks to Richard Swift for this point.

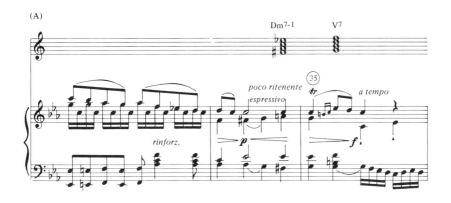

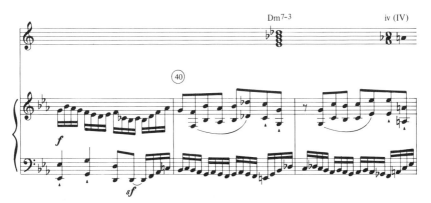

EXAMPLE 5.　Beethoven, Piano Sonata in C Minor, Op. 111. Allegro.

EXAMPLE 5 (*continued*)

EXAMPLE 5 (continued)

EXAMPLE 5 (continued)

present as a discipline even when it is concretized in fragments. Heroic discipline, however, is not always easy to tell apart from uncompromising rigidity. For all its formidable integrity, this music may be self-defeating in the end. Hence one of its most striking features: its extremely, even grotesquely, emphatic gestures of internal closure (Example 5c).

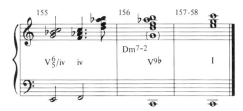

EXAMPLE 6.   Beethoven, Piano Sonata in C Minor, Op. 111. Closing measures of Allegro: outline.

As to final closure, the Allegro seeks it in a culminating gesture of
mastery that is deliberately astonishing—at once overwhelming and
not quite credible. The concluding measures do three things at once:
(1) they return to the resolution structure of the introduction; (2)
they detach the sonorities of the resolutions (V, I, and iv) from the
hegemony of the diminished-seventh aggregate; and (3) they state
these sonorities in a new order, corresponding to the unfulfilled
cyclical thrust that led from the introduction to the Allegro. The
process is outlined in Example 6. It begins with the diminished-
seventh aggregate, which enters forcefully over a tonic pedal and dies
away onto the subdominant major (mm. 146–49). The subdominant
minor then splits off on its own, assumes dramatic prominence, and
generates a cadence to the tonic major through Dm7-2, which is now
reinterpreted as a dominant. Thus the last tonic resolution in the
movement reenacts the first—a piece of unfinished business;[43] the
tonic major claims to quell the diminished-seventh aggregate, which
the minor could only perpetuate. In this context, all the C-minor
music and its extended derivatives appear to form little more than an
exaggerated episode—what the next chapter will identify as a dis-

43. I steal this term from Edward T. Cone, who explores its implications in his
"Schubert's Unfinished Business," *Nineteenth Century Music* 7 (1984): 222–32.

ruptive interlude. That the "interlude" amounts to just about the whole movement is, Beethoven seems to suggest, a mere detail.

The movement that follows is intended to make sense of that suggestion. Its variations seek to justify the (re)turn to the tonic major that closes the Allegro by expanding C major into a sonority so luminous and all-pervasive that it mirrors the return to the "elevated and pure source" evoked in Beethoven's 1815 diary entry. Behind this effort stands the traditional metaphor of the ideal mind or soul as harmonious music, as codified for the Middle Ages and beyond by Boethius. Boethius envisioned a *musica humana*: a perfect concord of body and spirit, reason and passion, formed by analogy to the *musica mundana*, the inaudible perfect harmony that governs the heavenly spheres.[44] Beethoven's variations set out to form a sustained elaboration of consonant harmonies, an "undisturbed song of pure concent," that can realize the figure of *musica humana* in actual sound: the *musica instrumentalis* that forms the third term in Boethius's system.

Beethoven may even have had Boethius specifically in mind. He composed Op. 111 while also working on the *Missa Solemnis*, and his work on the mass involved intensive research into the theory and practice of early music. As part of this project, he had a friend draw up abstracts from Boethius and other ancient authors.[45] Later, while at work on the Agnus Dei of the mass, he scribbled a note to himself: "Strength of the sentiments of inner peace above all."[46]

The same value governs the two-part form of Op. 111. At first, the Adagio seems simply to turn its back on the harshness of the Allegro; the contrast between the two movements could not be more extreme. Before long, however, denial turns to recognition and recognition to

44. "Boethius," *The New Grove Dictionary of Music and Musicians*, ed. Stanley Sadie (London, 1980), 2:844–45. See also John Hollander, *The Untuning of the Sky: Ideas of Music in English Poetry, 1500–1700* (Princeton, 1961), 3–51; and James Anderson Winn, *Unsuspected Eloquence: A History of the Relations Between Poetry and Music* (New Haven, 1981), 30–73. For an account of the workings of this conceptual matrix in another major work of Viennese Classicism, see my "Music and Representation: The Instance of Haydn's *Creation*," in *Text and Music: Critical Inquiries*, ed. Steven Paul Scher (Cambridge, forthcoming).

45. See Warren Kirkendale, "New Roads to Old Ideas in Beethoven's *Missa Solemnis*," in *The Creative World of Beethoven*, ed. Paul Henry Lang (New York, 1971), 163–99.

46. Ibid., 175n.

reenactment. The heroic discontinuities of the Allegro gradually submit to transfiguration by expressive doubling.

The recurrence of the diminished-seventh aggregate and its resolutions gives the first movement a basic periodic rhythm that cuts across the harmonic divisions of sonata form. The substance of this rhythm, however, is a series of disturbances, ruptures, shocks. Ruled by agitated fugal textures, the music repeats its fundamental pattern, its Schoenbergian *Grundgestalt*, in irregular surges, now sweeping, now constricted (Example 5a–c). No aspect of the music is left untouched by this process. The basic tempo of the Allegro is continually retarded and released; huge melodic leaps punctuate the texture at points of climax and closure; violent sforzandi on strong beats disrupt the metrical pulse in the act of affirming it. The unfolding of musical time, like the dissonant matrix that impels it, is at once unyielding and unstable.

In the wake of such turbulence, the limpid periodic rhythm of the slow movement, perfectly symmetrical in the theme, perfectly changeless through four variations, is extraordinarily consoling. The profoundly peaceful theme—Beethoven calls it an arietta, a little song—represents Classical binary form at its most transparent. Two eight-bar strains unfold in four-bar periods; each strain is repeated in the pattern AABB. The variations keep strictly to these proportions, and to much else. The underlying tempo of the arietta is never varied, even in passing—not a single accelerando or ritardando occurs in the whole movement—and the unvaried beat always falls three to a measure. The only dynamic element is the melodic motion, which continually quickens as the beat subdivides further with each variation. Countless sets of merely ornamental variations do the same thing, though rarely within such an austere framework. As Tovey liked to observe, however, Beethoven (like Bach) was never more serious than when he wrote such ornamentation, as the slow movements of the *Appassionata* Sonata, the Violin Concerto, the *Archduke* Trio, and the Ninth Symphony all attest.[47] In Op. 111, Beethoven reinterprets the "ornamental" increase in motion as a process that steadily enhances the expressiveness of the underlying harmony and

47. Donald Francis Tovey, *Essays in Musical Analysis: Symphonies and Other Orchestral Works*, rev. ed. (London, 1981), 110–17; idem, *Essays in Musical Analysis: Chamber Music* (London, 1944), 131–32.

rhythm. Something similar often happens in Wordsworth when objects are said to grow numinous while changing in no other way:

> Then sometimes in that silence, while he hung
> Listening, a gentle shock of mild surprize
> Has carried far into his heart the voice
> Of mountain torrents; or the visible scene
> Would enter unawares into his mind
> With all its solemn imagery, its rocks,
> Its woods, and that uncertain heaven, received
> Into the bosom of the steady lake.

> (*Prelude* [1805], 5.406–13)

The harmony of the arietta is simplicity itself. The tonic, dominant, and relative minor make up the structure, which is articulated by primary chords in the near absence of nonharmonic dissonance. The melodic lines elaborated over these harmonies match them in bareness; here, too, nonharmonic tones are extremely rare. The result is a basic sonority of crystalline purity and peacefulness. The successive variations strictly preserve the harmonic contours of the theme, but with each variation the melodic elaboration grows richer and more complex. On this level, new combinations of expressive dissonance evolve steadily, until the fourth variation pours them forth in unceasing profusion. By thus making the relationship between structure and ornament transparent, dynamic, and consummatory, Beethoven imparts a growing intensity to the primary harmonies—the imaginary sound, one might say, of brightening light as it scatters through a prism.

An analogous process enriches the periodic rhythm of the theme as the rhythmic surface of the music steadily grows more complex and agitated. Beethoven paces the changes in melodic motion so that the climactic fourth variation will inevitably arrive at what Rosen calls "almost undifferentiated pulsation," the borderline between melodic articulation and sheer continuity of sound. Heard against this barely rhythmicized trembling, the periodic rhythm sounds almost trance-like, the tidal swing of a musical wave motion. On both the smallest and the largest scales, the form of motion approaches the threshold of stillness.

In this way the consummation of the movement is prepared. The fourth variation overflows into a sort of cadenza in which everything changes at once (Example 7). The periodic rhythm dissolves, the harmony departs from C major for the first and only time in the movement, and the quickening motion crosses the border of measurable articulation into a series of trills—at the climax, a triple trill. Sustained over a dozen measures in unresolved dominant harmony (V and $V^7/\flat III$), the trills, as Rosen observes, suspend the flow of musical time[48]—though only, it must be added, on their own plane of action. Concurrently, a rapt strain of melody emerges, moving at the original pace of the arietta. This melody unfolds as an antiphony between bass and treble phrases that begin three octaves apart and draw closer by degrees. Bathed in the sound of the trills, the treble/bass exchanges form a perfect continuity, doubling and transfiguring the abyssal register leaps of the Allegro.

The closing downbeat of this process overlaps with the start of the triple trill, which holds the music perfectly static for two measures. The upper trill then detaches itself to form an unaccompanied unison with the melody; this rises in the treble until a forceful tone deep in the bass intrudes to herald a change. One more measure, and the trills resolve. The registral space expands to five open octaves, across which the treble and bass form a lyrical counterpoint based on measure 5 of the arietta. This counterpoint passes through dissonant combinations that would seem to place it worlds away from its origin, but the huge open interval virtually dispels the sensation of dissonance. The sonority intensifies with no loss of raptness or peace, expressively doubling both the pure consonance of the arietta and the harsh contrapuntal dissonance of the Allegro. It is worth noting that the association of "sentiments of inner peace" with wide registral separation seems to form Beethoven's privileged figure for divine revelation. Similar textures occur both in the Benedictus of the *Missa Solemnis* and the Adagio of the E-Minor String Quartet—a move-

---

48. Rosen, *Classical Style*, 448. Many commentators have stressed the effect of suspended time in these trills. As my qualifying remark above suggests, I take this effort to be a means to an end, not an end in itself. Beethoven, always the musician, seems to share T. S. Eliot's conviction: "Only through time time is conquered" ("Burnt Norton," 89). For a different view, see Wilfred Mellers, *Beethoven and the Voice of God* (New York, 1983).

EXAMPLE 7.   Beethoven, Piano Sonata in C Minor, Op. 111. "Cadenza" to Adagio.

ment, Beethoven told Carl Czerny, inspired by the sight of the starry sky and the thought of the music of the spheres.[49]

With the harmony and periodic rhythm of the arietta in abeyance, the consummatory passage of the Adagio doubles the surging temporality of the Allegro but frees it of all rigidity, rupture, tragic implacability. The ariettalike passage of musical time in a long, continuous arc of melody seems to give dynamic expression to something static in the trills—some all-pervasive presence of the kind that Wordsworth, in a remarkable act of transferred ambivalence, called "The sense of God, or whatso'er is dim / Or vast in [our] own being" (*Prelude* [1805], 13.72–73). This process culminates in the abrupt, but in no sense discontinuous, blossoming of the triple trill. Here the melody is reduced to a barely audible pulsation on a single pitch: not a contour traced in time, but the naked sound of passing time itself.[50] Like the "one life" that Wordsworth discovered at the apex of his Lake District boyhood, time reveals itself in this passage as a pure or primal music, an originary and ecstatic expressiveness:

> I was only then
> Contented when with bliss ineffable
> I felt the sentiment of being spread
> O'er all that moves. . . . Wonder not
> If such my transports were, for in all things
> I saw one life, and felt that it was joy;
> One song they sang, and it was audible,
> Most audible then when the fleshly ear . . .
> Forgot its functions and slept undisturbed.

(*Prelude* [1805], 2.418–21, 428–32, 434)

Song: arietta. Both Beethoven and Wordsworth substitute a figurative singing voice, a voice not heard by the ear, for the traditionally inaudible *musica mundana*. The voice finds its sounding medium in a distinctively Romantic version of *musica humana*: in "transports," overflows of joyous feeling, that become articulate in and through the rhythms of human time. Thus Wordsworth reinter-

49. Kirkendale ("New Roads," 188–90) connects the Benedictus with the quartet movement and cites Beethoven's often-quoted remark to Czerny.

50. For a discussion of such revelations of time, or "chronophanies," in Romantic works, see my *Music and Poetry*, 225–29.

prets "bliss ineffable" as expressive song; Beethoven restates the si-multaneity of the triple trill as the succession of melodic trills—three of them, each with a trilled upbeat. I would not put it past Beethoven to be thinking here in symbolic terms of triads and the Trinity. Given the self-consuming heroism of his Allegro, however, what matters most in the Adagio is something more immediate: an affirmation that the song of passing time is simple, radiant, and—astonishingly—benign.

The trills and their contrapuntal resolution aim at surpassing even the most idyllic mode of normal discourse. This more-than-utopian impulse is what compels the new harmonic color that emerges during the trills and continues through a dozen subsequent measures. The harmony here departs from C major only in order to prolong it with dazzling clarity. The structural purpose of the changing harmony is to defer an important cadence promised by the initial measures of trilling.[51] This deferral is realized as a progressive enrichment, a continuous assimilation of new sonorities in an accelerating har-monic rhythm. The trills establish temporal movement on the har-monic level as a plenitude: the plenitude continues—and expands—even after the trills have resolved. (One can hear in this a structural transcription of the accumulation of melodic dissonances in varia-tions 1–4). The outcome of this process is the reprise of the arietta, which coincides with the long-deferred cadence. The cadence itself is unobtrusive, rhythmically unmarked. Its effect is not to delimit, but to release; not to concenter the musical process that begins with the arietta, but to renew it.

The music that follows is meant to comprehend and affirm this act of renewal. In reprising the arietta, Beethoven also reprises the barely measurable pulsation of the fourth variation; the pulsation continues through a coda that once again floats away into twelve measures of trilling, this time in the tonic. As Rosen suggests, the latter passage forms "a synthesis of all that went before: the rhythmic accompani-ment of Variation IV (the fastest measured motion) and the theme in its original form (the slowest) are both suspended under the un-measured stillness of the trill."[52] The recapitulation of texture and

51. Tovey, *A Companion*, 278; Rosen, *Classical Style*, 447–48.
52. Rosen, *Classical Style*, 448.

resolution of harmony resembles the treatment of lyrical counterpoint in the finale of Op. 90, but here the recapitulation is more like a vivid memory, or even a metaphor, than like a new revelation. The harmony itself carries a secondary feeling. The earlier enhanced sonority is structurally dissonant, but its illocutionary force is to mirror a transcendent consonance. Like Wordsworth's spots of time, the consummatory passage is a nonpareil, recoverable only at a distance, in displaced forms. As the final trills draw to a close, a famous pair of exposed C–C♯ ninths make a wistful appearance, as if to acknowledge the necessity of this distance, this displacement.

The final trills have greater rhythmic definition than their earlier counterparts, but they are more than supple enough to consolidate the rhythmic work of the Adagio. In the secondary climax that the final trills provide, the expressive doubling of the Allegro's temporal character assumes a structurally stable form. As we know, the Allegro follows an irregular course set by the diminished-seventh aggregate. We might surmise, accordingly, that in doubling the irregularity Beethoven would also double the structural use of the aggregate. Diminished-seventh sonority is quite alien to the arietta: what role might it have as the variations proceed?

One answer is that a mere scarcity of diminished-seventh chords is refreshing after a movement rife with them; but more is at stake here than simple contrast. As Cooper and others have noted, the arietta and the first two variations form a continuous group. "Here," writes Cooper, "the music at first flows smoothly and then with a regular, gently dotted rhythm; and there are no forte . . . markings." With the third variation, "the mood changes suddenly. . . . If the mood of this variation is violent, it is a violent joy, a stamping dance of triumph."[53] As a sign of that triumph, Beethoven abruptly seizes upon the entire diminished-seventh aggregate and works it into the A section of the dance, where it adds a rather wicked insouciance to the general exhilaration (Example 8). The aggregate thus appears as what Bakhtin calls a "gay monster," a travesty of something terrifying by which carnivalesque jubilation casts all terror out.[54]

In the third variation, the contorted energy of the Allegro finds a

53. Cooper, *Beethoven*, 201.
54. Bakhtin, *Rabelais*, 91, 197.

catharsis, an explosive release from the struggle for heroic mastery. The antinomian festivity of this music, however, is in some ways as contorted as the Allegro itself. Its creative energy is too hard to separate from sublimated aggressiveness—a familiar problem in Romantic illocutions. The inspired figure at the close of Coleridge's "Kubla Khan" can serve as a literary parallel:

> And all should cry, Beware! Beware!
> His flashing eyes, his floating hair!
> Weave a circle round him thrice,
> And close your eyes with holy dread,
> For he on honey-dew hath fed,
> And drunk the milk of Paradise.

(49–54)

Gay monster or not, the diminished-seventh aggregate is still a source of blatant rupture here—so much so that the B section of the dance closes its eyes in holy dread and excludes all but a single fleeting appearance of Dm7-1. Nonetheless, certain terms have been set. The aggregate will be heard from again, and in music that will be called upon to reinterpret rupture as an image of transcendence.

The fourth variation resumes the serene unfolding of the movement. Here again, the A section sets forth the diminished-seventh aggregate, this time in the spirit of transferred ambivalence; stated and resolved off the beat, the chords ripple the flow of the music like stones lightly tossed in a stream. The diminished sevenths have a stronger, more lingering presence here than they do in the third variation, and some of their resolutions recall the resolution structure of the Allegro. As the music reaches the critical threshold between measured and unmeasured pulsation, its expressive doubling of the Allegro becomes richer, more explicit, more durable. Yet the reconciliation between the diminished-seventh sonority and the murmuring rapture of the music is also incomplete. In the fourth variation, the two halves of the theme are not simply repeated; they are varied further in the pattern AA'BB', with AB and A'B' in melodic parallel. In the A section, the full aggregate appears, but in the parallel B section, Dm7-3 is missing and Dm7-1 fails to resolve. More time must pass, or time pass differently, before the sonority of the variations can fully embrace a chromatic saturation by diminished-

EXAMPLE 8.   Beethoven, Piano Sonata in C Minor, Op. 111. Adagio: beginning of Variation 3.

seventh chords. Like a *Bildungsgeschichte*, the archetypally Romantic narrative of the self-education of consciousness, the musical process must find its way step by step.[55]

But the final steps are not far off. Following variation 4 the resolution of the consummatory trills leaves the music on the tonal plateau of E♭. At this point (m. 120) a transitional passage marked *espressivo* emerges (Example 9). Two more measures of E♭ assure a feeling of continuity; then the harmony begins to move. Simple sequences lead to C minor and A♭ major, then pass through further vicissitudes back to C minor again. Like the Rondo of Op. 90, the Adagio of Op. 111 plaintively revisits the parallel minor of its first movement, but in even more telling detail. A♭ major is the dominant-substitute of the earlier movement, and nestled in the circle of the interlude is something further: the diminished-seventh aggregate. Two of the diminished chords engage in the second swing to C minor; the third chord initiates a counterswing to C major and the reprise of the arietta.

In the aftermath of its consummation, then, the Adagio transfigures the diminished-seventh aggregate in the fullest possible terms. The final expressive doubling both incorporates and resolves the C-minor tonality in which the aggregate formed the nerve center of conflicting forces—turbulence and control, impulsiveness and rigidity. In turning to C minor, the Adagio reveals a previously unacknowledged gap in its effort to sublimate the tensions of the Allegro. In filling that gap, however, the C-minor music acts as a "plenitude enriching another plenitude"; it completes the harmonic enrichment of C major that originates during the trills. This is just the mode of ambivalence that Derrida calls the logic of the supplement.[56] And it is just this music of the supplement from which the arietta re-emerges in its original form, but supplemented in its own right by the accompaniment that pulses beneath it.

The *espressivo* passage reveals itself fully only in detail. On its three previous appearances in the Adagio, the diminished-seventh aggregate has been stated asymmetrically, and in successions unrelated to

---

55. On the successive stages of Romantic *Bildung*, see Abrams, *Natural Supernaturalism*, 187–95.

56. Derrida, *Of Grammatology*, 144–45.

EXAMPLE 9.   Beethoven, Piano Sonata in C Minor, Op. 111. *Espressivo* passage of Adagio.

the order of the chords established in the Allegro. On this occasion, however, the chords form a balanced pair of couplets, beginning with Dm7-3, the chord that disappeared from the fourth variation:

Measure:	126			127			128				129			130		
Beat:	1	2	3	1	2	3	1	2	3		1	2	3	1	2	3
Dm7:	Dm7-3		Dm7-2[a]				Dm7-2		Dm7-1[b]					Dm7-1[b]		
C/c:		IV⁶			i			i							V	

[a]Two notes missing.

[b]One note missing. (This fragmentary form of Dm7-1 carries over from m. 128³ to m. 130¹, resolving to V in m. 130². M. 129 isolates and accentuates the couplet

pattern of mm. 126–28 before the latter resolves; a G in the bass of m. 129^2 prefigures the resolution.)

The breaking up of the second chord in each couplet suggests a final end to conflict. In each case, the fragmentary chord is completed (and confirmed in its identity) by the chord following, the two together filling out a strangely consoling dominant minor-ninth. It is as if the aggregate were dissolving, blending into the "one song" all around it. Concurrently, the chords of the aggregate once more form a meaningful succession—the retrograde of their order in the Allegro. Even the earlier resolution structure (with changes of mode) returns in retrograde, each resolution set within the second beat of the measure: Dm7-3 resolves to IV, Dm7-2 twice progresses to I, and Dm7-1 begins (and frames) the final precadential progression to V. It is as if the emotional and structural violence of the Allegro were being undone, worked through in the Freudian sense, piece by piece. Each wound receives its balm, last to first, until a pristine motion and harmony—those of the arietta—are restored.

Perhaps the most important point that can be made about this restoration is that it leads to a chain of others. The reprise of the arietta overlaps into a free variation that combines the arietta's signature rhythm with the unforced rhythmic animation that doubles the animation of the Allegro (mm. 146–59). This in turn evolves into the reprise of the consummatory trills, which is also a second reprise of the arietta. The trilled reprise even leads to a miniature fantasy on the B section of variation 4 en route to the closing passage.

This chain of reprises can be understood both affirmatively and critically in relation to the program of Romantic esthetics. The utopian *Bildungsgeschichte* typically identifies its goal as the repossession and sublimation of a blissful origin. The origin, accordingly, achieves its originary value only when it is also an end, "comprehended essentially as result," in Hegel's phrase.[57] Beethoven exemplifies this type of return in the finale of his Piano Sonata in E Major, Op. 109, a set of variations that closes, after a long chain of trills,

---

57. Hegel's formulation appears in the Preface to his *Phenomenology of Mind*; the concept is one of the most widespread of the era. For discussion, see Abrams, *Natural Supernaturalism*, 179–187, 199–292. It should be noted, however (and often has been), that Abrams's account is insufficiently distanced from the concepts it addresses.

with an essentially literal reprise of its cantabile theme. In what may be a pointed contrast, the Adagio of Op. 111 ends by fragmenting the signature rhythm of the arietta—ends, that is, by undoing its origin. The Adagio defers a cyclical close on the model of Op. 109 in favor of a generalized, heterogeneous movement of reorigination. The effect is best conveyed by recalling once more Beethoven's 1815 diary entry: "I returned . . . to the elevated and pure source, to the Godhead. —And, to your art." One reprise entails another; no source is *the* source.

In large-scale terms, the recurrence of the diminished-seventh aggregate in the Adagio of Op. 111 can be said to find its extended resolution in the chain of reprises. This resolution coalesces with the exaltation of note motion that impels the series of variations; the "almost undifferentiated pulsation" that resumes with the reprise of the arietta continues unabated thereafter, ceasing only with the onset of the closing passage.

The cultural implications of this structure are highly charged. Romantic utopianism has been attacked by twentieth-century critics for harboring a latent absolutism. The argument runs that utopian esthetics can too easily be perverted into an "esthetic ideology" that is complicit with repressive and even totalitarian attitudes.[58] The esthetic ideology seeks to establish purity and elevation by repressing difference, heterogeneity, discontinuity. The results can be stifling for art; for history and society, they can be calamitous. The Adagio of Op. 111, however, with its thorough and rigorous traversal of the diminished-seventh aggregate, its heterogeneous chain of reprises, suggests that at least one version of Romantic utopianism is critical or vigilant enough to forestall the esthetic ideology. Far from repressing difference, the music insists on difference, and in so doing constitutes an implicit critique of the ideological tendency that may taint the utopian impulse.[59]

58. For discussion, see Jonathan Culler, " 'Paul de Man's War' and the Aesthetic Ideology," *Critical Inquiry* 15 (1989): 777–83. Richard Taruskin's "Resisting the Ninth," *19th-Century Music* 12 (1989): 214–56, raises similar issues in specific connection with Beethoven's Ninth Symphony. The Ninth is a crux of particular importance for Romantic utopianism, because its vehicle of progress is joy, a category (to use the psychoanalytic dualism) of pleasure rather than of reality.

59. For more on Beethoven's utopianism, see Solomon, *Beethoven*, 309–16, and *Beethoven Essays*, 214–15, 221–22.

A similar mixture of affirmation and critique can be taken to extend to utopian desire itself. The weight of diminished-seventh sonority in Beethoven's Adagio suggests that the desired "sentiments of inner peace" may be merely cherished illusions, even escapist illusions. Many of the works considered in this chapter find means to suggest the same thing: the easily shattered reflection of the ram in Wordsworth's "peaceful flood", the delicate lyrical counterpoint in the Rondo of Op. 90, the wind-blown images in Shelley's forest pool. There exists, indeed, an extended family of Romantic images in which the realization of desire all but coincides with the repression of disappointment. I have in mind those images of suspended loss, of deferred privation, that so often articulate moments of fullness in Romantic literature:

> Who hath not seen thee oft amid thy store?
>   Sometimes whoever seeks abroad may find
> Thee sitting careless on a granary floor,
>   Thy hair soft-lifted by the winnowing wind . . .
>   Or by a cyder-press, with patient look,
>   Thou watchest the last oozings hours by hours.
>   (Keats, "To Autumn," 12–15, 21–22)

> Grant me a single summer, you lords of all,
>   A single autumn, for the fullgrown song,
>   So that, with such sweet playing sated,
>   Then my heart may die more willing.
>   (Hölderlin, "To the Fates," 1–4)

> Four years and thirty, told this very week,
> Have I been now a sojourner on earth,
> And yet the morning gladness is not gone
> Which then was in my mind.
>   (Wordsworth, *Prelude* [1805], 6.61–64)

Images like these implicitly acknowledge that the process of idealization, the one indispensable element in all expressive doubling, all utopian esthetics, is an effect of desire before it is an effect of knowledge. The result is that the images demystify themselves in the very act of satisfying their audience—or, rather, they satisfy in the very act of demystification. To use the language of Paul de Man, as rhetoric these images mask loss as a metaphor of fullness, while as reference they arrest—but not indefinitely—the moment of loss.[60] Either way, their force is to preserve the possibility of idealization by giving disappointed desire the wherewithal to continue.

60. See Paul de Man, "Intentional Structure of the Romantic Image," in *The Rhetoric of Romanticism* (New York, 1984), 1–18.

3

IMPOSSIBLE OBJECTS:

Apparitions, Reclining Nudes, and Chopin's Prelude in A Minor

"Oh! no, indeed, this [Prelude in A Minor] is no concert piece," wrote André Gide. "I cannot see any audience liking it. But played in a whisper for oneself alone, its definable emotion cannot be exhausted, nor [a] kind of almost physical terror."[1] Gide's proposal to turn Chopin's baffling miniature into a pretext for private reflection is less a solipsistic gesture than a helpless one. The Prelude in A Minor positively resists both esthetic and analytic understanding. Much of it is deliberately ugly by early-nineteenth-century standards, and arguably by ours. Its harmonic processes are perplexing by any standards. Latent continuities can be teased out of the piece, as out of most others, but the value of doing so is questionable. The A-Minor Prelude is not enigmatic on a measure-by-measure basis, despite an important block of undecidable harmonies. It is not riddling but disruptive: it repeatedly breaks away from structural or textural patterns while maintaining a deceptive uniformity in melody and accompaniment. From a hermeneutic standpoint, the question that needs to be asked of this music is not what deep structure holds it together, but rather what motivates it to keep breaking apart. I will try to give some answers to that question in the present chapter,

1. From Gide's *Notes on Chopin*, cited in the Norton Critical Score: *Preludes, Op. 28*, ed. Thomas Higgins (New York, 1973), 96.

answers that gradually ramify to include the ill-assorted items named in my title. As one interpretive pathway after another opens up, so should most of the musical processes at work in the prelude—and so, too, should a group of culturally ascendant models for representing the very things that André Gide singles out in his little aperçu: the reflecting mind and the reflected body.[2]

I

Like several other pieces in Chopin's Op. 28, the Prelude in A Minor unfolds by negating its own apparent premises. It begins with two measures of glaringly dissonant accompaniment figuration; it ends after completing two strains of smooth, sinuous melody from which almost all accompaniment has fallen away (mm. 17–18, 20–22; Example 10). Taking this framework as a hermeneutic window, we might try to understand the prelude itself as a study in reversal or, more precisely, as a study in dialectic, conceived of in nineteenth-century terms as a series of dynamic oppositions that lead to reversals of meaning or value.[3]

Romantic writers tend to associate dialectical reversals with heightenings of subjective intensity—ideally, with advances in insight or self-possession, but more often with mental pain. The closing stanzas of Keats's "Ode to a Nightingale" are exemplary:

7.

Thou wast not born for death, immortal bird!
No hungry generations tread thee down;
The voice I hear this passing night was heard
In ancient days by emperor and clown. . . .
[Perhaps] the same that oft-times hath

2. For another attempt to link the problematical features of the A-Minor Prelude to nineteenth-century culture, see Rose Rosengard Subotnik, "Music as Post-Kantian Critique: Classicism, Romanticism, and the Concept of the Semiotic Universe," in *On Criticizing Music*, ed. Kingsley Price (Baltimore, 1981), 87–95. Subotnik carries her argument further in "On Grounding Chopin," in *Music and Society: The Politics of Composition, Performance, and Reception*, ed. Richard Leppart and Susan McClary (Cambridge, 1987), 105–32.

3. My formulation here is loosely Hegelian. For an overview of dialectical thought in the Romantic period, see M. H. Abrams, *Natural Supernaturalism: Tradition and Revolution in Romantic Literature* (New York, 1971), 174–77 and passim.

EXAMPLE 10. Chopin, Prelude in A Minor, Op. 28, no. 2.

Charm'd magic casements, opening on the foam
Of perilous seas, in faery lands forlorn.

8.

Forlorn! The very word is like a bell
To toll me back from thee to my sole self!

The chiasmatic structure of this passage is complex in detail but
clear in outline; it can be schematized roughly by saying that the pair
immortal bird/faery lands forlorn is reversed by the pair *Forlorn! The very
word/sole self.* Stanza 7 begins with an apostrophe to the nightingale
that posits a fantasy of immortality; as it closes, the stanza seeks to
stabilize the fantasy in the image of the faery lands forlorn that are
enchanted by the nightingale's song. Stanza 8 disrupts this effort by
turning the evocative term *forlorn* into a memento mori that "tolls"
the poet back to disenchantment and the sole (singular, solitary,
one-and-only) self. (Tolls: like a passing bell, a clock chime, or the
morning bells traditionally said to banish faery spirits.) The reversals
encompassed here are both psychological and epistemological. Fantasy gives way to consciousness of fantasizing; absorption in poetic
imagery, to consciousness of poetry as language; and consciousness
itself, to self-consciousness.

Dialectical reversals can also embrace unconscious processes,
though they typically do so with a certain transparency. The epilogue
to Coleridge's *Christabel* includes a good example:

A little child, a limber elf,
Singing, dancing to itself,
A fairy thing with red round cheeks,
That always finds, and never seeks,
Makes such a vision to the sight
As fills a father's heart with light;
And pleasures flow in so thick and fast
Upon his heart, that he at last
Must needs express his love's excess
With words of unmeant bitterness.

(656–65)

The surprising close of this passage derives from a double twist of dialectic. Wrought to excess, the father's love expresses itself in the form of anger. Pleasure comes all too "thick and fast"; it turns into a feeling of suffocation that demands a violent release. Meanwhile, the father's pleasure is vexed by more than its own excess. "Singing, dancing to itself," the child—who hovers imponderably between the fictional Christabel and Coleridge's own son, Hartley—acts out a blissful self-sufficiency. As the terms *fairy thing* and *elf* suggest, the father is enchanted by this, but he is also dispossessed by it, as if the child were a changeling. More than that, he is stricken with a pang of unconscious envy: the resentment of the adult who has lost the art of always finding and never seeking. Coleridge's term *unmeant bitterness* thus needs a certain Freudian revision. The bitterness is unmeant only by the father's conscious ego, which represses his defeated longing to become once more the "limber elf" of his own childhood. The father's words form an unconscious speech act; their aim is not so much to rebuke as to *address* the child, to intrude on the undivided self-address of its singing and dancing to itself.

A first approach to Chopin's A-Minor Prelude might link the music both to Keats's conscious and Coleridge's unconscious dialectics. Keats's contrast between the untroubled nightingale and his own much-troubled mind loosely resembles Chopin's contrast between plaintive melody and abrasive accompaniment. Both contrasts seem to raise the same question: Is pure songfulness a consolation or a lie? Meanwhile, the process by which Chopin arrives at the most basic reversal in the prelude—the reversal from unmelodized accompaniment to unaccompanied melody that frames the work—can be taken to suggest the same sort of unconscious conflict that Coleridge renders transparent. The accompaniment figuration plies its angular monotony for sixteen measures, then abruptly stops while the melody continues unimpeded. On its return (m. 18^3), the accompaniment seems damaged, uncertain; the tempo slackens, and the pedal, used only here, dulls the once hard-edged sonority. A silence quickly intervenes (m. 19^3); then the melody returns without accompaniment and leads the piece to a close. Given the expressive polarity that divides the melody from the accompaniment, it is tempting to hear the vacillation between the two as a musical analogue to the psychological defense mechanism known as doing and undoing—the classical manifestation of unacknowledged ambivalence.[4]

Taking these first surmises as points of orientation, we can begin to probe more deeply into the musical processes of the prelude. On the largest scale, dialectical movement appears in this piece as a gradually unfolding antagonism between melody and harmony. Melodically, the prelude consists of two parallel statements of a slowly descending theme, which itself consists of two parallel strains. During the first statement (Example 10, mm. 3–12), the melodic line is made up essentially of chord tones, and the melodic cadence of the first strain coincides with the first harmonic cadence (m. 6). As the second strain concludes, however, the accompanying harmony suddenly vaporizes into ambiguity just at the point where a cadence is expected (m. 11). The second melodic statement (mm. 14–21) is basically an elaboration of (local) dissonances, which, as we have seen, twice silences the previously implacable accompaniment. At first an articulation of the harmony, the melody evolves into the antithesis of the harmony.

This reversal rests on a group of important background processes.[5] In his analysis of the A-Minor Prelude, Leonard B. Meyer points out that the large-scale melodic design is based on the establishment, disruption, and resumption of a process—the linking of melodic phrases by common tones—while the harmonic design involves the "decisive" disruption of a process that is not resumed—the harmonic progression established at the outset (mm. 1–7).[6] Meyer calls this relationship between melody and harmony a parallelism, but it is more like an incongruity, and the prelude unfolds by turning it into a many-sided process of dissociation. Not only do the harmonic and melodic articulations of form pursue different courses, but they are also asynchronous—indeed, asynchronous twice over. Melodically, the breakdown of common-tone linkage divides the prelude at m. 14^2, where the disruptive melody-note, A, begins the process that

---

4. This defense mechanism was first described by Freud in his case history of the "Rat Man"; see Freud, *Three Case Histories*, ed. Philip Rieff (New York, 1963), 50–51.

5. The terms *background* and *foreground* are used throughout this chapter in a generalized, not necessarily Schenkerian, way to mark off relative degrees of structure and ornament.

6. Leonard B. Meyer, *Emotion and Meaning in Music* (Chicago, 1956), 93–97.

stabilizes the large-scale structure.[7] By contrast, the original harmonic cycle breaks down at m. 11 during a melodic cadence, where
the disruptive chord begins the process that *destabilizes* the large-
scale structure. Similarly, the melodic shape of the work is defined by
a pair of equal and parallel periods (mm. $1–12^2$, $12^3–23$). Each of
these begins with bare accompaniment figuration and overlays it with
the slowly descending melodic line. Harmonically, the piece divides
into unequal and complementary segments at the junction of mm. 14
and 15, where the tonic-to-be materializes for the first time out of
what has come to seem hopeless tonal ambiguity.

Only in the last two and a half measures are melody and harmony
realigned, but here they are not so much reconciled as fused together,
rendered indistinguishable from each other as the second melodic
statement becomes the upper voice of the block-chord progression
that acts as a coda. The arpeggios introduced at the last moment
(mm. $22^3–23$) dramatize this conflation of antithetical elements.
After teasing melody and harmony further and further apart, the
prelude closes by collapsing the difference between them. It is suggestive that only at this point of expressive collapse do we get a tonic
cadence,[8] so that in some sense the cadence completes the composition less than it negates it. This feeling of forced termination is
heightened by the rather intrusive effect of the unembellished block
chords, which usurp the place of the fantastically dissonant accompaniment figuration and thus call attention to the formulaic, in
context even archaic, quality of the closing cadential pattern.

The unresolvable clash between melody and harmony represents
Chopin's way of staging a larger dialectic between Classical authority
and Romantic innovation—a dialectic whose very definition preju-
dices it in favor of Romanticism. The melodic design of the prelude
pays homage to the Classical demands for balance and resolution,

---

7. $M. 14^2 = m.$ 14, beat 2. The details of large-scale stabilization (from m. 14^2)
and destabilization (from m. 11) are discussed below.

8. *Pace* Meyer, who calls the $ii_4^{6\sharp}–i_4^6$ progression in A minor at mm. 14–15
a cadence (*Emotion and Meaning*, 96). Even if one were not to argue about the
harmonies, there is no rhythmic articulation of a cadence at this point.

particularly the symmetrical resolution that Charles Rosen sees as central to the Classical style.[9]

The second melodic statement can be heard as a resolution of the first at two levels of structure. Ignoring a grace note in m. 10, the first statement uses only a single pitch, F♯, that is foreign to the eventual tonic, A minor. This F♯ becomes increasingly prominent, and the statement closes with four repetitions of it after descending a fourth from A to E (mm. 10–11). When the second statement begins, it repeats the A–E descent and proceeds to F♮, pointedly resolving the preceding F♯'s (mm. 14–16). Pointedly too, this F♮ is imposed as a dissonance on the tonic six-four harmony at this point, where it marks the decisive separation of melody and harmony in the work. It is striking that another resolution of F♯ to F♮ has occurred in the bass slightly earlier (m. 14^3), with the effect of stabilizing the harmony that has been disrupted since m. 11. The melody repeats and in effect appropriates the harmonic resolution to F♮, whereupon the F♮ turns into a source of harmonic tension.

At a more background level, the resolution of one melodic statement by another depends on the structural use of a single interval. As Michael Rogers has pointed out, the first melodic statement articulates the descent of a minor seventh (E to F♯), and the second statement mirrors this descent (as A to B) through measure 21.[10] In the little block-chord coda to the piece, the second statement is extended to fill out the entire tonic octave A–A (Example 11, p. 93). Given the tacked-on nature of the coda, we might expect Chopin to support the large-scale melodic resolution on another process, and this he does. The first descent of a seventh is a structural but not a registral event; the second descent is both. Resolution occurs when structure becomes perceptually explicit in the context of the tonic.

As my account may already have suggested, the melodic half of Chopin's dialectic in the A-Minor Prelude is itself conceived dialec-

9. Charles Rosen, *The Classical Style: Haydn, Mozart, Beethoven* (New York, 1972), 99.

10. Michael Rogers, "Rehearings: Chopin, Prelude in A Minor," *19th-Century Music* 4 (1981): 244–49.

tically. In keeping with its classicizing impulse, what might be called
the melodic prelude identifies dialectical reversal with structural resolution. In the process, it even approximates the figure of chiasmus
in its large-scale design. The chiasmatic pairs are formed by the tones
that outline the structural sevenths, E–F♯/A–B. The first pair is best
described by negation. The E is harmonized by the E-minor triad, a
sonority that could be, but is not, altered to form the dominant of A
minor; the F♯ is harmonically undecidable. The second pair fills in
the gaps imposed by the first. The A, the longest melody note in the
piece and the only syncopated one, banishes undecidability and affirms the tonic; the B is harmonized by the previously "missing"
dominant of A minor.

By casting his melodic reversals as resolutions, Chopin suggests
that even a music of doing and undoing can stabilize itself in the light
of tonal laws. And if dialectic always posits a subject, an "I," of the
dialectic, then that suggestion can be rewritten as the claim that
subjective intensity is not doomed to collapse into either self-
consciousness or unconsciousness.

The harmony of the prelude has other ideas. Like the melody, it
forms a dialectic in its own right, but not one much given to stabilizing itself. Anticlassical and antinomian, the harmonic prelude
carries the process of reversal to a dizzying extreme.[11]

Consider first the large-scale tonal plan. The prelude makes only
two full cadences, one in G major, the other in A minor.[12] The two
keys divide the piece, but only by disjunction; they must be understood as utterly unrelated to each other. In particular, G does *not*
represent the flat seventh degree of A, to be related to A via plagal

11. Rogers (ibid.) points to a latent Classical element by suggesting that the
harmony of the prelude is aligned with a formal segmentation based on golden
sections. If Rogers is right, Chopin may be tacitly (intuitively?) placing a limit on
the harmonic disruption that he explicitly cultivates.

12. The piece is sometimes said to begin in E minor, but it would be more
accurate to say that it begins *as if* in E minor. The E-minor triads of mm. 1–3 form
a static tonal level, not a key. Although they feint at marking a tonic, their only
confirmed function is vi of G—a fact that led Schenker to declare unequivocally that
the prelude begins in G major (Heinrich Schenker, *Harmony*, ed. and annot. Oswald
Jonas, trans. Elizabeth Mann Borgese [Cambridge, Mass., 1973], 252). Those with
a more monotonal view of tonal music than my own might prefer to speak of
cadences *to* G minor or other tonal levels.

movement through D major. Such a movement, initiated in mm. 9–10, is emphatically aborted by the harmonic mishap in m. 11, which begins with an alteration of D to D♯ and evolves into a series of undecidably ambiguous chords. The harmonic process is now driven implacably by the problematical D♯, which sounds on every beat in mm. 11–14. The harmonies are successively modified until the D♯ fits into a chord with directional value, a French sixth that flickers to life as m. 14 ends. A minor then simply emerges from the morass and demands to be considered the tonic.

Several dialectical determinations converge on these events. The harmonically undecidable chain of chords in mm. 11–14 represents an enhanced form of the most conspicuous feature of mm. 1–10, the grating nonharmonic dissonance of the accompaniment. With the appearance of the chain of chords, the normal relationship of structure to ornament is reversed. The dissonance can no longer be rendered coherent by subordination to an underlying harmony, while the harmony of the prelude as a whole is—in Classical terms—rendered incoherent by subordination to the dissonance. At best, the juxtaposition of G major and A minor that results might be understood, taking A as the tonic, as a harmonic articulation of the structural interval of the minor seventh that underpins the melodic design. The G-major cadence in mm. 5–6 can be heard to reach its long-term resolution (or at least its undoing) when its melody makes an essentially note-for-note return in mm. 20–21 in the context of A minor. In each case, the A–B step that brings about the melodic cadence also completes the large melodic descent of a minor seventh. The distribution of harmonies would thus seem to be modeled on the intervallic design of the melodies without reference to the principles of Classical tonality. And this produces yet another dialectical irony, since it is the melodic design alone that links the piece to the Classical style.

The harmonic details of the Prelude are no less vertiginous than its broad architecture. And whereas the melodic prelude tends to *identify* resolution with reversal, the harmonic prelude tends to *replace* resolution with reversal as the dynamic principle of the music.

In its first ten measures, the prelude follows what seems to be a cyclical harmonic process, more or less as described by Meyer:

G: vi I^6_4 V   I   iii

D: vi I^6_4 V

The submediant chords in this progression provoke uncertainty; the six-four chords impart clarity. The initial sonorities of G major and D major assume their submediant character only in the light of subsequent six-four harmony. The six-four chords, though unstable as local dissonances, orient and stabilize the larger harmonic structure.

Following the harmonic collapse of mm. 11–14, these values are reversed. Clarification now comes not from a six-four chord but from a fictitious submediant, namely the French sixth at m. 14^4, which stands in for the earlier submediant chords by the placement of its bass note on the sixth degree of the minor scale. The placement is emphasized by the important F♯–F♮ step in the bass at m. 14^{2-3}. A musical pun of sorts is at work here (Chopin reverts to it elsewhere in the preludes) that conceives of a technically supertonic sonority as an intensified submediant.[13] The French sixth now acts exactly as the six-four chords did in mm. 4 and 9—that is, as a dissonant point of arrival that gives the music its tonal bearings. Concurrently, the A-minor six-four chord of m. 15 surrenders that very same role: it joins the forces of destabilization by deferring the resolution of the French sixth.

This role reversal is subsequently compounded as the six-four harmony, which on both of its earlier appearances had resolved without much delay, is subjected to a long and dissonant prolongation. Chopin now opens out the inherent instability of the chord and converts it into a source of such drastic tension that the newly achieved tonic quality of A minor is actually thrown into doubt.

II

What motivates this web of dialectic reversals, this self-interfering mesh of ironies? One answer lies in the position of the A-Minor Prelude in the cycle of preludes as a whole. Part of Chopin's purpose in the cycle is to confront the classical foundations of musical co-

13. Other instances are noted in my *Music and Poetry: The Nineteenth Century and After* (Berkeley and Los Angeles, 1984), 94, 102.

herence by putting them under stress from a wide variety of sources.[14] With the A-Minor Prelude, he does this to the main principle of coherence of the cycle itself, the arrangement of the pieces around a double circle of fifths that pairs each major key with its relative minor. The cyclical process starts with the Preludes in C Major and A Minor. By holding back the identity of its tonic, the A-Minor Prelude defers the recognition of the inaugural major-minor pair. More than that, by suggesting G major as a tonic in its opening measures the prelude even makes a feint at the *wrong* circle of fifths, a single movement through the major keys.

Within the prelude itself, Chopin seems to be pondering the relationship between subjectivity—more particularly the too-keen subjectivity of dialectic—and musical time, which in this case means time as harmonized. By beginning in medias res with uncertain harmonies and employing six-four chords to resolve them, Chopin in mm. 1–7 highlights one of the distinct privileges of tonal music: the establishment of musical meaning by means of an integrative process that combines recollection and anticipation. The parallel design of mm. 7^3–9 confirms that this heightened shuttling before and after the immediate moment is, so to speak, the subtext of the G-major half of the piece. Recollective movement then shatters against the harmonic brick wall of mm. 11–14, and musical time now shapes itself by anticipation alone. The French sixth of m. 14 has no functional relationship to anything that precedes it. The chord can be recognized at all only because of its distinctive whole-tone sonority, and its only role is to issue the demand that A emerge as the tonic. The A-minor six-four chord that follows is, of course, equally proleptic; it arouses a harmonic expectation that rises in intensity to an almost anxiety-laden expectancy as the chord ceases to sound and the mandatory dominant resolution is deferred. The slowing of tempo that ensues as the first melodic strain leads *away* from the dominant adds a notable turn of the screw. But the peak of tension, and the astonishing climax of the piece, comes in the full silence that occupies the second half of m. 19, a moment in which the musical fabric is constituted entirely by the listener's heightened expectation of a

14. For a full discussion of this aspect of the preludes, see ibid., 92–95, 99–104.

dominant chord. The moment is so supercharged that more than one pianist has defended against it by holding the pedal down to the end of the measure.

Anticipation without recollection is a possible definition of desire. Romantic poetry in particular is full of passages that construe desire as pure prolepsis, from Wordsworth's definition of the human as "Effort, and expectation, and desire, / And something evermore about to be," to Goethe's injunction, "Schneller als die Gegenstände / Selber dich vorüberfliehn!" ("Swifter than the objects / Flee past your [present] self!"). In the same spirit, the structure of concentrated anticipation at the core of the A-minor Prelude refashions the tonic of the Classical style in the image of desire. There is no longer a "home key," a tonal center that is (or seems) intrinsic to the music; there is simply what the ear wants to hear, what it cannot bear not to hear. And yet, in one last reversal, the cadential pattern that closes the prelude is distinctly disappointing when it arrives, muffled by the motionlessness of its upper voice and depreciated by the conventionality of its block chords. The silence in m. 19 informs us that Keats was right: heard melodies are sweet, but those unheard are sweeter. Romantic desire always expects something . . . else.

III

To review our findings thus far, Chopin's dialectical design in the A-Minor Prelude relocates the focus of specific musical actions (not just general effects) from the object to the subject: in the melodic prelude by an idealized union, and in the harmonic prelude by a radical disjunction. Similar reorientations are basic, even in their similar internal contradictions, to most Romantic critiques of language and knowledge. The underlying attitude is epitomized by Wordsworth's claim that a world of objects uninformed by subjectivity constitutes "a universe of death" (*Prelude* [1850], 14.160). But other aspects of Chopin's design remain to be considered; we can go much further than this.

Why, in particular, does Chopin incorporate his multiple dialectical patterns within a single continuous texture? And why has he combined so many different patterns, superimposing them on one another in a kind of loose conceptual polyphony? One answer lies in the recognition of a structural trope that forms or pictures what might be called impossible objects—taking the term *object* to refer to the target of powerful feelings, as in the phrase *object of desire*. Objects in this sense are usually symbolic representations of persons, in which form they figure prominently in psychoanalysis. What I call an impossible object is a body or body-substitute (image, body part, sensory presence) with three salient characteristics: (1) it is excessive either in beauty or deformity; (2) it arrests an observer by its irrevocable strangeness; (3) it exerts a fascination that arouses desire, repulsion, or both at once. The curious magnetism of impossible objects has its roots in the same self-consciousness that propels Romantic dialectic; the objects act either as self-images or as erotic ideals for those who confront them.

An account of impossible objects in their own right will occupy us for the next several pages. The digression, however, is only apparent, a necessary corollary of the kind of study I am attempting here. What follows is meant to help establish a cultural position for the A-Minor Prelude, and to develop ways of understanding further musical details.

Perhaps the best introduction to the impossible object is a little parable by Kafka called "A Crossbreed," which tells of a "curious animal, half kitten, half lamb," who at times "insists almost on being a dog as well," and may also have "the ambitions of a human being." Among many remarkable things pertaining to his relationship with this animal, Kafka's narrator singles out one occasion

> when, as may happen to anyone, I could see no way out of my business problems and all that they involved, and was ready to let everything go, and in this mood was lying in my rocking chair in my room, the beast on my knees[.] I happened to glance down and saw tears dropping from its huge whiskers. Were they mine, or were they the animal's?[15]

The animal, as impossible an object as one could wish, is imbued with a surplus of the narrator's subjectivity. Continually touching him in intimate places—the lap, between the legs, on the ear—it

---

15. Franz Kafka, "A Crossbreed," in *The Complete Stories*, ed. Nahum Glatzer (New York, 1976), 427.

brings to life an unintegrated fragment of his psyche, symbolically set apart from him as a bodily incoherence. By embracing the animal while rocking in despair, the narrator is tacitly preparing to recover something of himself, something associated with the tears he should have shed, or has shed unknowingly. When he sees—recognizes—the tears, he acknowledges both his identity with the animal and the strong feelings that his apathy has disavowed.

The nineteenth century sometimes seems to have been overrun by impossible objects, many of them more equivocal than Kafka's animal. (Kafka himself, who counts here as an honorary nineteenth-century writer, has another one, an animate/inanimate biped/spool who/that is pure equivocation. Named "Odradek," a word of equivocal origins, the object may embody Kafka's texts; "[It] does no harm to anyone that one can see," he writes, "but the idea that [it] is likely to survive me I find almost painful.")[16] A glance at a few more instances will prove to be helpful with Chopin's prelude.

In Wordsworth's "Resolution and Independence," a speaker beset with anxiety—"the fear that kills; / And hope that is unwilling to be fed"—tries to restore an earlier state of joy through his encounter with an impossible object, an old leech gatherer who seems "not all alive nor dead, / Nor all asleep":

> Motionless as a cloud the old Man stood,
> That heareth not the loud winds when they call;
> And moveth all together, if it move at all.
>
> (75–77)

The rest of the poem traces a dialectic between the speaker's desire to draw "human strength" from this strange figure and his impulse to keep all of his subjectivity locked within himself. "Longing to be comforted," he puts some questions to the old man; when the answers come, he promptly wards them off—literally ceases to hear them as he withdraws to the privacy of his mind's eye:

> The old Man still stood talking by my side;
> But now his voice to me was like a stream
> Scarce heard; nor word from word could I divide;

16. Kakfa, "Cares of a Family Man," in ibid., 429.

And the whole body of the Man did seem
Like one whom I had met with in a dream.

(106–10)

Eventually, the speaker works through most of his resistances and adopts the image of the old man as a kind of magical charm against future anxiety. It is worth noting that when Lewis Carroll parodied "Resolution and Independence" in *Through the Looking Glass*, he seized unerringly on the themes of psychological deafness and the poet's "noble health."

A second literary instance can be taken from E. T. A. Hoffmann's "A New Year's Eve Adventure." The tale introduces us to Erasmus Spikher, a man who has lost his mirror image because of his infatuation with a daemonic mistress. (He also appears to have two faces, one young, one old.) Spikher is both a real person and an alter ego for the narrator, the Traveling Enthusiast. A victim of erotic delirium, Spikher embodies the Enthusiast's own supercharged and transgressive sexuality, together with a dread of sexual inadequacy.[17] These forces have almost destroyed the Enthusiast's ego, but he is able to subdue (if not master) them after a seemingly chance encounter with Spikher. Looking into a mirror, the Enthusiast sees an increasingly radiant image of his beloved, together with a reflection of himself so pale and tired he can barely recognize it. Shortly afterward, looking into the same mirror with Spikher at his side, he sees—and instantly recognizes—himself and no one else.

On Spikher's first appearance in the tale, his cloak undulates as if it were "a series of forms . . . dissolving and emerging from one another, as in Ensler's magic lantern show."[18] Hoffmann's allusion is to a highly popular form of entertainment that, for much of the nineteenth century, filled European cities with impossible objects. Based on the technology that would eventually produce slide and film projectors, magic lantern shows were purveyors of apparitions, most of them associated with supernatural terror or violent death. Though obviously "impossible," these ghosts and phantoms impressed con-

17. The Enthusiast repeatedly refers to the "dried-up" Spikher as "the little man," a term that would be suggestive enough even if it were not also a common German euphemism for the penis.

18. *Best Tales of Hoffmann*, ed. E. F. Bleiler (New York, 1967), 110.

temporary observers as astonishingly real, the more so as technology improved. Terry Castle, who has studied this phenomenon closely, suggests that the effects of the specter shows rested on an epistemological confusion. Developed when belief in spirits had "more or less definitively" begun to disappear under the pressure of scientific rationalism, the shows brought the spirits back as figments of the imagination. But not *mere* figments: the shows, writes Castle, "induced in the spectator a kind of maddening, irrational perception: one might believe ghosts to be illusions . . . but one experienced them here as real entities, outside the boundaries of the psyche. The overall effect was unsettling—like seeing a real ghost."[19] Unsettling though the effect may have been, however, its popularity tells us that it was also highly gratifying. The epistemological confusion seems to have been just what audiences wanted. For what the specter shows offered was a respite from demystification and rationality, a way to revisit the world lost to Enlightenment by perceiving apparitions both inside *and* outside the mind. The nostalgia satisfied thereby is a constant presence in the nineteenth century, from "Ode to a Nightingale" and the epilogue to *Christabel*, with their thwarted longing for faery things, to the later development of spiritualism and spirit photography.

In the broadest terms, impossible objects are products of an epistemological/topographical discourse in which human subjectivity ceases to be a common field and becomes, instead, a secret recess. No longer a shared sameness, the self is an essential difference; its watchword is a form of self-consciousness dramatically announced on the first page of Rousseau's *Confessions*: "I am made unlike anyone I have ever met; I will even venture to say I am like no one in the whole world."[20] Once conceived in these terms, the subject—call it the Romantic subject—is most often represented as an enclosure filled with conflicting impulses, a site "beset / With images, and haunted by itself" (Wordsworth, *Prelude* [1850], 6.159–60). This mental activity is so restless and prolific—and so like a specter show—that the subject is constantly threatened with separation from the outer world. And

19. Terry Castle, "Phantasmagoria: Spectral Technology and the Metaphorics of Modern Reverie," *Critical Inquiry* 15 (1988): 49–50.

20. Jean-Jacques Rousseau, *The Confessions*, trans. J. M. Cohen (Baltimore, 1953), 17.

not just in literature: the nineteenth century recognized excessive reverie as a medical disorder. Impossible objects mitigate the excesses of Romantic subjectivity by absorbing a piece of it. The objects are projected fragments of the subject's incoherence, fragments stabilized —or at least constrained—by the trope of embodiment. As such they assume an ambivalent fascination that, with luck, can reanchor the self to the world. The ego, to borrow a formula from Freud, creates in order to avoid falling ill.[21]

Impossible objects tend to disguise their origin in such desperate creation by seeming unmotivated, context-free, inexplicably present. Often enough, they simply turn up when most needed by a "peculiar grace," a "something given" ("Resolution and Independence"). That is why, uncanny though they are, the leech gatherer, the lamb/ kitten, and even Erasmus Spikher all possess a certain healing quality. The leech gatherer, for example, in keeping with his occupation, heals by wounding; he provides both an embodiment of Wordsworth's fears and the means to allay them. Yet impossible objects are hardly safe to idealize. All of them pose the risk of making subjective fragmentation worse, not better, and at worst, like the gigantic insect in Kafka's *Metamorphosis*, they can imprison the "whole" self in a symbol for one of its fragments. A startling example of such an all-too-impossible object appears in one of Théodore Géricault's anatomical studies (Figure 1). The painting shows two severed legs, placed crosswise and covered by an arm. That would be all, the stuff of the artist's field work in the dissection room, except for one thing: the arm is positioned so that it gives an uncanny impression of embracing, caressing, the legs. The erotic value normally thought proper to the body as a whole—especially to the painted figure—is displaced onto the body in pieces, so that whole and part, and even self and other, become arbitrary distinctions.

When it comes to music, we find impossible objects at their most familiar in the form of bravura pieces. The "transcendental" aspect of Romantic virtuosity, the satanic mystique of Paganini and the daemonic/erotic aura of Liszt, derived in part from the sense that these musicians were driven to create works of superhuman diffi-

---

21. Sigmund Freud, "On Narcissism: An Introduction," in Freud, *General Psychological Theory*, ed. Philip Rieff (New York, 1963), 67.

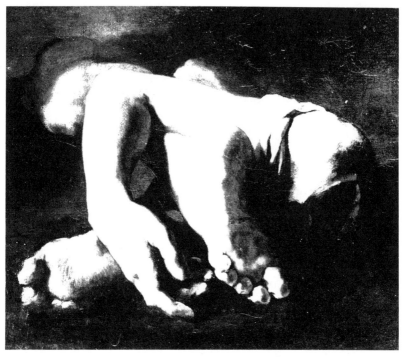

FIGURE 1.   Théodore Géricault, *Study of Dissected Limbs* (1818–19). Musée
Fabre, Montpellier.

culty—objects impossible to anyone but them. This makes the identification of the composer/performer as a charismatic, all but indescribable presence essential to the expressive situation. The esthetics
of bravura reduces music to sound production. What the audience
sees is a theatrical icon of the inspired musician; what it hears is a
highly charged extension of the performer's touch, breath, rhythm:
the body electric, in Walt Whitman's phrase. Hence the cultivation
of certain physical peculiarities (Liszt's long hair, Paganini's emaci-
ated pallor) and hence, too, the many cartoonlike caricatures of
musicians like Paganini, Liszt, Berlioz, and Wagner. (Composer/
conductors had a bravura of their own.) Robert Schumann recognizes
much of this syndrome when he remarks that "the Viennese, especially, have tried to catch the eagle [Liszt] in every way—through
pursuits, snares, pitchforks, and poems. But he must be heard—and
also seen; for if Liszt played behind a screen, a great deal of poetry

would be lost."[22] The performer at center stage, be it Liszt playing solos by Liszt or Wagner conducting Beethoven, acts out a scenario in which a figure like a rhapsodist exorcises the burden of his excessive passion or self-consciousness. Schumann describes Chopin's own playing in just these terms: "I [w]ould never forget how I had seen him sitting at the pianoforte like a dreaming seer, and how one seemed to become the dream created by him while he played, and how it was his terrible habit, at the close of every piece, to travel over the whistling keyboard with one finger as if to tear himself forcibly from his dream."[23] Not even Brahms was immune from the allure of this musical specter show. Clara Schumann did not call his "Paganini" Variations "Witches'" Variations for nothing; she knew what their difficulty signified.

Beyond the matter of performance lie questions of musical design. Some compositions are "impossible" not because they are abnormally hard to play but because they are musical Odradeks: they *sound* abnormal, and cannot be made to sound otherwise. By combining expressive insistence with formal perplexity, such works present themselves less as reworkings of a paradigmatic musical order than as concretizations, material em-bodiments, of the composer as a subject. (One historical index of this process is that composers identified with it tend to be snapped up as icons of subjectivity: the "stormy" Beethoven, the "sickly" Chopin.) Beethoven's "La malinconia" and Wagner's *Tristan und Isolde*, to select from works discussed elsewhere in this volume, are model instances of the impossible object in music, and so too, with its reiterative texture and crazy quilt of structures, is Chopin's A-Minor Prelude. We already know that the dialectical features of the prelude link it to the struggle of the Romantic subject to interpret and master its own intensities. By recognizing the prelude as an impossible object, we can move on to interpret what I characterized earlier as the conceptual polyphony of the music: its play of one dialectic against another, its multiplicity of superimposed patterns. This constructive incoherence can be taken as a trace (projection, embodiment) of the self-haunting incoherence that no Ro-

---

22. Robert Schumann, *On Music and Musicians*, ed. Konrad Wolff, trans. Paul Rosenfeld (New York, 1969), 156.
23. Ibid., 135.

mantic subject can escape, and that must be stabilized in order to bridge the gap between self-absorption and the social/material world.

Going further, we can ask what features of the prelude seem particularly expressive of the subjective incoherence that becomes articulate in impossible objects. The accompaniment stands out at once: a conspicuously abnormal and abrasive pattern, all the more compelling because it is played softly. The accompaniment is the feature that concretizes the effect of embodiment in the musical foreground. As we know, however, one of the basic processes in the prelude is the undoing of the accompaniment, something achieved negatively by abrupt curtailments and affirmatively by the little block-chord coda. The coda might be understood, accordingly, as a turn toward normalization, a repression of embodiment marked by a bland cadential formula. Dialectically understood, however, the coda sounds rather different. Implausible as its cadence may be, its block chords add a material fullness to the music: the warm sound, withheld until this point, of close-position harmonies. With this sonority (enhanced by registral placement and arpeggiation) the coda *preserves* the effect of embodiment—the chordal resonance being no less problematical and overintense than the intervallic friction it replaces.

Another effect of embodiment can be found in the structural background. Example 11 is a graph of the melodic prelude; it shows the two structural descents of a minor seventh in relation to the melodic foreground. What the graph reveals is that the first half of the work is founded on symmetry. The structural tones of the melodic strains marked *a* and *b* form the same intervallic pattern: major second, minor third. In the second half of the work, both the symmetry and the intervallic pattern break down. The strain marked *c* follows the intervallic pattern: major third, minor third; the last strain, *d*, condenses this to a minor third alone. This shift from fixity to dynamism has at least three consequences: (1) it establishes the minor third as the preeminent structural interval, and this in dynamic terms: the interval rises in value as the work proceeds; (2) it gives extra intensity to the tone F♮ at m. 16, which marks the change in intervallic design (the same tone, as we observed earlier, is already accentuated as a melodic and harmonic crux); and (3) it produces a telltale incoherence, a sort of signature, at the close of the work: for if strain *d* is extended into the coda, the result is the intervallic

EXAMPLE 11.   Chopin, Prelude in A Minor, Op. 28, no. 2. Melodic graph.

pattern minor third, major second—the retrograde of the pattern established by strains *a* and *b*. This resolution-by-reversal, however, occurs only outside the structural boundaries of the minor-seventh descents—occurs, that is, as a disruption. By thus problematizing a boundary and accentuating a tone and an interval, the melodic prelude invests its structural background with an overdetermined effect of embodiment. That is to say: the discourse of the Romantic subject penetrates this music to a level of structure that its composer lacked a vocabulary to describe, the level, so to speak, of the musical unconscious.

IV

The harmonic prelude, too, offers a further provocation to commentary. The harshest passage in the work (mm. 11–14), where the melody freezes and the harmony stops making sense, can be heard as a disruptive interlude between one melodic descent of a minor seventh and the other. Similar disruptive interludes, both brief and extended, are frequent in music between Beethoven and Mahler, and probably trace their lineage to the Romanza of Mozart's D-Minor Piano Concerto. The interludes destabilize the recapitulated material that follows them, in feeling or texture if not in structure. Even the Cavatina of Beethoven's String Quartet in B♭ Major, Op. 130, subtly heightens the dissonance of its voice-leading after it emerges from the weird passage marked *beklemmt* that intrudes on the movement near the close.

Thus in the Andantino of Schubert's late Piano Sonata in A Major, the plaintive opening gives way to a middle section that mounts steadily to a climax of extreme violence. The violence gradually ebbs away, but when the opening returns it is doubly disturbed: by a stabbing counterpoint above it and a new, uneasily rocking accompaniment below. The closing measures avoid—or more exactly, dispel—a cadence and die away deep in the bass on a nerveless plagal progression (iv–i [prolonged]–i). The harmony forms an intimation that the seemingly bygone violence is cyclical, unexhausted. The plagal progression, right down to its voice-leading, is identical to the earlier progression that forms the transition to the disruptive interlude (mm. 65–68).

Perhaps the most extravagant instance of this structural trope occurs in Berlioz's *Symphonie fantastique*, where the body of the entire third movement can feel like a disruptive interlude between the English horn solos that frame it.[24] As Schumann notes, the movement reaches its climax as the idée fixe "undertakes to express the most fearful passion, up to the shrill A♭ [mm. 96–109], where it [the idée fixe] seems to collapse in a swoon."[25] The alienating difference made by the fearful passion is then dramatized by the muttering chorus of four timpani that envelops the closing solo, replacing the earlier answers of an offstage oboe.

Literary versions of the disrupted interlude are based on reflection—both the mind's and the eye's; they depict some kind of

24. Beethoven, as I noted in Chapter 2, provides the prototype for this kind of extravagance in the opening movement of the Piano Sonata Op. 111.

25. Robert Schumann, "A Symphony by Berlioz," trans. Edward T. Cone, in Berlioz, *Fantastic Symphony*, the Norton Critical Score, ed. Edward T. Cone (New York, 1971), 237.

mirror image that is distorted when the surface in which it appears is approached or breached. In most cases, the spectator idealizes the original sight of the image, but the disturbance brings about a change in value, so that the image afterward comes to evoke loss or frustrated desire. The disrupted image has the potential to grow increasingly seductive, even persecutory, as the desire that it elicits becomes insatiable. Its role, however, is complicated by the fact that the Romantic subject often shows a compulsion to disrupt idealized reflections precisely in order to set its own desire beyond all limits. Another way to describe this is to say that the interlude transforms the original reflection into an impossible object.

In the "Witches' Kitchen" scene of Goethe's *Faust*, for example, Faust stands mesmerized before a mirror, "now approaching it, now standing off":

> What do I see? A form from heaven above
> Appears to me within this magic mirror!
> Lend me the swiftest of your wings, O Love,
> And lead me nearer to her, nearer!
> Alas! but when I fail to keep my distance,
> And venture close to where she rests
> Her image dims as if enwrapped in mist!
>
> (2429–35)[26]

The impetus for Faust's mirror play is his demand as a subject for insatiable desire, which he can gain only if the reflection remains unattainable, an erotic ideal. Ignoring Mephistopheles' offer to "track down such a sweetheart" for him, Faust keeps his place at the mirror. He soon admits, "I'm going completely crazy" ("Ich werde schier verrückt"), but he cannot tear himself away.

A similar pattern appears in Coleridge's "The Picture." This poem is narrated by a split subject, an "I" who declares himself to be free of a hopeless love, and a "he" who persists in loving. "I" recalls that "he" once spied the reflection of the beloved in a stream, only to have her disrupt it with beheaded flowers (!):

---

26. Johann Wolfgang von Goethe, *Faust*, ed. Cyrus Hamlin, trans. Walter Arndt (New York, 1976), 59. Translation modified.

> Then all the charm
> Is broken—all that phantom world so fair
> Vanishes, and a thousand circlets spread
> And each mis-shapes the other. Stay awhile,
> Poor youth, who scarcely dar'st lift up thine eyes!
> The stream will soon renew its smoothness, soon
> The visions will return! And lo! he stays:
> And soon the fragments dim of lovely forms
> Come tumbling back, unite, and now once more
> The pool becomes a mirror.
>
> (91–100)

When the mirroring surface renews itself, however, the idealized image is gone. "I" then addresses "he" ironically, urging the "ill-fated youth" to intensify his misery until it becomes a madness that will reinstate the image as an impossible object:

> Go, day by day, and waste thy manly prime
> In mad love-yearning by the vacant brook,
> Till sickly thoughts bewitch thine eyes, and thou
> Behold'st her shadow still abiding there,
> The Naiad of the mirror!
>
> (107–11)

The irony of these lines is obviously double-edged: "I" has been busily doing what he projects for "he," and the startling catachresis, "The Naiad of the mirror," can be read *against* "I" as a sign of his reenchantment. It comes as no surpise when "I" collapses back into "he" at the end of the poem. Desire is prized here, ultimately by "I" and "he" alike, exactly to the degree that it consumes the desiring subject. In this connection, it is worth recalling the fragment by Wordsworth that we encountered in the last chapter. When Wordsworth wants to preserve an idealized image from subjective excess, what he does is preserve a reflection from being shattered.

Like these episodes from Goethe and Coleridge, Chopin's A Minor Prelude makes a disturbed reflection the sign of subjective extravagance. The parallelism between the work's two melodic statements highlights the role of the second as a skewed mirror image of the first: disjunct in key, locally dissonant where the first is consonant, dynamic in structure where the first is rigid. The significance of this melodic mirror relationship derives from the harmonic activity of the disruptive interlude. The interlude begins by negating the cadential process that precedes it, and ends by dialectically calling forth the deferral of a cadence: the all-too-prolonged six-four climax of the work. The climax, as we observed earlier, has a purely expectant, purely desiring character; and its expressive vehicle — its largely *unaccompanied* expressive vehicle — is nothing other than the second melodic statement. The disruptive interlude may thus be taken to invest Chopin's Romantic subject with something of the same unqualified longing that drives both Faust and Coleridge's lovesick youth. What we hear in the harmonic mis-shapings that fill the interlude is the sound of a willful self-alienation, the tone of voice of a subject impatient to establish itself as transcendental, as incapable of final satisfaction or unity.

This suggestion is greatly enhanced by Chopin's management of expectancy-laden harmonies once the interlude has reached its all-important French sixth. Since the normal resolution of the French sixth is to the dominant, the six-four harmony that follows this one has its own impetus toward a dominant resolution powerfully reinforced. As I noted earlier, this impetus reaches its peak in the silent half of m. 19, where heightened expectancy alone literally becomes the music. The failure of m. 20 to provide a resolution is thus particularly cruel, and exacerbates desire past the point of satiability. The distorted image constituted by the melody of this passage, like the feminine images in Faust's mirror and Coleridge's stream, appears only to cheat the desire that it sustains.

V

A chapter devoted to incoherence should not tie things up too neatly. A final group of hermeneutic moves, however, may round our topic off without closing it. My analysis has suggested that nineteenth-century tropes of embodiment serve primarily to limit the interiority of the Romantic subject. Why, we might ask, must the bodiliness put to this purpose be concretized as excess or disruption? Why must it appear as an impossible object?

One answer may lie with a massive historical shift in the social disposition of mind and body. Michel Foucault has suggested that modern techniques of social observation and regimentation originated in the eighteenth century, taking hold through the design of prisons, barracks, schools, and other spaces of confinement. The historical aims of these techniques included the control of unchecked bodily activity—activity associated with both social and physical lower strata, with urban crowding, infectious disease, messes, orifices, and sex.[27] As Wordsworth declares in *The Prelude*, a world swarming with lower-bodily activity, "buffoons against buffoons / Grimacing, writhing, screaming" ([1805], 7.672–73), is paralyzing to subjectivity; it lays "the whole creative powers of man asleep" (655).[28] The Romantic subject experiences unlimited bodiliness as unlimited blockage.

A small dose of poison, however, can be medicinal. Impossible objects act on this principle: they limit bodily excess by putting it into discourse. Mediated through the trope of embodiment, lower-bodily activity becomes accessible to the subject—ideally as a means of self-restraint or self-possession, but in any case in a framework of dialogue.

Some impossible objects make this process explicit. Consider, for example, Edouard Manet's notorious painting *Olympia* (Figure 2), a work that will also prove pertinent in the next chapter. The "impossibility" of this reclining nude is obtrusive, and was recognized as such by both Manet's friends (Mallarmé: "[the figure is] captivating and repulsive at the same time") and his enemies (Gautier: "*Olympia* can be understood from no point of view").[29] Olympia belongs candidly, even aggressively, to the lower-bodily sphere, in pointed con-

27. Michel Foucault, *Discipline and Punish: The Birth of the Prison*, trans. Alan Sheridan (New York, 1979), esp. 195–217.

28. For a fuller discussion of this topic, with special reference to Book 7 of Wordsworth's *Prelude*, see Peter Stallybrass and Allon White, *The Politics and Poetics of Transgression* (Ithaca, N.Y., 1986), 1–27, 118–24; and my "Gender and Sexuality in *The Prelude*: The Question of Book 7," *ELH* (*English Literary History*) 54 (1987): 619–38.

29. Jean Collins Harris, "A Little-known Essay on Manet by Stéphane Mallarmé," *Art Bulletin* 46 (1964): 560; and Théophile Gautier, article in *Le moniteur universel*, June 24, 1865; cited by J. Lethève, "Impressionists and Symbolists and Journalists," *Portfolio and Art News Journal* 2 (1960).

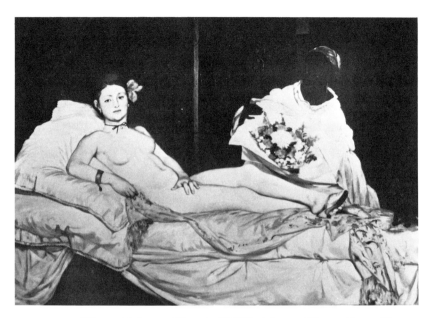

FIGURE 2.   Edouard Manet, *Olympia* (1863). Musée d'Orsay, Paris. Photo: Musées Nationaux.

trast to Titian's Venus of Urbino, whose pose she parodies. Given the allusion to Venus, Olympia might even be taken to personify the lower-bodily, as a profusion of details attests: the rumpled sheets; the flowers wrapped in newspaper (an icon of the Paris streets); the provocative splay of Olympia's hand over her genitals, which parodies the gesture of concealment typical of Renaissance Venuses; and above all the stretching cat, a visual pun on *la chatte*, French slang for those same female genitals. (No one missed this detail; as Anne Coffin Hanson observes, "Olympia was rebaptized 'The Venus with the Cat' . . . and a spate of cartoons quickly made the cat into Manet's special symbol.")[30]

The way that Olympia is painted, however, suggests a restraint rather than a release of the lower-bodily. As Carol Armstrong puts it, Manet's "stark, unmodulated contrasts and broad, harsh areas of signboard paint . . . refuse . . . the transformation of painted surface

30. Anne Coffin Hanson, *Manet and the Modern Tradition* (New Haven, 1977), 98.

into the fleshy thicknesses of the female body."[31] This style, like the little choker around her neck, binds and regulates the force of Olympia's unabashed nakedness. Manet's refusal to enflesh her figure, as Titian had enfleshed the less dangerous (because more idealized) figure of his Venus, fixes Olympia as an object for consumption. Like her black servant, she belongs to a visual order that is also an order of domination. For the unseen master in that order, be it her client or the spectator, she represents—embodies—the overlap between the will to power and sexual desire.

Olympia occupies a border zone between the body as tangible, fleshy, weighty matter and the body as imaginary form, substanceless image. The reclining nude in Faust's magic mirror does just the same thing. These figures are perfect microcosms of the impossible object. They entangle the Romantic subject with the body and release the dialectical energies of both. They collapse rigid distinctions between social, material, psychological, and epistemological forces. They disturb hierarchies of value.

As we have seen, all these are also the activities of Chopin's A-Minor Prelude, activities that the music carries out with a complexity and a depth of cultural resonance that bear comparison with those of Goethe's text and Manet's painting.

In closing, I would like to return to the music one last time and venture a speculation—the typical reward of more rigorous hermeneutic work. It is possible that the effect of embodiment in the prelude refers less to the body in the abstract than to the much-troubled body of the composer himself. During November and December 1838, Chopin worked on the preludes in Palma de Mallorca under conditions of severe physical discomfort. After a while he began to cough up blood, which made him an object of "horror and fright" to the local populace; the Mallorcans were phobic about consumption.[32] In early March 1839, two months after finishing the preludes and a week after leaving Spain, he let drop a revealing remark in a letter to his friend Julian Fontana. Referring to his

31. Carol M. Armstrong, "Edgar Degas and the Representation of the Female Body," in *The Female Body in Western Culture*, ed. Susan Rubin Seleiman (Cambridge, Mass., 1985), 234.

32. George Sand, *Un hiver à Majorque*; cited in the Norton Critical Score of Chopin's Preludes, Op. 28, 5.

Polonaise in C Minor, a highly disruptive work, Chopin comments: "It is not my fault if I am like a mushroom which seems edible but which poisons you if you pick and taste it, taking it to be something else."[33] In writing strange, problematical music, then, Chopin finds a way to revalue the object of horror and fright that his body has so recently been. He becomes a poison mushroom: fleshy, deceptive, alluring, and dangerous.

33. *Selected Correspondence of Fryderyk Chopin*, coll. and ed. Bronislaw Edward Sydow, trans. and ed. Arthur Hedley (London, 1962), 171.

4

LISZT, GOETHE,
AND THE DISCOURSE OF GENDER

The finale of Liszt's *Faust* Symphony is supposed to be a setting of the "Chorus Mysticus" that concludes Goethe's *Faust*. Liszt's repetitions of the text, however, suggest that the movement is primarily a setting of just two lines: the famous closing couplet, "Das ewig Weibliche / Zieht uns hinan." As this emphasis informs us, Liszt is attempting here to represent Woman under the aspect of eternity. Another way of saying that might be that he is just trying to keep women out of history. He would certainly not be the first male artist to come up with that idea. In this chapter, I propose to bring history, with women in it, into dialogue with the expressive rhetoric of the *Faust* Symphony. Liszt's celebration of a certain eternal feminine can be understood as part of a broad cultural project for the representation of sexual difference. In manifold ways, the musical processes of the symphony overlap with the techniques by which nineteenth-century literature and painting idealize—and sometimes resist idealizing—the rigid but unstable gender system of bourgeois patriarchy.

This chapter, accordingly, has two subjects: the *Faust* Symphony, and the cultural discourse in which it participates. The symphony will anchor the discussion that follows, but it will also serve repeatedly as a lens through which a wide variety of representational practices can be brought into focus—through which, indeed, it becomes possible to rethink the representation of gender in the nineteenth century.

I

Liszt's *Faust* Symphony originally consisted of three movements, each one a musical portrait of a leading character in Part 1 of Goethe's *Faust*: Faust himself, Gretchen, and Mephistopheles. In 1857, three years after completing this version, Liszt added the choral finale. The movements are full of the thematic interweaving that is characteristic of Liszt's large-scale works. Faust's themes reappear in the "Gretchen" movement, and Gretchen's motto theme returns first in the "Mephistopheles" movement and then in the finale, where it provides the melody for the key phrase, "Das ewig Weibliche." The "Mephistopheles" movement famously realizes Goethe's conception of Mephistopheles as the spirit of negation by confining itself to parodies of the motives, themes, and structure of the first movement.

I will be referring to the themes of the symphony fairly often, so it will be best to begin by characterizing them (not a neutral activity: a gradually expanding process of interpretation will begin at the same time). The "Faust" movement, a sonata form with an extended slow introduction, begins by stating a pair of primary motives.[1] The first of these, the Faust motive proper, is all-pervasive. It occurs at all the most important structural junctures of the movement and eventually appears as a counterpoint to all three of the themes assigned to Faust in the exposition. The motive accentuates two cardinal elements: the tone G♯ (A♭), particularly in the relation of a half-step to G♮, and the augmented triad. After a dramatic initial descent from A♭ to G, a sequence of four augmented triads descends by half-step until all twelve tones of the chromatic scale have sounded. The sequence ends with the augmented triad E–G♯–C, which establishes itself by rep-

1. On sonata form in Liszt, see Richard Kaplan, "Sonata Form in the Orchestral Works of Liszt: The Revolutionary Reconsidered," *19th-Century Music* 8 (1984): 142–52. Although I find the analyses in Kaplan's essay convincing, it will be obvious that I disagree with his claim that "if we are fully to appreciate Liszt's music, we will surely have to hear it and understand it not merely as a vehicle for the depiction of characters, events, or ideas, but in and of itself " (152). For me, this is a distinction without a difference.

etition as a referential sonority in the form C–E–G♯. (Note the return to G♯ at the close of the melodic process, m. 3.) The second motive, *dolente*, is joined seamlessly to the first and harmonized by the latter's augmented triads.

The first Faust theme of the exposition, Allegro agitato ed appassionato, derives from the Faust motive. Like the motive, it is structured by groups of descending semitones—initially the same semitones that structure the motive itself (Example 12). The second theme, Affetuoso, is a straightforward expansion of the *dolente* motive. Liszt seems to associate this theme with Faust's passion for Gretchen; it is the first of Faust's themes to recur in the "Gretchen" movement, and the one most fully developed there. Part of the sense of longing that the theme carries for most listeners may come from the striking division of its two-bar phrases between winds and strings—in the first instance between clarinets and horns and solo viola. The third Faust theme, Grandioso, is a relatively independent element, though its contour and rhythm derive loosely from the Faust motive.

Liszt is more parsimonious in the second movement, at least as far as Gretchen is concerned; he gives her only two themes. Gretchen's motto is evidently conceived as a restrained and spiritualized counterpart to Faust's Affetuoso theme. The link between the two is drawn by parallels in structure and scoring. On its first appearance, Gretchen's motto is sung by a solo oboe against accompaniment figuration on solo viola, with the rest of the orchestra silent. Faust's earlier antiphony of winds and solo viola in paired two-measure phrases is echoed and sublimated in Gretchen's unbroken homophony of solo viola and oboe in paired four-measure phrases. Gretchen's second theme, Dolce amoroso, is little more than a pendant to the first; the two share the same key and phrase structure. By introducing some register shifts in its second half, the Amoroso theme intensifies the musical processes associated with Gretchen, but otherwise it simply repeats them.

In grouping the themes that characterize Faust and Gretchen, Liszt, consciously or not, follows the terminological convention that identifies the beginnings or endings of melodies as masculine if they are accented, feminine if they are unaccented. Both of Faust's germinal motives begin on a syncopated accent that is tied over the bar

EXAMPLE 12. Liszt, *Faust* Symphony. Analysis of Agitato theme, "Faust" movement.

line, as if to suggest the unyielding dynamism at the core of his character. The three Faust themes run the gamut of masculine possibilities: a masculine beginning (the Affetuoso theme), a masculine ending (the Grandioso theme), and both (the Appassionato theme). Gretchen's two themes are feminine both at the beginning and the end. I do not want to give undue weight to this metrical gendering of themes, but it does show Liszt mobilizing, or being mobilized by, the cultural codes that support the standard terminology. Certainly the traditional representation of femininity as a form of lack—as masculinity with a minus sign—hovers behind this melodic grouping. In the same vein, Gretchen's themes can be said to behave like the nondeveloping second theme of a first-movement sonata form: the theme that nineteenth-century theorists, once more spotting a lack, customarily called feminine.[2]

Liszt's sorting of Faust's and Gretchen's themes according to gender extends beyond metrical convention into a whole series of stylistic oppositions, the stuff of a rigid and exhaustive binary logic that

---

2. My thanks to Richard Taruskin for pointing this out to me. On the origin of the masculine/feminine usage for themes, see the communication by Peter Bloom in *Journal of the American Musicological Society* 27 (1974): 101–2. My thanks to Ruth Solie for drawing this document to my attention.

is itself marked as masculine in patriarchal culture.[3] Where implacable semitones rule Faust's Appassionato theme, Gretchen's motto traces a placid diatonic pattern—a transparent articulation of the A♭-major triad. (The Amoroso theme does much the same thing.) Faust's melodic material freely mixes rising and falling contours. Gretchen's themes consist wholly of descending phrases: they droop sweetly, all the more so when one phrase begins higher than the last. Faust's themes are based on disjunct motion within the phrase, with special emphasis on melodic leaps of a sixth or seventh; Gretchen's themes are studies in almost unbroken conjunct motion. Faust's material is contrapuntally active; Gretchen's is limpidly homophonic. Faust's themes divide into disparate halves, with the second half less stable than the first; the two halves of Gretchen's themes do little more than repeat each other. Faust's themes and motives, in whole or part, undergo sequential development throughout the sonata exposition; the Appassionato theme even runs through a full reprise in a distant key (♭ii) as a kind of mock exposition repeat.[4] Gretchen's themes recur only at fixed pitches (the motto) or fixed pitches and octave transpositions (the Amoroso theme). There is one exception to this last point—something seemingly insignificant but worth keeping in mind. On two occasions, Liszt gives Gretchen's motto a short-lived transposition (starting on ii, moving to vi) that adds a touch of the minor mode. This hint of vitality aside, Gretchen's themes are simply inert.

These formal oppositions can easily, almost glibly, be thematized in terms that conform to patriarchal representations of sexual difference. Liszt's Faust and Gretchen radically separate strength from sweetness, passion from tenderness, vitality from stability, force from beauty. Faust's thematic diversity suggests a masculine Becoming that divides from and idealizes the Being embedded in Gretchen's thematic redundancy. Faust's restless mind, assuming its identity in the tonal void of parallel augmented triads, strives after the repose of nature locked within a perfect major triad.

---

3. On binary thought as a patriarchal institution, see Hélène Cixous, "Sorties," in Hélène Cixous and Catherine Clément, *La jeune née* (1975), in English as *The Newly Born Woman*, trans. Betsey Wing (Ithaca, N.Y., 1986), 63–130.

4. Kaplan ("Sonata Form," 148) notes this episode, which he calls a "false exposition repeat." I prefer the term *mock repeat* because the episode is not deceptive.

Liszt plainly invites us to understand these suggestions, which are supposed to be unproblematical within his cultural framework. But the symphony carries other suggestions, too, suggestions more equivocal, more fully engaged with the cultural practices that define and regulate gender. We can understand much more.

The most consistent element in Liszt's binary logic is the portrayal of Gretchen in terms that suggest almost complete immobility in opposition to Faust's dynamism. If I had to name the chief representational practice by which nineteenth-century ideology tries to regulate femininity, symbolic immobilization would be my choice. Like most cultural icons, the immobilized woman forms a vehicle for numerous and conflicting meanings, among them sexual purity, erotic passivity, self-abnegation, commodification, and—perhaps above all—availability to be gazed at. (Of the last, more later.) The immobility of Liszt's Gretchen initially seems to suggest an ideal purity of character: the unworldly sweetness of the Victorian Angel in the House. As daughter, wife, and mother, the domestic angel was supposed to preside over a "place of Peace" set apart from the contested spheres of historical time and public life. To achieve this, she was asked to practice self-renunciation in order to cultivate qualities that were supposedly hers by nature: simplicity, altruism, moral beauty.[5] "Above all," wrote Virginia Woolf, "—I need not say it— she was pure. . . . If there was chicken, she took the leg; if there was a draught, she sat in it."[6] Woolf's description applies poorly to Goethe's Gretchen, whose love for Faust takes at least the whole chicken and destroys her family in the process. Liszt's Gretchen is another matter. With its exhaustive opposition between Gretchen's thematic redundancy and Faust's protean diversity, Liszt's music projects Gretchen as unself-conscious and psychologically whole, Faust as re-

5. The classic statement of this ideology appears in John Ruskin's *Sesame and Lilies* in the essay "Of Queen's Gardens" (1865); Coventry Patmore's volume of poems *The Angel in the House* appeared in 1854. Bram Dijkstra, in his *Idols of Perversity: Fantasies of Feminine Evil in Fin-de-Siècle Culture* (Oxford, 1986), 1–24, surveys the nineteenth-century literature on this topic. Dijkstra's work must be used with caution, however. Though invaluable as an archive, it is (with intermittent exceptions) crude, glib, and very often misleading as commentary—largely incapable of grasping what is complex, self-divided, or problematical about any text whatever.
6. Virginia Woolf, "Professions for Women," in *Collected Essays*, vol. 2 (London, 1960), 285.

flective, self-divided, and conflict-laden. Where Faust's themes sig-
nify diverse aspects of his character, which transcends all of them,
Gretchen's themes portray—or capture—her essence. As Gounod
was to do in his nearly contemporary *Faust*, Liszt idealizes Gretchen
by representing her in terms more suited to bourgeois melodrama
than to Goethe's radically heterogeneous text. His musical portrait of
Gretchen implicitly belongs to a *Sinfonia Domestica*, with a figure of
vestal simplicity at its center.

Liszt's Gretchen is also implicated in an immobility that might be
called hermeneutic: the separation of women from the cultural production of meaning, the prohibition of woman as subject from par-
ticipation in the interpretive practices that invest her with meaning
both for herself and for others. Under this rule of exclusion, women
become subjects only insofar as they are taken as objects of male
interpretation.[7] Their subjectivity is not abolished, but it is reduced
to what may be signified to a man by the woman's body, gesture, or
behavior. Women are thus rendered all surface, like images in a
picture plane; hence Nietzsche's notorious remark that women are
not even shallow.[8] (The latent association between the "profundity"
thus denied and the maternal/erotic "depths" traditionally ascribed to
women is worth pondering.) Liszt's Gretchen is hermeneutically immobilized by the structural process at the heart of the movement
named for her: the juxtaposition of her music with Faust's. Barred
from any development of their own, Gretchen's themes become
significant only in and through the lyrical new forms that their
proximity evokes—evokes abundantly—from Faust's. Gretchen's
music "attracts" Faust with its unchanging surface; Faust's music
explicates that attraction by continually transforming its own expressive character.

The ideological and hermeneutic types of feminine immobility

---

7. On discourse and rules of exclusion, see Michel Foucault, *The Archeology of
Knowledge and the Discourse on Language*, trans. A. M. Sheridan Smith (New York,
1972), 215–20.

8. In full: "Women are considered profound. Why? Because one never fathoms
their depths. Women aren't even shallow" (from *Twilight of the Idols*, trans. Walter
Kaufman in his *Portable Nietzsche* [New York, 1962], 470). On Nietzsche and femininity (and much else), see Jacques Derrida, *Spurs: Nietzsche's Styles*, trans. Barbara
Harlow (Chicago, 1979).

overlap in one of the most important of patriarchal institutions, a specifically visual form of domination that also, as we will see, takes on musical form in the *Faust* Symphony. I am speaking of the gaze: a prolonged or repeated look, often from a concealed position, by which a man scrutinizes a woman's body, gesture, or intimate (private, secret) behavior. This structure of looking may be recreated by a painting, represented in a text, or practiced in various social spaces from the bedroom to the marketplace.[9] It may have private or neurotic motives in a given instance, but it is always authorized as a privilege of gender. The gaze has its most familiar tradition in the painting of the female nude, though it also has a literary tradition, especially in the form of poetic inventories of women's "beauties," a rhetorical technique of fragmentation that derives its highest authority from the example of Petrarch.[10] In the nineteenth century, the gaze moves into a position of unusual preeminence as the male's power to scrutinize the female body is everywhere institutionalized, from the crass commodification of Degas's brothel monotypes to the sublimated voyeurism of Keats's "The Eve of St. Agnes":[11]

> Anon his heart revives: her vespers done,
> Of all its wreathed pearls her hair she frees;
> Unclasps her warmed jewels one by one;
> Loosens her fragrant bodice; by degrees
> Her rich attire creeps rustling to her knees:
> Half-hidden, like a mermaid in sea-weed,
> Pensive awhile she dreams awake.
>
> (226–32)

9. For a further exploration of the gaze in nineteenth-century discourse generally, and music in particular, see my "Culture and Musical Hermeneutics: The Salome Complex," *Cambridge Opera Journal* 2, no. 3 (1990).

10. On Petrarch's rhetoric of feminine fragmentation, see Nancy J. Vickers, "Diana Described: Scattered Women and Scattered Rhyme," *Critical Inquiry* 8 (1981): 265–80.

11. Charles Bernheimer relates the gaze to the Degas monotypes in his essay "Degas's Brothels: Voyeurism and Ideology," *Representations* 20 (1987): 158–86. Degas's work has become something of a crux in the history of the painterly gaze; see Carol M. Armstrong, "Edgar Degas and the Representation of the Female Body," in *The Female Body in Western Culture*, ed. Susan Rubin Suleiman (Cambridge, Mass., 1985), 223–42.

As Keats's imagery suggests, a strong culturally coded complicity plays between immobility and the gaze. The gaze ordinarily catches or places its object in a condition of immobility, as if to defer the reconcealment of what has been revealed. Conversely, immobility is instituted as the paradigmatic feminine position in order to perpetuate the structure of the gaze across the whole cultural field.

For twin icons of the nineteenth-century gaze, one can hardly do better than to choose Manet's *Olympia* and the first chapter of the novel that Flaubert called "the moral history . . . of the men of my generation," *Sentimental Education*.[12] Commenting on *Olympia*, Norman Bryson notes that "the image addresses two extreme, and incompatible, codes, in this case codes of sexual representation: woman as Odalisque, *objet de culte*, woman presented for consumption as spectacle, woman as image; and woman as Prostitute, available physically and not only visually, woman as sexuality in its abuse, as sexually exploited."[13] What is even more disturbing than the conflict between these codes, however, is the ease with which they overlap and blend, at once lending the glow of art to prostitution and casting the glare of prostitution over art. (But then, "What is art?" asked Baudelaire, and answered: "Prostitution.")[14] More disturbing still in this conflation of looking and "possessing" is the suggestion—a suggestion hard to resist—that for the nineteenth century the sexuality of looking, or scopophilia, rivals genital sexuality as a means of satisfying male desire. It is no accident that *Olympia* also invokes a third code that synthesizes the two mentioned by Bryson: the novel code of pornographic photography.[15]

Perhaps this trend is so strong because the gender system of the nineteenth century is so unstable, or perhaps because the association of gender and power is at once more thoroughgoing and more contested at this period than ever before. Be that as it may, the preem-

12. Gustave Flaubert to Mme Leroyer de Chantepie, *Correspondance de Gustave Flaubert* (Paris, 1928), no. 800.

13. Norman Bryson, *Vision and Painting: The Logic of the Gaze* (New Haven, 1983), 145.

14. Charles Baudelaire, *Intimate Journals*, trans. Christopher Isherwood (1930; rpt. New York, 1977), 3.

15. On this topic see Gerald Needham, "Manet, Olympia, and Pornographic Photography," in *Woman as Sex Object*, ed. Thomas Hess and Linda Nochlin (New York, 1972), 81–89.

inence of the gaze and of its scopophilic force is fully explicit in the
episode that impels Flaubert's novel: Frédéric Moreau's "vision" of
Mme Arnoux, the *ne plus ultra* of love at first sight:

> As she stayed in the same position, he took a few turns to right
> and left, in order to conceal the purpose of his movements; then
> he stationed himself near her sunshade . . . and pretended to be
> watching a launch on the river.
>
> He had never before seen anything to compare with her splen-
> did dark skin, her ravishing figure, or her delicate, translucent fin-
> gers. He looked at her workbasket with eyes full of wonder, as if it
> were something out of the ordinary. What was her name, her
> home, her life, her past? He longed to know the furniture in her
> room, all the dresses she had ever worn, the people she mixed
> with; and even the desire for physical possession gave way to a pro-
> founder yearning, a poignant curiosity that knew no bounds.[16]

Everything is here: the immobilized woman, the privileged and concealed position of the spectator, the shift from erotic to scopophilic
desire—or more exactly, *through* erotic to scopophilic desire—in a
look that seems to touch the body fixed before it.

The hegemony of the gaze is often attributed to male fears of
female sexuality, but while this suggestion is undoubtedly persuasive,
it does not go very far. The most venturesome work on the gaze has
called attention to male narcissism as a social and cultural agency. In
the language of Jacques Lacan, what the gazer both seeks and is
authorized to find is a "specular" image: an image in which the
subject's privileged sense of self is crystallized.[17] The immobilized
woman is appropriated, not only as an object in which to take

---

16. Flaubert, *Sentimental Education*, 18.

17. Lacan's account appears in *Four Fundamental Concepts of Psychoanalysis*,
trans. Alan Sheridan (New York, 1981), 67–119. Luce Irigaray extends the concept
of the specularization of woman to Western tradition as a whole in *Speculum of the
Other Woman*, trans. Gillian C. Gill (Ithaca, N.Y., 1985). Other discussions will be
found in the essays by Bernheimer ("Degas's Brothels") and Armstrong ("Edgar
Degas"), and in Naomi Schor, "The Portrait of a Gentleman: Representing Men in
(French) Women's Writing," *Representations* 20 (1987): 113–33. Not surprisingly,
the gaze has been much discussed in film theory. For the classic statement, see Laura
Mulvey, "Visual Pleasure and Narrative Cinema" (1975), in her *Visual and Other
Pleasures* (Bloomington, Ind., 1989), 14–28.

pleasure, but also as a covert image of the pleasure taken. She serves as an extension of the gazer's own sexualized body, as a measure of his masculinity, and as a confirmation of his idealized self-knowledge. It follows that the object of the gaze must be both arrestingly visible, her privacy or private parts exposed, and yet subject to an unacknowledged effacement by the gaze itself. In "Turning" ("Wendung"), a poem about the gaze, Rilke accordingly suggests that the gaze alone brings women fully into the masculine realm of the visible—and in so doing defeminizes them, imprisoning them in a repertoire of images that reflect masculine knowledge and desire. (Visibility here is polarized against invisibility, as the male to the female genitals.)[18] In sum, the gaze is the paradigmatic means by which women, as Virginia Woolf wryly put it, "have served all these centuries as looking-glasses possessing the magic and delicious power of reflecting the image of man at twice its natural size."[19]

Detached and controlling, the gaze uses its specular structure not only to gain pleasure but also to keep power. The patriarchal gender system requires men to maintain social power over women and rewards them with sexual pleasure from women. Yet the demands of power, the overlapping needs to police, to defend, and to symbolize power, have a way of deferring the pleasure, even of spoiling it. Problems caused by this disparity were particularly vexing in the nineteenth century, when masculine power typically sought to delegitimize a key factor in its destined pleasure: feminine sexuality itself. All such problems, however, vanish before the gaze. For the gaze is the privileged act through which power and pleasure are harmonized. In his *History of Sexuality*, Michel Foucault observes that the nineteenth century used physical examination and insistent observation to compile an elaborate medical/psychiatric inventory of sexual "perversities." The aim of this practice, he suggests, was not only to "say no to all wayward or unproductive sexualities," but also to produce "perpetual spirals of power and pleasure." The medical power that took charge of sexuality, writes Foucault,

---

18. Irigaray develops this theme throughout the first section of *Speculum*, "The Blind Spot of an Old Dream of Symmetry."

19. Virginia Woolf, *A Room of One's Own* (1929; repr. New York, 1957), 35.

set about contacting bodies, caressing them with its eyes, intensifying areas, electrifying surfaces, dramatizing troubled moments. It wrapped the sexual body in its embrace. . . . Power operated as a mechanism of attraction; it drew out those peculiarities over which it kept watch. Pleasure spread to the power that harried it; power anchored the pleasure it uncovered.[20]

I would like to give this argument of Foucault's a deconstructive twist and suggest that the spiral of power and pleasure created by observation is not a special case, exterior to normalized sexualities, but rather the most privileged form of normalized nineteenth-century sexuality itself. "Wine," wrote the early Yeats,

> comes in at the mouth,
> And love comes in at the eye;
> That's all we shall know for truth
> Before we grow old and die.
> I lift the glass to my mouth,
> I look at you and I sigh.

("A Drinking Song")

To look: to enjoy: to consume. Perhaps the famous blinding of Charlotte Brontë's Mr. Rochester allows Jane Eyre to marry him precisely because he will never be able to absorb her into the sexual economy of looking that Yeats takes to be a cardinal truth.

Goethe's Faust never really gets to exercise the gaze on Gretchen, though it is almost the first thing he wants to do, and he even hides in her empty bedroom to do it in imagination. Goethe in *Faust* is both preoccupied with the gaze and deeply suspicious of it. He withholds Gretchen from Faust's eye in the bedroom scene, yet before the scene ends he offers her as a spectacle to the reader (or to himself as author). Slowly undressing, Gretchen sings the ballad "Es war ein König in Thule."[21] The song of undying love makes her an especially seductive specular image—all the more so when she stands, un-

---

20. Michel Foucault, *The History of Sexuality*, vol. 1: *An Introduction*, trans. Robert Hurley (New York, 1980), 44.

21. My thanks to Cyrus Hamlin for drawing my attention to the importance of the "König in Thule" scene.

clothed but adorned with jewelry left in her room by Mephistopheles, in front of a mirror. Later, in the dungeon scene that closes Part 1 of *Faust*, Goethe confronts the violence always latent in the gaze when he has Gretchen, at daybreak, imagine herself at the public spectacle of her execution.

It is tempting to speculate that Liszt's musical "portrait" of Gretchen stems from the association of singing and looking in Goethe's "König in Thule" scene. Be that as it may, Liszt's Gretchen is represented in terms that faithfully reproduce the structure of the gaze. She belongs in the company of Donna Elvira in the balcony scene of *Don Giovanni*, of Brünnhilde as Siegfried breaks the ring of magic fire, of the nymphs that Mallarmé and Debussy "perpetuate" through the eyes of a faun. The movement named for Gretchen is the implicit incidental music for a scene of gazing.

A closer look at the structure of the movement will show in what sense this is true. The music follows an ABA' design. The A section, in the key of A♭, unfolds Gretchen's themes; one brief, premonitory passage also introduces a fragment of Faust's Affetuoso theme (Example 13). The B section, in shifting tonalities, consists of lingering soft-focus transformations of Faust's Appassionato and Affetuoso themes, with Gretchen's music excluded. The A' section recapitulates A, but the reprise of Gretchen's motto is truncated, partly edited out by two mysterious chords. When the Affetuoso fragment returns, it leads to a further return of the Affetuoso material in a new form and a foreign key. A reprise of Gretchen's Amoroso theme follows, but the movement goes on to close with an ethereal transformation of the only Faust melody unheard so far, the Grandioso theme.

On this description, the two essential activities of the "Gretchen" movement are the displacement of Gretchen's music and the lyrical softening of Faust's. Each of these procedures serves as a trope that conforms to a key dimension of the gaze: displacement to narcissism, and softening to the spiral of power and pleasure. In the first case, the music does quite literally what the structure of the phallicized gaze prescribes: it immobilizes the feminine by means of representation and receives back an image of the masculine in idealized, libidinally rewarding form. By the A' section of the movement, where Gretchen's music explicitly keeps dissolving into Faust's, Liszt's musical portrait of Gretchen confesses itself to be—to have been from the

(A) oboe solo

(B) oboe solo

EXAMPLE 13.   Liszt, *Faust* Symphony. Faust's Affetuoso theme. (A) "Faust" movement. (B) "Gretchen" movement.

start—no more than a trope for the narcissistic self-reflection that a man derives from idealized scopophilic love. What we have been calling Gretchen's music is really Faust's—hence perhaps the intrusion of that Affetuoso fragment in the A section. What the movement does as a whole is to trace Faust's specular image as it merges with and emerges from its feminine surface.

What is all-important to note about this narcissistic pattern is that it is not presented as a sign of private perversity, but as an instance of cultural normality, fully authorized and highly valued. Faust's musical interventions in Gretchen's movement are all constructive, not compulsive. They alone give the movement its tonal and thematic dynamism; they alone impart an intelligible large-scale structure to the static repetitions of Gretchen's melodies. Faust's music does cultural work, even in the act of gazing.

Within this framework of sanctioned narcissism, the spiral of power and pleasure ascends. In the B section of the "Gretchen" movement, Faust's melodic material exchanges the ardent, somewhat hectic propulsiveness of its original form for something slower, more sensuous, unclenched enough to be erotic. Though broad in its thematic range, the music proceeds by dwelling on one block of repeated melodic figures after another; its foremost activity is to protract the pleasures of its own sonority. Liszt's thematic transformations involve details of tempo, articulation, dynamics, and contour, but above all it is his orchestration that makes the difference. The Appassionato theme, introduced in the "Faust" movement by first and second violins in unison against tremolos and sforzandi in the lower strings, now sounds on first violins alone against murmuring string triplets and sustained or slow-moving chords on the oboes and bassoons. From the outset, the Faust of this episode flushes with a "feminine" luxuriance that belongs, not to Gretchen, but to the pleasure of fantasizing about her. The Affetuoso theme no longer divides its phrases between winds and strings, but sounds in continuous lines that constantly change in tone color—first scored lightly against harp arpeggios, then enveloped in a pianissimo tutti passage complete with delicate strokes on the cymbal. Between these two episodes Liszt interposes a kind of serenade in which a continuous accompaniment on triple flute rises and falls while solo string combinations repeat a fragment of first-movement melody based on the Faustian sonority of the augmented triad (Example 14).

This music, then, concentrates intensively on the material pleasures of mixed tone-colors and transparent instrumental textures. And these are pleasures inextricably linked with the power of Faust's music to displace Gretchen's, whose themes no more participate in the erotic *scena* they provoke than a gazed-at body shares in the pleasure the gazer takes in it. Like concealment in the space of the gaze, Liszt's musical displacement—the endless deferral of a counterpoint between Faust's themes and Gretchen's—transfixes Gretchen's music as a term of reference, an object of interpretation that is always the same whether it sounds or not. With Gretchen's themes held in abeyance, Faust's music recasts the conflict-laden complexity that empowered it heroically in the first movement as a conflict-free power of self-delighting metamorphosis. By the final measures of the movement, Gretchen's music has dwindled to a void that Faust's music fills in the act of completing itself. Gretchen's Amoroso theme loses its tonal stability, its contour blurring as it subsides onto an A♭ six-four chord (Z19–30). Faust's music then appropriates the tonic harmony and moves to a close in its crystalline new transformation.

EXAMPLE 14.   Liszt, *Faust* Symphony. "Faust" section of "Gretchen" movement. Note how the violins "persuade" the cellos to shift (on
their last appearance) from a perfect to an augmented triad—
indeed, to the primary augmented triad C–E–G♯, continued
from the common tone A♭/G♯. (Rehearsal numbers refer to the
Eulenberg study score.)

The musical gaze, asserting its full privilege, exhausts and consumes
its object.

For a literary counterpart to Liszt's Gretchen, we might look to the
artist's model of Christina Rossetti's poem "In an Artist's Studio"
(1856). With her sister-in-law, Elizabeth Siddal, in mind, Rossetti
describes a woman who has yielded herself up to the gaze of an artist

who fills all his canvases with an unchanging image of her, so that "every canvass means / The same one meaning, neither more nor less" (8–9). The artist sees his model as willingly, indeed joyfully, immobilized in an identity that fulfills his wishes and underwrites his symbolism. He does not see that he consumes her, "feeds upon her face," or that his portraits show her "Not wan with waiting, not with sorrow dim; / Not as she is . . . / But as she fills his dream" (12–14).

The situation is not perfectly simple, however. Rossetti's poem is far from denying the peculiar power of the victimized model, the half-esthetic, half-erotic allure that makes her the object of male wonder, fascination, and even obsession. Taking a cue from the work of Nina Auerbach, we can locate the source of that power in a metamorphic fluidity that the artist takes as his own, a fluidity that allows the model to become a queen, an angel, and "a nameless girl in freshest summer-greens" with equal perfection.[22] In isolation, each of the artist's paintings forms an attempt to limit and appropriate the model's metamorphic power. Taken together, though, the long series of paintings inevitably constructs a sign of her resistance. Paint her as he will, the artist can never fully retrieve her from the position she often took, "hidden just behind [the] screens" that were used to block naked models from unauthorized eyes.

Liszt's "Gretchen" movement allows a similar equivocation to sound in the fleeting transpositions of Gretchen's motto, their minor mode rendered especially poignant by abruptness and isolation. For a moment, Liszt's Gretchen slips out of focus, blurs her portrait: and in that moment the movement named for her half concedes its technique of domination. Like the paintings of Rossetti's artist, the movement pays tribute to the fascinations of the immobilized woman by taking as its own her all-too-mobile power to fascinate.

This insight, however, is withdrawn almost as soon as it is tendered. As the first transposition concludes on a somewhat clumsy "feminine" ending, it is interrupted by a snatch of Faustian melody—the Affetuoso fragment we considered earlier. Shortly afterward, the motto returns in "proper" form, as if to correct or undo the deviant transposition. Gretchen, like Lizzie Siddal, is made to hold still.

22. Nina Auerbach, *Woman and the Demon: The Life of a Victorian Myth* (Cambridge, Mass., 1982).

II

Thinking back over what has been said so far, we might observe that the process by which Liszt consumes or derealizes his Gretchen is the same as the process by which he idealizes her. We can hear as much in the sheer sound of her music, music that begins each A section with a texture of arresting idiosyncrasy and grows steadily more conventional in scoring as it grows more ardent. This mode of idealization, which invests women with erotic or spiritual charisma in and through a form of privation, is basic to nineteenth-century discourse on gender. Women become erotic ideals when they arouse desire in men before they can feel or recognize desire in themselves—the case of Liszt's Gretchen. And they become spiritual ideals, agents of redemption, through their limitless capacity to suffer the consequences of the desires they arouse in men or, worse yet, find transmitted to them, implanted in them, by male desire—the case of Goethe's Gretchen. (Transmitted: like what used to be called a venereal disease, as if sexuality itself were the prototype for syphilis. Implanted: like a child. Hence the sickly or ill-fated children of so many "fallen women" in fiction: Hardy's Tess of the D'Urbervilles christens her short-lived son "Sorrow.")

Formed out of these negations, the bourgeois equivalents of Adam's rib, the idealized woman embodies a tenderness and beauty that can restrain and shape masculine energy, an energy that is inherently excessive, that would expend itself in meaningless rough-and-tumble unless it were confronted by a woman with the pathos of a lack. Rilke, summing up this iconology in quasi-Freudian terms, appeals to the woman to cure the man of an infatuation with his own precultural, psychosexual interior:

> . . . how could you know
> what primordial time you stirred in your lover. What passions
> welled up inside him from departed beings. What
> women hated you there. How many dark
> sinister men you aroused in his young veins. Dead
> children reached out to touch you . . . Oh gently, gently,
> let him see you performing, with love, some confident daily task, —
> lead him out close to the garden, give him what outweighs

the heaviest night . . . . . . Restrain him . . .

(*Third Duino Elegy*, 76–85; ellipses Rilke's)

Only under the woman's restraining hand does the man have access to the garden, the space of order, fertility, innocence, and sweet labor, for which his restless energy searches. It is idealized femininity alone that makes masculine energy available for cultural work.

But ideals cast shadows. It is generally acknowledged, at least by those who understand cultural discourse as inevitably gender-marked, that feminine ideals are always paired with dangerous contraries. The gazed-at woman, for example, has an obverse often figured by the Medusa: the woman who transgresses the visual order, who returns the gaze and immobilizes the gazer.

In its most extreme form, the splitting of woman into ideal and contrary creates the notorious opposition of angel and monster, madonna and whore, a division so ingrained in late-nineteenth-century male mentality as to produce an epidemic neurosis that makes virulent misogyny the precondition of sexual potency.[23] More generally, the ideal/contrary relationship seems to embed in cultural discourse an early-infantile defense against ambivalence: the division of the object of love, in the first instance the parents, into "good" and "bad" versions.[24] As a result, men in patriarchal culture find themselves polarized not against one lopsided version of femininity, but against two: one fixed, the other mobile, one a figure of restraint, the other of excess. Liszt is no exception. As we will see in a few pages, the Gretchen of the *Faust* Symphony is really two Gretchens.

The practical trouble with splitting women according to the terms of male ambivalence is that cultural defense mechanisms do not work any better than their psychological counterparts. The system of po-

23. On the angel/monster syndrome, see Susan Gubar and Sandra Gilbert, *The Madwoman in the Attic: The Woman Writer and the Nineteenth Century Literary Imagination* (New Haven, 1979), 1–44. The classic account of the neurotic overlap of potency and misogyny is Freud's essay "The Most Prevalent Form of Degradation in Erotic Life" (1912), reprinted from the *Standard Edition* in Freud, *Sexuality and the Psychology of Love*, ed. Philip Rieff (New York, 1963), 58–69.

24. First proposed by Freud, this concept of defensive splitting was developed most fully by Melanie Klein. See her "A Contribution to the Psychogenesis of Manic Depressive States" (1934), in Melanie Klein, *Contributions to Psychoanalysis* (London, 1950).

larizations is intrinsically, almost impulsively, unstable; its feminine terms cannot reliably be told apart. Goethe's Faust makes that discovery during the Walpurgisnacht, when he sees a pale and shackled girl whom he takes for Gretchen. Mephistopheles warns him off: the girl is the Medusa, he says; every man thinks she's his sweetheart. Faust does not deny it, but neither can he cease gazing at this beautiful Medusa, nor cease desiring her. Knowing who she is, he continues to see Gretchen's "dear, sweet body" in her (Goethe pointedly elides any reference to her head). Faust goes on to justify his continued gaze by invoking the twin conditions of the privative ideal: "What suffering! and what delight! / I can't tear my eyes from that sight" (1.4201–2).[25]

For the nineteenth century, the doubling of women into ideal and contrary almost always plays itself out in terms keyed to bourgeois sexuality. The feminine ideal domesticates sexuality by separating desire from pleasure. As a virgin, she desires marriage without reference to the pleasures—or disappointments—of consummation. As a wife, she may receive sexual pleasure—covertly, if she's lucky—but must not set herself up as a subject who desires. The feminine contrary rules over a seductive but terrifying social space that breaks all bourgeois bounds: a carnivalesque scene of frenzy, perversion, adultery, prostitution, impotence, and castration. (Here we encounter Wagner's Venusberg and any room whatever occupied by Zola's Nana. Joyce's Nighttown is a belated version of the same thing.) This is not necessarily a space to be shunned; it is more a space to be mastered by a combination of masculine self-possession and economic power. Its danger is the threat of reversal: an addiction to its pleasures that ends in erotic and economic enslavement.

Given these dangers and instabilities, it is inevitable that the relationship of the man to his feminine ideal would be shadowed, sometimes even overshadowed, by the need to defend the ideal against contamination by the contrary. If the gaze, for instance, marks a scene of power folded into pleasure, it is also marked by the anxious traces of voyeurism and fetishism, in which an always-deferred pleasure is predicated on the dread of impotence.[26] Thus

25. Adapted from Goethe, *Faust I & II*, trans. Charles E. Passage (Indianapolis, 1965).
26. On this subject, see Bernheimer, "Degas's Brothels."

Goethe's Faust, enchanted with Gretchen, almost immediately de-mands a fetish, a bosom cloth or garter, and asks to be concealed in her bedroom where he can "see her, have her"—terms his rhetoric comes close to merging.

Each side of the feminine ideal has its own requisites of cultural/ psychological defense. With the female sufferer, the man must deny that suffering is a form of empowerment that can invest the feminine subject with authority and charisma. In her novel *Villette*, Charlotte Brontë dwells on that power and its ambivalence. Drawing on her experience of a performance by Rachel, Brontë writes of an actress in whom "what hurts becomes immediately embodied":

> Swordsmen thrust through, and dying in their blood on the arena sand; bulls goring horses disembowelled, make a meeker vision . . . than Vashti [Brontë's sobriquet for the actress]. . . .
>
> Pain, for her, has no result in good. . . . On sickness, on death itself, she looks with the eye of a rebel. Wicked, perhaps, she is, but also she is strong; and her strength has conquered Beauty, has overcome Grace.[27]

Perhaps it is to negate this strength, to reclaim its territory for beauty and grace, that nineteenth-century male artists notoriously find their ultimate image of the suffering woman in her dead body: the Mignon of Goethe's *Wilhelm Meister*; Robert Browning's Evelyn Hope; the Ophelia of John Everett Millais's much-imitated painting, whose floating corpse is so intimate a part of the landscape that envelops it that the beauty of the body blends seamlessly into the beauty of the scene.[28]

On the erotic side, the idealizing man must protect his ideal from internalizing the very desire that she inspires. Here the issue is not so much sexuality as a function of the body, but the role of sexual desire as a culturally authorized signifier of psychological and social power.

---

27. Charlotte Brontë, *Villette* (Harmondsworth, Eng., 1979), 339, 340.

28. On Ophelia in the nineteenth century, see Elaine Showalter, "Representing Ophelia: Women, Madness, and the Responsibilities of Feminist Criticism," in *Shakespeare and the Question of Theory*, ed. Patricia Parker and Geoffrey Hartman (New York, 1985), 77–96. Dijkstra (*Idols*) has a chapter on the cult of the sick and dying woman's body (25–63) which contains striking illustrations, some of them of a really frightening extremity.

The right to desire, we might say, is the reward of power successfully maintained. But desire, like money, is hard to take out of circulation; it passes inexorably from hand to hand and is sometimes repaid with interest. The dilemma wrought by desire finds a perfect illustration in Torvald Helmer, the husband of Ibsen's *A Doll's House* and a walking compendium of middle-class values. Torvald must somehow reconcile his strong sexual desire for his wife, Nora, with his more distanced idealization of her as his "little lark," a merry and irresponsible creature who lives on his social and economic largesse. His solution is to imagine her recurrently as his virgin bride on their wedding night, the helpless girl who knows nothing of either money or sex:

> I pretend that you're my young bride, that we're just coming from
> the wedding, that for the first time I'm bringing you into my
> house—that for the first time I'm alone with you—completely
> alone with you, your trembling young beauty. All this evening I've
> longed for nothing but you. When I saw you turn and sway in the
> tarantella—my blood was pounding till I couldn't stand it.[29]

Torvald's defensive technique executes a kind of triple play. It incorporates the structure of the gaze, with the accompanying circle of narcissistic reflection and spiral of power and pleasure; it establishes Nora's virginity as a renewable resource, thereby securing the bourgeois separation of feminine pleasure and desire; and it isolates Nora from the position of social and economic empowerment to which her actual desire would—does—lay claim.

As Brontë's bloodthirsty imagery for Vashti and Torvald's conflation of sexual and economic domination suggest, the bedrock issue in the preservation of the feminine ideal is the preservation of sexual difference itself as an inviolable absolute. Not only do the ideal and the contrary repeatedly blur into each other, but the contrary also encroaches dangerously on masculine identity. Swordplay and making money are for men to do; if women can do them (and even overdo them), then cultural masculinity does not require biological maleness for its embodiment. When the feminine ideal is disrupted, women inevitably gain in psychological, social, and economic power. Linked together by phallic representations of authority, these three terms

29. Henrik Ibsen, *Four Major Plays*, trans. Rolf Fjelde (New York, 1965), 101.

constitute the traditional sphere of masculinity itself. For nineteenth-century men, it seems as if women's entry into that sphere would immediately feminize it altogether or, more radically, appropriate its phallic power on behalf of an enigmatic, metamorphic femininity that would shift men toward the "feminine" positions symbolized by lack of desire and abundance of suffering. Deny sexual difference, deny any part of it, and the feminine would at once replace the masculine as the core gender of humanity. To prevent this, the hegemonically masculine culture erects a law: male and female may couple, but they must not mix. Their mixing, as the medical sexology of the period affirms, breeds only perversion.[30]

We can now return to Liszt and ask how the defense of the feminine ideal against its contrary is articulated by the *Faust* Symphony. By confining Gretchen musically to the same one meaning, neither more nor less, Liszt wards off the beautiful Medusa; yet in that very act he invites her, even impels her, to make an appearance. The effect is one of repression, and we can detect it in part by recalling Goethe's Gretchen and noting what Liszt fails to see in her: everything that is bold, impassioned, corruptible, erotically awakened, guilty, masochistic, irrational. In a word: almost everything. In more specifically musical terms, however, we might hear the inviolable purity of Liszt's Gretchen as a proleptic defense against the kind of mocking transformation of her music that Berlioz wrote in the "Witches' Sabbath" movement of his *Symphonie fantastique*, a work that had a profound impact on Liszt. In Berlioz's famous episode, the beloved escapes from the composer-hero's idealization of her, his immobilization of her in an idée fixe represented by a single recurring

---

30. On this subject see Peter Gay, *The Bourgeois Experience, Victoria to Freud*, vol. 2: *The Tender Passion* (New York, 1986), 219–327; George Chauncey, Jr., "From Sexual Inversion to Homosexuality: Medicine and the Changing Conceptualization of Female Deviance," *Salmagundi* 58–59 (1982): 114–46; and Christopher Craft, " 'Kiss Me with Those Red Lips': Gender and Inversion in Bram Stoker's *Dracula*," *Representations* 8 (1984): 101–33. According to the period's theory of "sexual inversion," male homosexuality is the result of a female psyche in a male body. Sander Gilman cites a complementary trend in late-nineteenth-century medicine that regards (female) prostitutes as "hidden" males; see his "Black Bodies, White Bodies: Towards an Iconography of Female Sexuality in Late Nineteenth-Century Art, Medicine, and Literature," *Critical Inquiry* 12 (1985): 204–42, esp. 223–29.

melody, and returns to him in the "base, trivial, and grotesque" form of a dance tune to take part in a raucous orgy.[31]

The threat of such a Berlioz-like travesty is raised explicitly by the parody technique of the "Mephistopheles" movement. That same threat is laid to rest (or so it would seem) when Gretchen's motto does indeed return, but without any mocking distortions, and for a moment suspends Mephistopheles' wild parade of negations.

But what if we were to listen to the "Mephistopheles" movement in disregard of the conventional wisdom about it, as represented by the introduction to the Eulenberg study score: "Gretchen alone remains completely untouched by this wild and obscene ado: her theme always appears entirely unaltered in its original purity"?[32] Example 15a shows Gretchen's motto in its original form; Example 15b shows what happens to it in the "Mephistopheles" movement, where it appears at the close of the development. The "Mephistopheles" version is, and is meant to be, the most lyrically entrancing statement of Gretchen's motto in the entire symphony. It becomes so, however, only by utterly violating the melodic and harmonic stillness at the core of the original music. The theme does not return in Gretchen's key of A♭. Instead, A♭ returns destabilized, as a dominant, in high string tremolos from which the theme materializes in D♭. Other discontinuities quickly follow. Just as the first half of the theme approaches its closing phrase, it is interrupted by a solo horn that calls forth a glowing enharmonic modulation to E major. The unprepared shift in tonal and instrumental color imbues the music with an unmistakable feeling of sensuous yearning. That feeling intensifies as the melody expands from 3/4 to 4/4 time, adds an expressive new phrase with a broad melodic leap at its center, and—inflected by a Faustian chain of semitones—lingers uncharacteristically over dominant harmony. To round things off—or, rather, *not* to—the dominant is prolonged until the conclusion of the episode and left unresolved (Example 15b).

Amid this play of discontinuities, Gretchen's music steadily undoes its own celestial rhetoric. The high shimmering strings of the

---

31. Quotation from Berlioz's program, reprinted in *Fantastic Symphony*, the Norton Critical Score, ed. Edward T. Cone (New York, 1971), 24.

32. Franz Liszt, *Eine Faust-Symphonie* (London and Zurich, n.d.), v.

EXAMPLE 15. Liszt, *Faust* Symphony. (A) Original form of Gretchen's motto. (B) Gretchen's motto in "Mephistopheles" movement.

EXAMPLE 15 (*continued*)

beginning gradually descend through three octaves and shed their tremolo; the motto theme itself deepens in timbre, its penetrating sweetness on the oboe giving way to the more sensuous color of the solo horn. The Gretchen of this episode has all the subjective force that Goethe gave her but that Liszt has earlier repressed. She is roused from her rigid sweetness, released into self-transformation, imbued with a restless eroticism. Far from being untouched by Mephistopheles' wild and obscene ado, Gretchen is demystified by it. Her music breaks the delicate membrane of sexual difference: it takes as feminine the tonal and melodic dynamism, the freedom of contour, and the pleasure in tone color that are characteristic of Faust's musical style—and of Liszt's.

No sooner is Gretchen evoked in these terms, however, than she is swept away in the rush of more Mephistophelian mockery. The uncanny return à la Berlioz cannot be prevented, after all—but it can be repudiated, and with a vengeance. The episode does not bring back Gretchen alone, but also the deconstructive (affirmative, self-questioning) impulse that earlier prompted the minor-mode trans-position of her motto. What makes her return disturbing is not an explicit danger, not the gross obscenity that Berlioz memorably evokes in the squeals of the piccolo clarinet. The disturbing force is precisely the impassioned dynamism that Liszt associates with cultural hegemony.

III

Within the tonal plan of the symphony, Gretchen's return in the "Mephistopheles" movement forms a large-scale dissonance of special importance. As I noted earlier, the primary Faust motive is centered on the augmented triad C–E–G$\sharp$(A$\flat$). The three tonalities that play the largest role in the symphony represent the three possible resolu-tions in which one tone of this triad becomes a tonic.[33] The "Faust" movement, in C major, takes E as its dominant substitute for the second and third theme groups; the second theme is recapitulated in E just before its recapitulation in the tonic. Gretchen's peculiar affinity for A$\flat$ we know about. In the C-major "Mephistopheles" movement, the three-key exposition passes through G minor before again taking E major as a dominant substitute. In this context, we can see that the tonal and structural placement of Gretchen's music in the "Mephistopheles" movement profoundly subverts Liszt's earlier con-struction of the feminine ideal. By conveying Gretchen to E, the active member of the structural augmented triad, and by doing so at the close of the development section, Liszt brings Gretchen into the dynamic core of sonata form. Her music is allied with the most basic

---

33. In an essay contemporaneous with this chapter, R. Larry Todd also calls attention to certain structural projections of the augmented triad C–E–G$\sharp$ in the *Faust* Symphony; see his "The 'Unwelcome Guest' Regaled: Franz Liszt and the Augmented Triad," *19th-Century Music* 12 (1988): 93–115.

of structural tensions; that it be overwhelmed by Mephistopheles' becomes essential to the resolution of large-scale harmonic tension. The tonal order of sonata form—and of the symphony—bluntly demands that the E-major Gretchen be repudiated. Liszt complies by moving quickly to the retransition, which leads to the tonic through the same quasi-dominant E major that Gretchen has briefly appropriated and "feminized." The resolution is decisive: E major is not heard from again.

Gretchen, however, is not the only object of repudiation here. It is arguable that Liszt's recapitulation in this movement undoes his own earlier representation of Mephistopheles as the spirit of pure negation, and thereby also undoes the heroization of Faust. There is no mistaking the malicious parody that rules Mephistopheles' exposition and development as Faust's themes are literally taken apart and tossed in fragments from one instrumental group to another. But parody and transformation are both forms of metamorphosis, and the recapitulation here does much to blur the distinction between them. Especially as the second and third theme groups return in C major, the music assumes a straightforwardly festive and ebullient character, with only intermittent patches of grotesquerie. One episode even gives the third theme a light-footed playfulness that borders perilously on the Mendelssohnian, a quality far more puckish than diabolical. We might speculate that as the recapitulation proceeds, Mephistopheles gradually metamorphoses from the spirit of negation into the spirit of virtuosity, inventiveness, untrammeled fantasy. This shift from a musical Walpurgisnacht to carnival festivity is strikingly confirmed when the second and third groups reverse their order in the recapitulation, and the second—originally a cacaphonous G-minor fugue—comes out as a miniature scherzo, built sequentially of fragments of the fugue subject, minus the grating counterpoint. Mephistopheles thus evolves into a fantastical, charismatic figure who resembles no one so much as the Liszt of the virtuoso years, the Paganini-inspired Liszt who delighted in a certain studied *diablerie* as a part of his artistic persona.

In his private life, Liszt experienced that *diablerie* in consistent opposition to the two women he loved and admired the most: Marie D'Agoult, who endlessly belittled his virtuoso career, and Carolyne Wittgenstein, with whom he associated his retirement from the concert stage. Liszt's renunciation of his diabolical persona, however, could not be expected to happen overnight, and it may be that in the "Mephistopheles" movement of the *Faust* Symphony the diabolical Liszt returns for a last hurrah.

If so, that would suggest a more than esthetic reason for Liszt's revision of the symphony. In the original ending, Gretchen's motto, again on the horn, makes a short-lived reappearance in F, the tonality in minimum tension against the tonic. A brilliant C-major crescendo follows, based on a nonparodic variant of Faust's Grandioso theme. The original symphony thus ends with a rhetorical triumph in which antinomian genius overrides a feminine call to order. In the revised version, the crescendo becomes a diminuendo, a transitional passage that interprets the reappearance of Gretchen's motto as a Beatrice-like revelation of the feminine principle. The finale promptly heeds that revelation, and in so doing allows Liszt to make reparation for his earlier gynophobic gesture. Yet no reparation can fully escape the gender-based logic that rules the symphony as a whole. Like the "Gretchen" movement, the "Chorus Mysticus" can celebrate woman only by negating her. Liszt's hymn of praise to the eternal feminine is unmistakably fervid, but it is also specular, in the manner of the gaze: a thinly disguised celebration of the eternal masculine.

This internal contradiction appears both expressively, in Liszt's choice and disposition of vocal resources, and formally, in the disruption of large-scale harmonic and melodic activity.

The most obvious element of male-centeredness in the "Chorus Mysticus" is the fact that the music is for male chorus and solo tenor. In contrast, the "Chorus Mysticus" of Goethe's *Faust* is deliberately left ungendered at the conclusion of a slowly evolving antiphony of male and female voices. Goethe's chorus removes sexual difference from the sphere of persons to the sphere of principles: the eternal feminine is precisely that which beckons, leads onward, an "us" that is both male and female. But the "us" of Liszt's "Chorus Mysticus" is explicitly and exclusively male. The feminine may lead this "us" to the fulfillment of "our" energetic striving, but she can do so only as a rhetorical figure within the discourse of a band of brothers in which she has no part.

Similarly, at the end of Goethe's play, Faust remains mute, while "a penitent, formerly called Gretchen," eloquently celebrates his ascent. In the symphony it is Gretchen who is mute, or muted, her melody sung by a solo tenor who, in his sudden individuation from the choral mass, inevitably seems to embody Faust himself. Like the earthly Gretchen, whose significance can articulate itself only in the Faustian music that displaces her own, Liszt's eternal feminine is quite literally indistinguishable from the male conception, the male expression of her. She can make herself heard only in the tones of a male voice.

Even at that, it is not clear whether she is heard at all. The tenor part repeatedly calls attention to itself at the expense of the text, a process that begins with its opening gesture: the transformation of Gretchen's motto into a long, sensuous melisma. As we will see shortly, the tenor plays a destabilizing role in this movement. His principal action seems to be to keep on singing, to prolong the ecstatic contour of his melodic line, which soon expands to incorporate Faustian melodic leaps. Closely akin to the Faust of the "Gretchen movement," he appropriates where he adores. For the tenor, to praise the eternal feminine is to form a specular image for masculine depth of feeling.

In formal terms, what I am tempted to call Liszt's deconstruction of his own celebratory pattern turns on the question of closure for the symphony. Here again the structural augmented triad C–E–G♯(A♭) plays a fundamental role. By the time the finale begins, E major has been thoroughly integrated with the tonic C major through the dynamics of sonata form. A♭, however, has been left in a realm of its own. The purpose of the "Chorus Mysticus" is to build a bridge between A♭ and C, both as structural and as allegorical tonalities. To achieve this, Liszt calls on a close meshing of harmonic and melodic processes.

The finale begins with the chorus slowly arpeggiating the tones of the C-major triad until all but the last few lines of Goethe's lyric have been heard. With the phrase "Das Unbeschreibliche, hier wird es getan" ("The indescribable here is attained"), the music moves emblematically onto Gretchen's tonal level of A♭. This point of arrival, which also completes a harmonic elaboration of the structural augmented triad (Example 16), turns out to be the keystone of an arch. Immobile as ever, but in revalued terms, Gretchen's sonority now

EXAMPLE 16.   Liszt, *Faust* Symphony. Opening of "Chorus Mysticus."

becomes the turning point through which the symphony finds large-scale resolution, the "attainment" spoken of in the text. The music passes from A♭—a sort of "transcendental" A♭ represented mainly by its subdominant and dominant-seventh chords—through a B-major sequence and back again to C. Once completed, this arch pattern reoccurs more broadly, dividing the main body of the movement into two quasi-strophic sections.

Both strophes are governed by an important division of labor. Only the solo tenor sings the phrase "Das ewig Weibliche"—and each time he sings it he pauses, strangely reluctant to go further. The chorus, meanwhile, softly interjects "Zieht uns hinan" into the pauses, as if to prompt the tenor to complete his affirmation. As far as the text goes, the tenor eventually complies; he begins to sing "Zieht uns hinan" on the dominant of C, thus linking transcendental attainment with a future tonic cadence. Musically, however, completion is just what the tenor seeks to avoid. All his melodic phrases but the last end inconclusively, most of them on a half cadence—the musical icon of incompletion. Heard in A♭ and B, tonal levels that the chorus sets through deceptive cadences, the tenor's half cadences seem like refusals of premature closure. Heard in the tonic, however—a tonal level the tenor must set for himself—the half cadences begin to sound like an affirmation of pure mobility, a refusal of closure itself. This eminently Faustian attitude is at odds with the submissiveness demanded by the text. And even when the tenor does at last submit, the gesture he uses is so indirect, so tentative, as to affirm and resist the eternal feminine in equal measure.[34]

34. A few details omitted in this paragraph must be mentioned here. The deceptive cadences of the chorus are modeled on the A♭ arrival at "getan," which takes the form of a progression from C^7 to the A♭ triad. This progression can be thought

The crucial passage ends the second strophe. After a breathless buildup, with harp arpeggios swirling through sustained blocks of wind and string sonority, the music breaks off abruptly. The harmony at this juncture is governed by a C-major German sixth. The tenor then enters unaccompanied and slowly, ambiguously draws two tones from the German sixth to sing "Zieht uns" one last time: A♭ descending to C. A♭ and C, as in Gretchen and Faust: this is a pair—a couple—of tones in which the whole of the "Chorus Mysticus" lies condensed. Another pause follows; then the tenor's final "hinan" resolves the German sixth with an elliptical C-major cadence: $iv^{6\sharp}_{5\flat}$–I for $iv^{6\sharp}_{5\flat}$–I^6_4–V–I (Example 17). The tenor, however, continues to resist even this limited degree of closure. To bring his melodic line to rest, he need only complete his final phrase on a doubled root of the all-important cadential triad. He begins the word *hinan* on the upper neighbor, D, as if preparing to do just that—then rises instead to the third of the chord, thereby enervating a cadence that is already shaky enough.

It remains for the chorus to stabilize the sonority by taking up the tenor's missing C and reiterating it in unison over a pair of plagal cadences. The tenor, we might say, acts as if he were setting only the word *hinan*, taking it as a sign of the mobility that he cherishes throughout the movement. The chorus, whose allegiance is to unity, not mobility, reintegrates the phrase "Zieht uns hinan" and recloses the circle that links "hinan" to "Das ewig Weibliche." The climax of the movement follows accordingly as the chorus expands its vital unison C into a full tonic triad while arpeggiating the same triad melodically. This resolution forms an answer to the structural augmented triad of Example 16, then leads us onward to a fortissimo outburst on the organ that proclaims the close.

In their divergence, the chorus and the tenor act out a troubling duality that no social ideal can escape: the ideal as myth, object of belief, self-present value, versus the ideal as ideology, instrument of

---

of as borrowed from F minor, the relative minor of A♭, where it would function as V^7–III; like the more traditional deceptive cadence V–VI (V–IV), this one employs leading-tone resolution to create the needed sense of limited finality. The tenor's last phrase on "Das ewig Weibliche," an elliptical subdominant progression from C^7 to F^6_4, alludes to this hypothetical F minor; the chorus then alters the F^6_4 to form a German sixth that brings the tenor part to its crisis (discussed below).

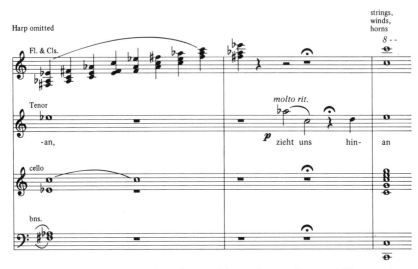

EXAMPLE 17.   Liszt, *Faust* Symphony. Close of tenor line in "Chorus Mysticus."

power, rhetorical construct. For the generic masculinity represented by the chorus, a redemptive submission to the eternal feminine is possible. The cultural order that idealizes woman by privation is, it seems, strong enough to restrain the metamorphic power, the deviant mobility, by which she threatens the bounds of gender. But the individuated male represented by the solo tenor can never quite believe in that restraint, and so can never quite yield to the illusions of his own ideal. His hesitation may find a gloss in one of Nietzsche's cautionary aphorisms about those "quiet, magical beings . . . *women*": "The magic and most powerful effect of women is, in philosophical language, action at a distance, *actio in distans*; but this requires first of all and above all—*distance*."[35] Reluctant to utter the words of redemptive submission, Liszt's tenor finally pronounces them with a profound scruple of reservation, the undertone of a psychosexual resistance that is also a cultural privilege. Though touched by the hope that the eternal feminine leads us onward, he acts on the principle that she merely leads us on.

35. Friedrich Nietzsche, *The Gay Science*, trans. Walter Kaufmann (New York, 1974), 124 (aphorism 60).

5

MUSICAL FORM
AND FIN-DE-SIÈCLE SEXUALITY

It is the union of man and woman, in other words, love, that creates
(physically and metaphorically) the human being. . . . [No one] can
[ever] again surpass that act whereby he became human through love;
he can only repeat it . . . and it is this repetition which alone makes
possible the unique nature of this love whereby it resembles the ebb
and flow of the tide, changing, ending, and living anew.

—Richard Wagner to August Röckel, January 5–26, 1854

In the preceding chapter we treated music as an agent in the
history of gender. In the present chapter we will treat it as an agent
in the history of sexuality. Wagner's *Tristan und Isolde* and Wolf's
song "Ganymed" will be the chief objects of study; the study itself will
situate these pieces in a network of discursive and representational
practices that draws to a focus in Sigmund Freud's *Three Essays on the
Theory of Sexuality*. Freud enters this picture because his three essays
(re)articulate certain radical changes in the concept of sexuality that
emerge in late-nineteenth-century culture. I will soon be arguing that
the structural processes of Wagner's opera and Wolf's song do the
same thing. To prepare my case, however, I have to begin with
Freud—and to get to him will require a whirlwind tour of sex in the
nineteenth century. As so often in this book, my approach to the

135

music will involve more and closer attention to nonmusical issues than is customary. As so often, however, I hope to show that this is an advantage, not a drawback, where musical understanding is concerned.

I

At the beginning of the nineteenth century, quipped Virginia Woolf, a great dark cloud changed the climate of England.[1] Much the same can be said for the climate of sexuality. The change found its most formal expression in medical discourse, especially in two new areas: (1) the theory and typology of sexual "deviation" and (2) the study of sexuality as a function—with women, often a dysfunction—of gender. The medical account, however, was influential in part because it codified developments in mentality and practice that had already begun to find representation in other cultural fields, from dress codes to the arts.[2]

The new sexual dispensation involved a double shift in the ruling paradigms of desire. What had been physical became biological; what had been moral became psychological. In what might be called the "classical" situation, sexual desire, together with its occasional counterpart, erotic love, appears as a physical disposition kindled in one person by another. It may then be either subdued as a rebellion of flesh against spirit, or extinguished through the act of physical love. Desire in this classical model is a function of generic human nature, not of individual character; it operates on the body, not the person. In representational practice, its foremost trope is a metaphor of fire. Thus Milton's Adam, speaking to Eve after the Fall:

> . . . Never did thy Beauty since the day
> I saw thee first and wedded thee, adorn'd
> With all perfections, so inflame my sense
> With ardor to enjoy thee, fairer now
> Than ever, bounty of this virtuous Tree.
>   So said he, and forbore not glance or toy

1. Virginia Woolf, *Orlando* (1928; rpt. New York, 1973), 225–26.
2. Here, and throughout my account, I draw substantially on Michel Foucault, *The History of Sexuality*, vol. 1: *An Introduction*, trans. Robert Hurley (New York, 1980).

> Of amorous intent, well understood
> Of *Eve*, whose Eye darted contagious fire.

(*Paradise Lost*, 9.1030–36)

(Note the etymological play on "ardor" and "inflame," which acts as an analysis/critique of the traditional language of desire.) Medical discourse, taking its cue from Galen, understood sexual "ardor" as a literal effect of bodily heat, the prime mover of life itself. "In this model, sexual excitement . . . in both men and women [signified] a heat sufficient to concoct and commingle the seed, the animate matter, and create new life."[3] The same model also understood deviations from the "normal" path of heterosexual love to follow from perversities of moral will rather than from changes in the nature of desire itself.

The psychobiological model of desire that emerges in the nineteenth century differs from its classical predecessor in only one essential respect, but that one is explosive. Instead of understanding desire as a recurrent disposition of the body, the nineteenth century understands it as a persistent force within the personal subject. Desire becomes a basic component of subjectivity itself, one of the cluster of basic forces that establishes subjectivity as the chief institution of personhood. Here is Shelley in a fragmentary essay, "On Love" (1818):

> There is something within us which from the instant that we live and move thirsts after its likeness. It is probably in correspondence with this law that the infant drains milk from the bosom of its mother; this propensity devlopes [sic] itself with the devlopement of our nature. . . . [We wish for] an imagination which should enter into and seize upon the subtle and delicate peculiarities which we have delighted to cherish and unfold in secret, [for] a [bodily] frame whose nerves, like the chords of two exquisite lyres strung to the accompaniment of one delightful voice, vibrate to the vibrations of our own.[4]

---

3. Thomas Laqueur, "Orgasm, Generation, and the Politics of Reproductive Biology," *Representations* 14 (1986): 5. I have also borrowed—unconsciously—Laqueur's opening gambit: an allusion to Woolf's *Orlando*.

4. From *Shelley's Poetry and Prose*, selected and ed. Donald H. Reiman and Sharon B. Powers (New York, 1977), 473–74.

Biologically, desire in the postclassical model is understood to follow from a sexual instinct that aims at the preservation of the species. Shelley's proto-Freudian speculation about breast-feeding carries a hint of this notion; Schopenhauer's debunking claim that in "love-affairs . . . the will of the individual appears at an enhanced power as the will of the species" carries more than a hint.[5] Psychologically, the same instinctual desire is understood as a sign of the hidden, innermost character of the personal subject. Shelley's talk of interpenetrating secrecies exemplifies this view; Michel Foucault's *The History of Sexuality* theorizes it. Foucault points to a triangulation of knowledge, sex, and power; sex is asked to reveal "the deeply buried truth about ourselves," but this is a truth that must be deciphered rather than merely read, interpreted (often by qualified experts) rather than merely observed.[6] One is, in short, as one desires. And it is in this context, as Arnold Davidson has suggested, that classes of persons known as "deviants" can appear: people whose character is supposedly formed as the result of abnormalities in the sexual instinct.[7]

By importing desire into the structure of both character and knowledge, the nineteenth century produced (constituted, invented) what we call sexuality. This "deep" subjective force has unheard-of mobility; it can be interpreted in a limitless number of ways, assume any value, become attached to everything from political and racial violence to transcendental aspiration.[8] At one extreme, personified in the figure of the syphilitic prostitute, sexuality can typify an abyss of contamination widely supposed to form the core of the nineteenth-century city. At the other extreme, the ideal of a regenerate sexuality

5. Arthur Schopenhauer, *The World as Will and Representation*, trans. E. F. J. Payne (New York, 1966), 2:534.

6. Foucault, *History: An Introduction*, 69.

7. Arnold I. Davidson, "How to Do the History of Psychoanalysis: A Reading of Freud's *Three Essays on the Theory of Sexuality*," *Critical Inquiry* 13 (1987): 252–77. My account of Freud's text has been generally influenced by this important essay.

8. For examples, see Neil Hertz, "Medusa's Head: Male Hysteria Under Political Pressure," in *The End of the Line: Essays on Psychoanalysis and the Sublime* (New York, 1985), 161–93; and Michael Rogin, " 'The Sword Became a Flashing Vision': D. W. Griffith's *The Birth of a Nation*," *Representations* 9 (1985): 150–95.

can play an essential role in utopian movements like those of Fourier and the Saint-Simonians.[9]

These possibilities, however, were not realized evenhandedly. Despite its innovativeness, the instinctual model of desire was both socially repressive and historically conservative. Socially, the supposed need to regulate the anarchic force of sexuality produced a vast population of "deviants," "neurotics," and "debauchees" (the latter mostly slum dwellers) from whom "normal" people had to be protected. The bourgeois paterfamilias was especially vulnerable: "If he look[s] from his window he sees the pavement—*his* pavement—occupied by the flaunting daughters of sin, whose loud, ribald talk forces him to keep his casement closed."[10] The protection of the pavement could be ruthless: witness the British Contagious Diseases Acts of the 1860s—laws that empowered the police to "arrest women, subject them to internal examination and incarcerate them in lock-hospitals if they were suffering from gonorrhoea or syphilis."[11] Historically, instinctual desire preserved most of the external features of its classical forerunner. Desire is still aroused in the subject by a specific sexual object, and still seeks extinction like a flame in its physical consummation. Sexual deviation is still proscribed, its moral taint now reinforced by its biological freakishness. In particular, the structure of desire remains resolutely heterosexual, the sexual instinct being "naturally" drawn to the attractions of an opposite sex.

No system so preoccupied with the threat—and the lure—of transgression can be stable for very long. Already by midcentury the instinctual model of desire is beginning to mutate. The result is not a decisive or hegemonic replacement, but a rival, a countermodel that would gather strength as the century advanced. Here again,

9. On contamination in the city, see Peter Stallybrass and Allon White, *The Politics and Poetics of Transgression* (Ithaca, N.Y., 1986), 125–48. On Fourier and the Saint-Simonians, see Frank Manuel and Fritzi Manuel, *Utopian Thought in the Western World* (Cambridge, Mass., 1979).

10. From the *Lancet* (1857), quoted by E. Trudgill, "Prostitution and Paterfamilias," in *The Victorian City*, ed. H. J. Dyos and M. Wolff (London, 1973), 694; cited by Stallybrass and White, *Politics of Transgression*, 137.

11. Judith Wallkowitz, *Prostitution and Victorian Society: Women, Class, and the State* (Cambridge, 1980), 1–2; cited by Stallybrass and White, *Politics of Transgression*, 133.

medical discourse provides a site of articulation for more sweeping cultural changes. And in this case, the medical discourse is that subversive and intractable thing called Freudian psychoanalysis.

Freud's *Three Essays on the Theory of Sexuality* (1905) literally takes the instinctual model to pieces.[12] In the process, the tenacious survivals from the classical model also disappear. Instead of a single "genital" instinct, Freud theorizes a tangled web of highly specific sexual drives that begin with infancy and are gradually, but not very firmly, united under the primacy of the genitals. Sexuality is interpreted, not as a force of nature, but as a primary means for departing from nature, a critical threshold between the biological and the psychological.[13] The concept of a "normal" sexuality evaporates, except as a social contract; sexual "deviations" are traced to various phases in sexual development, the ultimate origin of which is a state of "polymorphous perversity." Most importantly, Freud suggests that sexual desire is decidedly *not* awakened by, or dependent on, or naturally bound up with, its objects. "We have been in the habit," he writes,

> of regarding the connection between the sexual [drive] and the sexual object as more intimate than it in fact is. Experience of the cases that are considered normal has shown us that in them the sexual [drive] and the sexual object are merely soldered together—a fact which we have been in danger of overlooking in consequence of the uniformity of the normal picture, where the object appears to form part and parcel of the [drive]. We are thus warned to loosen the bond that exists in our thoughts between [drive] and object. It seems probable that the sexual [drive] is in the first instance independent of its object; nor is its origin likely to be due to its object's attractions.[14]

12. A cautionary word is in order here. The standard edition of Freud in English is full of talk about "instinct" and the "instinctual." This, notoriously, is a mistranslation. Freud does not speak of *Instinkt* but of *Trieb*: drive, impetus, impulse. The concept is deliberately loose; Freud once identified the drives posited by psychoanalysis as its mythology.

13. For a full account of this important concept, see Jean Laplanche, *Life and Death in Psychoanalysis* (Baltimore, 1976).

14. Sigmund Freud, *Three Essays on the Theory of Sexuality*, trans. James Strachey (New York, 1962), 13–14.

In this model, desire is a free, unattached force that seeks objects but for which no object is natural or privileged. This force, the famous Freudian libido, always exists in excess of its objects, and it cannot be fully satisfied by any object whatever. Its career is unpredictable; it may attach itself to a single object, perhaps one beyond its reach, or to partial objects, or to an endless series of objects. Its fundamental character, insofar as it has one, is a capacity for transformation. Within less than half a page of the *Three Essays*, Freud describes the libido as increasing and diminishing, distributing and displacing itself, concentrating on objects, becoming fixed on them, abandoning them, moving between objects, and directing the subject's sexual activity.[15] Libido, in short, is preeminently *fluid*, and indeed Freud's favorite metaphors for it are figures of fluidity, of currents that flow within and between persons. The fire of classical desire is replaced by that endlessly circulating, endlessly rhythmic, medium—water.[16]

It is an old and essentially anti-Freudian cliché to relate these metaphors to nineteenth-century hydraulics. Their more vital relationship is to the emergence of fluidity as the primary figure for sexual desire, a desire that cannot be bounded by those things that offer it temporary satisfaction. The imagery that closes Isolde's Transfiguration should come to mind at once here, since *Tristan* will shortly be our main concern:

> In dem wogendem Schwall
> in dem tönenden Schall
> in des Welt-Atems
> wehendem All—
> ertrinken—
> versinken—
> unbewußt—
> höchste Lust!

---

15. Ibid., 83.

16. In her essay "On the Mechanics of Fluids" (in *This Sex Which Is Not One*, trans. Catherine Porter [Ithaca, N.Y., 1985], 106–18), Luce Irigaray observes that Western culture traditionally identifies solids with rationality. She errs, however, in suggesting that Freudian psychoanalysis repeats rather than challenges this identification.

Both this text and Wagner's music for it certainly came to Kate Chopin's mind when her novel *The Awakening* (1899) needed a central image of "höchste Lust." Chopin exploits the vital ambiguity of Wagner's final term—"Lust" being capable of meaning both bliss and longing:

> Edna did not know when the [Frédéric] Chopin [Fantasy-] Impromptu began or ended. She sat in the sofa reading [her beloved] Robert's letter by the fading light. Mademoiselle had glided from the Chopin into the quivering love-notes of Isolde's song, and back again to the Impromptu with its soulful and poignant longing.
>
> The shadows deepened in the little room. The music grew strange and fantastic—turbulent, insistent, plaintive and soft with entreaty. The shadows grew deeper. The music filled the room. It floated out upon the night, over the housetops, the crescent of the river, losing itself in the silence of the upper air. [17]

A strange but persistent offshoot of this liquefaction of desire is a struggle for power between gender-marked instances of the figure. As a province of femininity, desire is represented preeminently by the sea, the ebb and flow of tides, Isolde's *wogender Schwall*. This usage is common to both male and female artists; here is Kate Chopin again:

> Beside the sea, absolutely alone, she cast the unpleasant, pricking garments from her, and for the first time in her life she stood naked in the open air. . . . She walked out. The water was chill, but she walked on. The water was deep, but she lifted her white body and reached out with a long, sweeping stroke. The touch of the sea is sensuous, enfolding the body in its soft, close embrace. [18]

In his drawing *Fish Blood* (Figure 3), Gustav Klimt shows the danger (and allure) that men see in such a feminized libido. Klimt's women are ecstatically merged with their watery medium; their hair rhymes with the swirl of its current, in which they float as if weightless. Their bodies both attract the gaze of masculine desire (mirrored

17. Kate Chopin, *The Awakening*, ed. Margaret Cully (New York, 1976), 64. The (punning) identity between Robert's letter and the "love notes" of Isolde's song is worth pondering.

18. Ibid., 113.

in the drawing by the rigid eye of the fish) and collapse it, deny it the stability of a single bounded object. (None of the overlapping bodies is quite complete.) The juxtaposition of the women's legs and thighs with the fish's head suggests an implicit inversion of the mythic image of the mermaid. The inversion acts as an analysis or critique. What makes the mermaid seductive, Klimt seems to say, is that her fabled tail denies (disguises, effaces) the female genitals, the sight of which is fraught with anxiety for traditional masculinity.[19] *Fish Blood* itself equivocates on this point, representing the lower bodies of the women in such sketchy terms that the male spectator may, if he wishes, see nothing there.

Masculinized libido is commonly represented by two processes that are supposed to be under male control: the circulation of money and the (metaphorical) flow of semen. These two images frequently unite in variations on the myth of Danae, the woman whom Zeus visited in a shower of gold.[20] (The identification of the shower with the god's semen goes back to antiquity.) Klimt's painting *Danae* (1907–8; Figure 4) is exemplary here. As Carl Schorske observes, the "golden stream of love" finds Klimt's reclining nude "blissfully curled in receptivity."[21] This Danae, however, is also a woman in bondage; her feet are wrapped together, as if to make sure she does not uncurl. Two further instances of this motif may be taken, with minimal commentary, from D. G. Rossetti's "Jenny" and Zola's *Nana*:

> I think I see you when you wake,
> And rub your eyes for me, and shake
> My gold, in rising, from your hair,
> A Danae for a moment there.
>
> ("Jenny," 376–79)

19. See Freud's highly influential two-page essay "Medusa's Head" (1922), in Freud, *Sexuality and the Psychology of Love*, ed. Philip Rieff (New York, 1963), 212–13.

20. For more on Danae, see Bram Dijkstra, *Idols of Perversity: Fantasies of Feminine Evil in Fin-de-Siècle Culture* (Oxford, 1986), 369–71. (But see above, Chapter 4, n. 5.)

21. Carl Schorske, *Fin-de-Siècle Vienna: Politics and Culture* (New York, 1980), 272.

FIGURE 3.   Gustav Klimt, *Fish Blood (Fischblut)*, pg. 6 from *Ver Sacrum.*
Vienna, Vol. 1, Feb. 1898. Photomechanical reproduction,
printed in olive green, 11 9/16″ × 10 3/4″. Collection, Museum
of Modern Art Library, New York.

This was the period of her life when Nana lit up Paris with redou-
bled splendour. She rose higher than ever on the horizon of vice,
dominating the city with her insolent display of luxury, and that
contempt of money which made her openly squander fortunes. . . .
What astonished the young woman was that in the midst of [the]
river of gold which flowed between her legs, she was constantly
short of money.[22]

22. Emile Zola, *Nana*, trans. George Holden (Harmondsworth, Eng., 1972),
409, 411–12.

FIGURE 4.   Gustav Klimt, *Danae* (1907–8). Private collection, Graz. Photo: Galerie Welz, Salzburg.

Rossetti's lines seem to play on a Victorian colloquialism that underlines the link between sexuality and money. Where we speak of "coming," Rossetti's contemporaries spoke of "spending." The speaker in these lines addresses a prostitute whose services he declines; he decides, so to speak, to spend instead of spending. As to Zola, his is a cautionary tale; it shows what can happen when Danae uncurls with a vengeance.

Freud's libidinal model is a conceptual reproduction of the way that Wagner, Kate Chopin, Klimt, Rossetti, Zola, and their contemporaries represent desire, put desire into discourse. To summarize, the model has three essential features. First, it produces a desire that is originally independent of its objects and forever transcendent of them. Second, it produces a desire that is independent in particular of its object's gender. Libidinal desire invariably deconstructs gender. (Kate Chopin's bathing scene, for example, realizes an earlier fantasy in which the bather is a man. Wagner's letter to Röckel includes the claim that "the true human being is both man and woman.")[23] Third, libidinal desire is conceptualized as a force and is generally represented as a fluid in metaphors of surging, ebbing, and flowing.

The last point needs one elaboration. Unlike its instinctual predecessor, libidinal desire can be narcissistic, that is, it can take the subject's own ego as its object. Freud represents the fluctuations of love and desire between two persons as a process in which libido freely streams back and forth between the self and the other as objects.[24] An important consequence is that a profound erotic fulfillment can occur when libido is released from the other and allowed to flow back onto the self, as if the other were only a detour that desire takes on its way home. For an exemplary image, we can once more turn to Klimt's *Danae*. With her unseen left hand positioned suggestively as if to precede or overlap the phallic stream at her genitals, with her powerful thigh blocking the gaze of the viewer, Danae partly reclaims as her own the flow of libido otherwise inflicted on her.

We are now in a position to ask how the music of Wagner and Wolf represents libidinal desire. Before proceeding, however, I want to state emphatically that my use of terms like *object*, *libido*, and *narcissism* in what follows is meant neither to depreciate the music nor to suggest that it can be reduced to a crude sexual essence, or indeed to any essence whatever. (Freud, by the way, would be the first to agree.) Instead, my claim is that the discourse on sexuality begun in the mid-nineteenth century can open hermeneutic windows for *Tristan und Isolde* and for "Ganymed"—compositions in which that discourse, that sexuality, are both exemplified and produced.

---

23. *Selected Letters of Richard Wagner*, trans. and ed. Stewart Spencer and Barry Millington (New York, 1988), 303.

24. See Freud, *Three Essays*, 83–84, and the concluding pages of the essay "On Narcissism: An Introduction," in Freud, *General Psychological Theory*, ed. Philip Rieff (New York, 1963), 56–82.

II

The features that give *Tristan und Isolde* its libidinal character are well known, and in its early phases my argument can advance on the commonplace only by describing these familiar features in terms that emphasize their cultural identity. I have already alluded to Isolde's crowning metaphor of *höchste Lust* as a *wogender Schwall*. Beginning with Wagner's own program note to the concert version of the Prelude, *Tristan und Isolde* has always been understood to represent desire as an endless ebbing and flowing, "forever renewing itself, craving and languishing."[25] The musical realization of this idea depends on a cluster of distinctive effects: melodic motion by semitones, ambiguous or indefinite harmonies, a texture dense with appoggiaturas, many of which "resolve" to unstable referential sonorities. As to Tristan and Isolde themselves, they crave and languish as subjects because they necessarily find each other frustrating as objects. Each appears to the other as a gateway—an entry and a barrier—to "the miraculous world of Night,"[26] a condition in which the boundary between subject and object collapses and desire is no longer doomed to survive its satisfaction. In order to achieve what Freud calls "an actual happy love . . . the primal state in which ego-libido and object-libido cannot be distinguished,"[27] Tristan and Isolde sidestep physical consummation and woo death more than they woo each other. Isolde's Transfiguration, which consummates her love and brings closure to the opera, occurs—and can only occur—once her desire is free to proliferate in the absence of its object. Like their descendants in Rilke's *Eighth Duino Elegy*, Tristan and Isolde are always "blocking the view" that they reveal to each other; the fulfillment of desire appears to them only "behind" the other, "as if by some mistake" (*Eighth Duino Elegy*, 26–27).

25. From Wagner's program note, as reprinted in Wagner, *Prelude and Transfiguration from Tristan and Isolde*, ed. Robert Bailey (New York, 1985), 47. I should add that the final scene of the opera is referred to here by its correct name, Isolde's Transfiguration, rather than by the commonly misapplied term *Liebestod*.

26. Ibid., 48. As will become evident below, the metaphor of the gateway is Wagner's.

27. Freud, "On Narcissism," 80.

All that is missing from this alignment of *Tristan und Isolde* with the libidinal model of desire is a suggestion that the gender of Wagner's lovers is only marginally important. That suggestion will come. In the meantime, we might simply note that Tristan and Isolde's language about each other, together with the music that conveys it, does little or nothing to articulate the polarity of masculine and feminine—an elision that is drastically at odds with normal nineteenth-century practice. If we forget the pronouns, the dialogues between the lovers could be reversed, or exchanged between persons of the same sex, without making any appreciable difference.

And now for the music. How does Wagner incorporate the dynamics of libidinal desire into the musical processes of *Tristan und Isolde*? The answer depends on a structural trope that corresponds to the pregnant ambiguity of Isolde's last word, *Lust*. The trope occurs where two illocutionary forces overlap, one suggesting the fulfillment of desire, the other suggesting a deferral of fulfillment. For Wagner, this typically involves a passage that reaches a climactic melodic cadence at the same time as it defaults on a full harmonic cadence. As a general technique, the overlap of closure and continuation is basic to Wagner's mature style, but its use in *Tristan* in the form of what we might call the *Lust*-trope is nonpareil.

Like most things in the opera, the *Lust*-trope finds its prototype in the Prelude, and in particular in the first cadence, which occurs in m. 17 (Example 18). The territory here is familiar, though it may become less so as we proceed. After intimating A minor as a tonic by successive arrivals on the dominant-seventh chords of A, C, and E, Wagner dwells on V^7 of E, prolongs it by appoggiaturas that resolve to its fifth degree, and then—with a powerful pizzicato on the lower strings—moves by way of resolution to V^7 of A, which thereupon generates a deceptive cadence to the F-major triad. This triad is attacked with a sudden fortissimo under a B♮ appoggiatura in violin octaves; when the fortissimo dies away to piano, the B resolves downward to A. Everything conspires to make this cadence deeply satisfying: the gradual buildup, the heart-thump of the pizzicato, the climactic entry of the first bowed notes on the double basses in combination with horn octaves—and yet the cadence is an evasion. The feeling of satisfaction arises because the prominent melodic resolution from B to A replaces the harmonic resolution that the

EXAMPLE 18.   Wagner, *Tristan und Isolde*. Prelude, mm. 1–17.

deceptive cadence defers, without on that account allowing the ear
to forget that it has been cheated. What counts as a fulfillment is
actually a rapturous occasion of unfulfillment.[28]

Set in motion by textual claims of bliss, the *Lust*-trope of *Tristan
und Isolde* punctuates the lovers' discourse so that each release of
desire, no matter how entrancing, becomes a further accumulation,
a slippage of desire beyond its object. Three passages from act 2 can
serve to illustrate this process.

The love duet that opens scene 2 reaches its first peak of intensity as Tristan and Isolde join in the phrase "Himmelhöchstes,
Weltentrücken! Mein!" (Example 19). Starting with staggered en-
tries on "höchstes," the lovers' voices ascend in parallel steps. On the
second syllable of "entrücken," Isolde reaches the chromatic lower

28. Apropos of this passage of the Prelude, special note should be taken of the
root movement by fifths (B^7 to E^7) that precedes the E^7–F cadence and limits the
latter's tendency to assume an autonomous cadential value. Wagner reverts to this
technique elsewhere in the opera, e.g., in the $G\sharp^7_{5\flat}$–$C\sharp^{(9)}_7$–$D\sharp$m cadence that closes
the line "O ew'ge Nacht, süsse Nacht" in act 2.

EXAMPLE 19.   Wagner, *Tristan und Isolde.* Act 2, "Himmelhöchstes."

neighbor of G (as $\hat{5}$ of C) and holds it for two measures, while Tristan does the same for the diatonic upper neighbor. As they finish singing "entrücken," the lovers hold back from the G that forms their melodic goal while the harmony turns (more exactly, turns back) to the dominant seventh of C. A vocal pause follows while the orchestra reiterates the harmony; then the lovers arrive at G together on the triumphant word "Mein!" The arrival is reinforced by a fortissimo dynamic, but it is also partly baffled by the harmony, which just goes on affirming the dominant seventh.

Shortly after this, a further peak of intensity occurs as Tristan and Isolde sing "Ewig, ewig ein!" in octaves (Example 20). Their vocal line reduces to a pair of resolutions: A♭ to G (at "Ewig . . .") and A♮ to G (at ". . . ewig ein"). The second "ewig" brings us around again to the dominant seventh of C; this harmony "resolves" at "ein" to a C-major six-four chord—which is to say that it does not resolve at all. (The six-four chord forms a perfectly explicit extension of the dominant seventh, with which it begins to oscillate while the voices sustain their climactic G.) Here, as in the previous example, the textual and melodic affirmation of closure forms no more than a momentary eddy in a musical process that is all continuation.

The most dramatic instance of the *Lust*-trope in the opera is also the most famous: the interrupted cadence that curtails act 2, scene 2, as Brangäne shatters the lovers' idyll with a piercing shriek. On a first impression, it seems absurd to speak of mere deferral here, and still more absurd to speak of fulfillment. Brangäne's shriek is really a displaced death cry, the voice of the wound that Tristan will soon invite from Melot's sword. The disruption of the authentic B-major cadence in which the lovers seek a musical consummation is both brutal and unanswerable. Yet both Tristan and Isolde sustain their climactic melody note—in Isolde's case, a strong high-B—against Brangäne's shriek and its attendant cacophony. For a tenacious moment of deafness, a moment in which the lovers "keep their positions as if entranced," the force of *höchste Liebeslust* seems to prevail. In a sense, the whole rest of the opera exists to recuperate and expand that moment. The B-major cadence that Brangäne's shriek revokes, even including the fall of the cadence on the words "höchste Lust," will be summoned back later—displaced, rendered more fluent, re-echoed—as Isolde completes her Transfiguration.

EXAMPLE 20.   Wagner, *Tristan und Isolde*. Act 2, "Ewig ein!"

The Transfiguration forms Wagner's means of opening what he calls, in his program note to the Prelude, "the breach that will reveal . . . the path into the sea of love's endless rapture."[29] Yet here a problem emerges—or, rather, *the* problem on which the whole opera turns. As we have seen, Wagner's *Lust*-trope concretizes the rhythms of a desire that has always already begun to resume even in the act of finding what Freud, with calculated irony, calls its "partial and temporary extinction."[30] Yet what Wagner seeks in Isolde's Transfiguration is the full and permanent extinction typical of classical, not libidinal, desire. His problem is to find a musical realization for this "final redemption" *within* the sphere of the fluid and never-final libido.[31] By common consent, he succeeds in doing this; as Joseph Kerman observes, the cadences that close the opera come with "unparalleled weight."[32] But where does this weight come from?

For a preliminary answer, we might focus on a series of cardinal moments in the opera, all of which center on the pitch b^2. The series begins with the cadence at m. 17 of the Prelude (which is also recapitulated at several critical junctures), continues with the catastrophe of Brangäne's shriek, and closes with the B-major cadences of the Transfiguration. These moments chart the course of ultimate fulfillment as b^2 metamorphoses from a preeminent appoggiatura to an unrealized tonic to a cadential tonic. The pitch gathers weight as its structural force is slowly clarified; large-scale resolution emerges from a process of intensification. Intensification, then, is the breach that Wagner requires: libidinal desire is rewarded not by extinction, but by an indefinite expansion "in measureless space, without barriers."[33]

Wagner concretizes this process by restructuring the *Lust*-trope in the Transfiguration. Where text and melody had once combined to reward a desire cheated by the harmony, harmony and melody now combine to reward a desire cheated by the text. To put this another way, most of the opera puts deferral and fulfillment into a narrative relationship; deferral acts as the means by which the story of desire

29. Wagner, *Prelude and Transfiguration*, 47.
30. Freud, *Three Essays*, 83.
31. Wagner, *Prelude and Transfiguration*, 48.
32. Joseph Kerman, *Opera as Drama* (New York, 1956), 212.
33. Wagner, *Prelude and Transfiguration*, 48.

is prolonged. In the Transfiguration, the relationship becomes not narrative but figurative: deferral becomes a trope for the consummation of desire. As Wagner puts it in his program note, "the gates of union are thrown open" as the dying Isolde sinks onto Tristan's body.[34]

I would now like to take a closer look at the process of intensification by which Wagner arrives at Isolde's Transfiguration and its consummatory force—a process that the career of the pitch b^2 epitomizes but by no means exhausts. Here again, the heart of the matter lies in the first seventeen measures of the Prelude, this time in the deployment of two basic sources of structure: the Desire motive and the *Tristan* chord. Heard on the oboe in mm. 2–3, the Desire motive consists of a semitonal ascent from G♯ to B. The *Tristan* chord, which is conventionally described as a half-diminished seventh, appears on the downbeat of m. 2 in the form F–B–D♯–G♯ (hereafter T), and on the downbeat of m. 6 in the form A♭(G♯)–D–F♯–B (hereafter T′). Drawing on the work of Robert Bailey and Allen Forte, I will try to show that an impelling musical process of *Tristan und Isolde* is the progressive reinterpretation of T, T′, and the Desire motive—the outcome of which is nothing other than Isolde's Transfiguration.[35]

The Prelude opens with a model (mm. 1–3) and a sequential statement (mm. 4–7). According to the standard account that I invoked earlier in this chapter, the model presents T as a local dissonance that resolves to the dominant seventh of A, whereupon the sequence presents T′ as a local dissonance that resolves to the dominant seventh of C. Robert Bailey, mindful of the fact that the operatic version of the Prelude, unlike the concert version, ends in C, argues that the opening resolutions to E^7 and G^7 intimate what he calls a double-tonic complex, a situation in which two keys a minor third apart have equal claims, though at different times, to be the tonic. Bailey also demonstrates that it is at least possible to hear T and T′ as structural sonorities, in particular as minor triads of A♭ (G♯) and B with added major sixths. As Bailey observes, when the

---

34. Ibid.

35. Robert Bailey, "An Analytical Study of the Sketches and Drafts," in Wagner, *Prelude and Transfiguration*, 113–46; Allen Forte, "New Approaches to the Linear Analysis of Music," *Journal of the American Musicological Society* 41 (1988): 315–48.

Desire motive and its sequential continuation return during the love duet of act 1, Wagner "actually replaces the earlier *Tristan* chords with the straightforward A♭ and B triads, changing their mode to major."[36] If we accept Bailey's reading, the "E⁷" and "G⁷" chords of mm. 3 and 7 change their spots; they become German sixths of A♭ and B. In essence, that is to say that they remain dominants, only with alternate roots. Hence Bailey's double-tonic complex acquires a shadow, a parallel complex a semitone lower.

The juxtaposition of the A♭(G♯)-minor and B-minor triads in the two basic forms of the *Tristan* chord can be taken as a harmonic projection of the Desire motive. The tones G♯ and B are the cardinal points of the motive, and as Example 21 shows, the model and sequence that open the Prelude arpeggiate G♯–B as a structural interval. G♯ and B are further accentuated by the fact that they are the only tones that T and T′ have in common: they form the nucleus of the *Tristan* chord itself.

A♭(G♯) and B, however, whether as tones or harmonies, do not carry equal structural weight. B is the melodic goal of the Desire motive — and of the act 2 love duet; B major is the harmonic goal of the opera. Accordingly, if T′ is taken as a decorated triad of B minor, we would expect it to receive special accentuation in mm. 1–17 of the Prelude. Another look at Example 21 will reveal not only that this happens, but that it happens doubly. Measures 1–16 form a structural arpeggiation of T′, a configuration we might just as well call the tonic added-sixth. Furthermore, the deceptive cadence of m. 17 takes off from a dominant-ninth chord of A, which, as Allen Forte observes, can be regarded as a composite of T′ and the E⁷ of m. 3.[37]

The large-scale impact of T, T′, and the Desire motive crystallizes when we recall that Isolde's Transfiguration not only ends in B, but also begins in A♭. With this in mind, we can sketch the overall movement of the opera about as follows:

36. Wagner, *Prelude and Transfiguration*, 121–23; quote 123.
37. Forte, "New Approaches," 328. Forte actually hears the composite *instead* of the dominant ninth, in keeping with a general claim that linear processes in the Prelude are primary, tonal ones secondary (or even tertiary). My own position is that the music raises this question of primacy, but only in order to dramatize its undecidability.

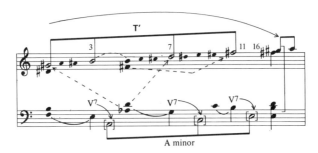

EXAMPLE 21.   Wagner, *Tristan und Isolde*. Prelude, mm. 1–17: graph. Derived from Wagner, *Prelude and Transfiguration from Tristan
and Isolde*, ed. Robert Bailey (New York, 1985), 127–29,
by Christopher Lewis, "Mirrors and Metaphors: Reflections
on Schoenberg and Nineteenth-Century Tonality," *19th-
Century Music* 11 (1987): 30.

1. The Prelude establishes the double-tonic complex A/C,
together with its shadow A♭(G♯)–B. The shadow remains
more or less marginal while the A/C complex governs the act
as a whole.[38]

2. Act 2 begins to accentuate the shadow, to give it a
more dynamic presence. The reunion of Tristan and Isolde at
the beginning of scene 2 gravitates toward climaxes in C, but
the comsummatory love duet that begins with the phrase "O
sink' hernieder, Nacht der Liebe," seeks closure in B. "O
sink' hernieder," which marks the midpoint of the opera,
also begins in A♭ —an A♭ that emerges, as Bailey observes,
by splitting off from an extended section in A♮.[39]

3. Act 3 begins in F minor—the relative minor of A♭
—and ends with the decisive replacement of the A/C complex by A♭(G♯)/B in Isolde's Transfiguration. At its close,
the Transfiguration circles back to mm. 2–3 of the Prelude
and states the Desire motive, at pitch, on the oboes and English horn. With this gesture, Wagner encourages us to hear
the Transfiguration as a tonal projection of the Desire motive
in the latter's primary structural form, the dyad G♯–B. The

38. Wagner, *Prelude and Transfiguration*, 121–22.
39. Ibid., 140.

effect of intensification, of expansion on the largest scale, also extends to the harmonic projection of the motive that occurs when we hear T and T′ as added-sixth chords. To go a step further: if we think of the F-minor opening of Act 3 as an allusion to the F-major cadence at m. 17 of the Prelude, then the overall movement of the act forms a retrograde of the first two structural "sentences" of the opera: mm. 8–17, which evolve the cadence to F, and mm. 1–7, which establish the double-tonic complex(es) and set forth G♯–B as a structural motive.

A further perspective on the Transfiguration can be drawn from the work of Allen Forte. Forte demonstrates that the Prelude is ruled by linear projections of T, T′, and other collections, all of which represent the pitch-class set 4–27. For this reason, he regards the *Tristan* chord as "a self-standing musical object, not dependent for its meaning upon a resolution to some other sonority."[40] Considered in these terms, the Transfiguration gains its intensity not by expanding or clarifying previous tonal implications, but by reinterpreting linear events in tonal terms, releasing a flood of tonal meanings that has previously been dammed up. Forte's position would seem to rule out Bailey's, not to mention the standard account, but it is neither necessary nor desirable to decide among the three. On the contrary, the triple ambiguity is precisely what this music seeks. The lack of definite structural boundaries, like the achievement of closure through intensification, conforms to the rhythm of libidinal desire.

The accentuation of the G♯–B dyad accumulates through a series of cardinal moments. Example 22 is adapted from Forte's graph of mm. 79–89 of the Prelude, where the Desire motive overlaps with the supreme climax of the music and ushers in a recapitulation of the opening. As the beamed notes show, this passage forms an interlocking linear statement of two forms of set 4–27: the *Tristan*-chord T and the inversion represented by the E^7 first heard in m. 3. The common tones in this process are G♯ and B, which are accentuated not only by this commonality itself but also by the two-octave leap that conjoins the close of T and the opening of $E^{7}*$. (The asterisk

40. Forte, "New Approaches," 327*n*.

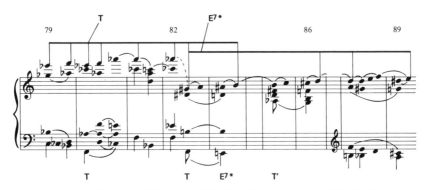

EXAMPLE 22.   Wagner, *Tristan und Isolde*. Linear graph of Prelude, mm. 79–89. From Allen Forte, "New Approaches to the Linear Analysis of Music," *JAMS* 41 (1988): 333.

identifies the chord as an inversion of T instead of/as well as a dominant seventh.)

The lovers' apostrophe, "O sink' hernieder, Nacht der Liebe," at the midpoint of act 2 brings a similar interlock closer to the foreground. Tristan's vocal line for this phrase is an explicit ascending arpeggiation of T; Isolde's line is a more decorated descending arpeggiation (Example 23; Isolde closes with an octave displacement that also embraces an ascending form of T). The two lines overlap so that Isolde enters descending from C♭ (B) to A♭ just after Tristan has finished ascending from A♭ to C♭; at the moment of transition, Tristan attacks C♭ as Isolde attacks A♭. This manner of intertwining the lovers' voices once again accentuates the critical interval of Desire that will, when projected tonally in Isolde's Transfiguration, grant the descent of the longed-for "Nacht der Liebe."

Before that can happen, however, Tristan must die. It is at Tristan's death that Wagner begins the restructuring of the *Lust*-trope that will come to fruition in the Transfiguration. Isolde, arrived from Cornwall at last, holds the dying Tristan in her arms while the Prelude is recapitulated from the Desire motive to the F-major deceptive cadence and a little beyond. At first the music is very loud and agitated; Tristan, after all, is dying at the very moment of reunion. Yet the clamor and agitation steadily subside, as does the tempo, yielding at last to a tranquillity that irradiates the cadence. In another instance of expansion into "measureless space," Wagner

EXAMPLE 23.   Wagner, *Tristan und Isolde*. Act 2.

gives the cadence an unprecedented breadth, sustaining its B♮ appoggiatura many times longer than he does in the Prelude. The swell
of desire is correspondingly fuller, its melodic resolution more gratifying, its accentuation of the pitch b^2 the more telling. The lovers
may be cheated of each other after agonies of anticipation, yet their
separation draws to a focus in the primary form of the *Lust*-trope,
music that embodies the life, not the death, of libidinal desire.

As Tristan dies, Wagner intimates that the A/C complex of act 1
dies with him. In the Prelude, the deceptive cadence is followed by
a C-major progression from the dominant side that ends with a
cadential downbeat (mm. 18–20); this is answered by a quasi-

cadential plagal progression to the triad of A major (mm. 20–21). (The progressions are linked by introductory D-chords in modally altered roles, V^6_5 [V^4_3]/V and iv, respectively.) At Tristan's death, the C-major progression reappears, but the A-major answer does not follow; the bond between the two keys has begun to crumble.

What does follow at this point is Isolde singing the strangely affirmative words "Ich bin's." She sings them twice: first to the step A–G♯, then to the step C–B. And having thus melodically trans-formed the tones of one complex into the other, she takes the once-more accentuated G♯–B as a cue to project a linear statement of T' as a "self-standing musical object."

The Transfiguration, where all such processes culminate, is less something that Isolde does than something she embodies. In musical terms, the essential action occurs in the orchestra. Isolde's role is to reperform that action as a speech act, the force of which is to cancel the impression of tragedy, to construe intensity of passion as a reli-gious illumination—as what Kerman calls "the compelling higher reality of our spiritual universe."[41]

The music itself is, famously, a recapitulation of two passages, one in A♭, the other in B, from the big love duet of act 2. In their original form, these passages are separated by a group of intervening keys. By skipping over the latter, Wagner at last enfranchises the elective affinity between the keys of A♭ and B that has been latent ever since the Desire motive first sounded in the Prelude. As Example 24 shows, the A♭ portion of the Transfiguration begins with a two-measure phrase, the downbeats of which are occupied by the chords of A♭ and C♭ (B). This in turn becomes the model for a sequence that opens on C♭, thus rearticulating the conjunction of A♭ and C♭ on the next structural level. In act 2, these processes form little more than local accentuations of the Desire motive in its structural form. In act 3, they represent the gradual expansion/intensification of the motive into the harmonic design of the Transfiguration, which will also unfold—*is* also unfolding—by conjoining the previously separated sonorities of A♭ and B. After a few measures of deferral and remi-niscence, this process culminates as Isolde's vocal line passes from A♭

41. Kerman, *Opera as Drama*, 195.

EXAMPLE 24.   Wagner, *Tristan und Isolde*. Opening of Transfiguration.

as $\hat{1}$ of A♭ major to C♭, now genuinely B, as $\hat{5}$ of E major (IV of B). A plagal cadence to B major follows at once.

The crowning process of the Transfiguration centers on two rhythmically variant versions of the same theme, identified as *x* and *x'* in Example 25. At the words "Heller schallend," *x* makes a climactic arrival and sounds three times over plagal cadences. Related melodic figures then project an ascent by semitones from G♯^{2} to G♯^{3}. At this point a steadily mounting crescendo reaches its peak, and *x'* emerges, sounding twice over two more plagal cadences. More subdominant harmony leads on to the climactic full cadences grouped around Isolde's final words, "höchste Lust," where *x* reappears twice in its original form and once more in augmentation. The expressive force of this music lodges in the details—as if Nietzsche had been right to call Wagner a great miniaturist:

> 1. Both *x'* and the "Heller schallend" statement of *x* form projections of B and G♯ as structural tones: $\hat{5}$ and $\hat{3}$ of E major (IV), respectively. G♯ also manifests a quasi-libidinal mobility by sounding in ardent combination with the B-major triad (Examples 25a,b). The sonority that results can (or, rather, should) be interpreted in complementary ways. On the one hand, it constitutes a suspension of $\hat{3}$ of E major into the tonic triad. On the other (as Bailey notes),[42] it constitutes a reinterpretation of T', the tonic added-sixth, as major rather than minor.

42. Wagner, *Prelude and Transfiguration*, 146.

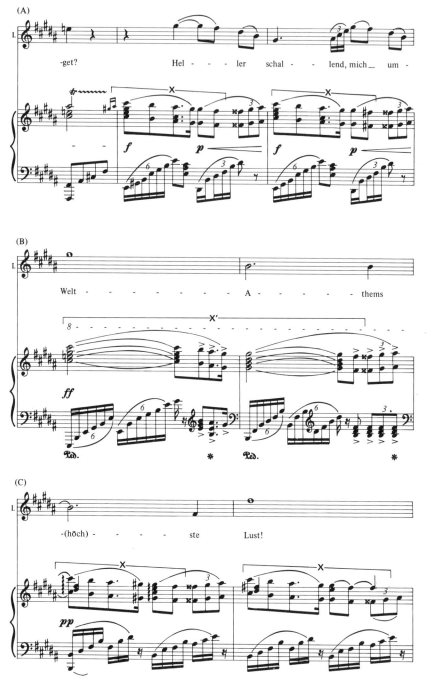

EXAMPLE 25.   Wagner, *Tristan und Isolde*. Transfiguration.

2. The prominence of E major as IV throughout the closing pages of the opera also bears more than one meaning. It represents both an expansion of the plagal cadence that effects the transition between the A♭ and B portions of the Transfiguration and a reinterpretation of E^7*, which precedes T′ in mm. 3–6 of the Prelude.

3. The "höchste Lust" version of x completes the restructuring of the *Lust*-trope by reinterpreting the master tones G♯ and B. G♯, its work finished, surrenders its structural role to become a simple appoggiatura to the dominant. B, as the reward of its many accentuations, at last emerges—wells up—in the form of the pitch b^2 as $\hat{1}$ of B major. And just as this happens, "Isolde" (so runs Wagner's stage direction), "as if transfigured, sinks gently in Brangäne's arms onto Tristan's body."[43]

In dramatic terms, this transfiguration comes to Isolde not merely in but by means of Tristan's metamorphosis from a real to an imaginary object of desire. Isolde's text begins with the fantasy that Tristan is alive, is smiling, is awakening. This fictitious Tristan is then dissolved into a fluid element, explicitly identified with the music we are hearing, that pours from Tristan to Isolde and finally envelops her, its origin forgotten:

Höre ich nur diese Weise,	Can it be that I alone
die so wundervoll und leise,	hear this wondrous, glorious tune,
Wonne klagend,	softly stealing,
alles sagend,	all revealing,
mild versöhnend	mildly glowing,
aus ihm tönend,	from him flowing,
in mich dringet,	through me pouring,
auf sich schwinget,	rising, soaring,
hold erhallend	boldly singing,
um mich klinget?	round me ringing?
Heller schallend,	Brighter growing,

43. Ibid., 97.

mich umwallend,   o'er me flowing,
sind es Wellen   are they waves
sanfter Lüfte?   of tender radiance?[44]

This passage conforms in every detail to the Freudian language of love. The ego-libido that was invested in the beloved as object-libido now flows back onto the subject and becomes ego-libido once more, yielding a flood of narcissistic pleasure so overwhelming that the ego drowns in it. The transitional moment in this process is the dissolution of Tristan's image: the moment that Isolde sings "Heller schallend" while theme x makes its first climactic appearance.

The movement of psychosexual regression is also embodied in the "regressive," that is, the recapitulatory character of the Transfiguration as a whole. The music returns Isolde to the scene of her fullest earlier rapture and completes in fantasy the cadence/consummation that was shattered in reality. Even the material omitted from the recapitulation plays a role in this. In act 2, the future A♭ portion of the Transfiguration ends with an intrusion: one of the series of warnings that Brangäne, from her tower, sends down to the lovers. The intrusion vanishes in act 3, its omen of unfulfillment revoked by the flood of final bliss.

Isolde's dispersal of Tristan's image—and her own awareness—into the unqualified movement of "höchste Lust" also testifies to a weakening of gender boundaries. In its original form, the A♭ portion of the Transfiguration is first sung by Tristan. Isolde follows with a parallel passage, omitted in the Transfiguration, in which she repeats virtually the whole of Tristan's vocal line. This strophic articulation of the lovers' desire acts as a denial of sexual difference—and its inequalities. As desiring subjects, Tristan and Isolde are indistinguishable. (Wagner's only concession to contemporary sexual ideology is that Isolde takes instruction from Tristan and affirms herself by repeating his words. This is not, however, a process of contamination, as its counterparts almost inevitably are in nineteenth-century love scenes.) By returning to Tristan's strophe but omitting her own, Isolde reaffirms that the subject of desire is indifferent to gender, that the true human being, to recall Wagner's dictum, is both male and

44. Ibid., 96–97; translation by Andrew Porter.

female. It may even be that the subject expressing itself in Isolde's voice is Desire itself, impelled, as Foucault says it must be, to reveal itself as the truth.

Throughout the opera, as has often been noted, Wagner portrays Tristan and Isolde in terms that reverse certain deeply entrenched gender roles. Tristan, the most passive and masochistic of heroes, occupies a traditionally feminine position. Constantly wounded, he ought to embody male anxieties about castration, dependency, and impotence; instead he assumes the traditional feminine power to attract, to entrance, the other. Isolde is the more active, the more traditionally "masculine" of the lovers. When she brandishes and then extinguishes the hymeneal torch in act 2, she appropriates, seemingly with no resistance from Wagner, an age-old masculine position, not to mention the phallus itself.

The apostrophe, "O sink' hernieder, Nacht der Liebe," perfectly epitomizes the mobility of gender between Tristan and Isolde. The crisscrossing arpeggiations of T in the vocal lines intimate a sexual difference that is also a sexual sameness. Masculine and feminine overlap as mirror images of each other, and this just as the lovers ask for a forgetfulness in which their separate identities will fade away ("gib Vergessen, daß ich lebe"). Not that Tristan and Isolde could be anything other than a heterosexual couple. Wagner's own sexuality (or its idealization) is plainly embodied in Tristan, and besides, the convention is inexorable; Tchaikovsky, too, wrote heterosexual operas. Nonetheless, Tristan and Isolde are constituted as subjects in terms that scuttle the concepts of instinct, of the primacy of the object, of sexuality as a force of nature, even of Nature itself. They are constituted as subjects by a desire that overflows all boundaries, and for which gender is finally no more than a pretext.

III

Tristan und Isolde, then, is a radical work not only in its musical procedures but also in its sexual ideology. Yet for all that, it does not make a perfectly clean break with prelibidinal modes of thought. The desire that it celebrates can only find satisfaction through the loss of an object, but there is still only *one* object in the world whose loss can, so to speak, inflict that satisfaction. And although the desire that speaks through Isolde's Transfiguration is neither masculine nor feminine, Isolde still embodies it as a woman who dies into the image of a beloved man—as, indeed, she has been taught to do by that man himself in the original form of her A♭ music. Only in its representation of desire as a tidal force that in large measure constitutes the personal subject does *Tristan und Isolde* commit itself unconditionally to the libidinal model. That is, of course, a rather large "only." Large enough, in any case, to underwrite the signature effect of the opera: the "end of the world" fantasy that dominates the love duets of act 2 and reaches its peak in Isolde's Transfiguration. Freud suggests that this fantasy typically arises when the subject concentrates all of its (ego- and object-) libido on a single love object, and in so doing depreciates or derealizes everything else.[45] The example he gives— presumably with act 2 in mind—is *Tristan und Isolde*. Act 3 adds the converse. The Transfiguration shows that the end of the world can come, and come most forcefully, when the totality of desire rushes back in a flood from the object to the subject.

Hugo Wolf's "Ganymed" (1888) is less apocalyptic but more thoroughgoing in its commitment to libidinal desire. We will need to begin here with the text (by Goethe), from which the music diverges in principled ways—a technique, as I have argued elsewhere, that is basic to the Lied as a genre.[46]

Ganymede is a marginal figure in classical mythology: a comely Trojan youth carried off to Olympus by an eagle of Zeus, or by the enamored Zeus himself in the form of an eagle. From the fifteenth to the seventeenth centuries, Ganymede's rape by the eagle was a fairly widespread icon of homosexual love, both in poetry and (especially) in the visual arts.[47] By the eighteenth century, this tradition was in eclipse, but some trace of it seems to have guided Goethe when he

45. From Freud's case study of the famous paranoic Daniel Paul Schreber, in Freud, *Three Case Histories*, ed. Philip Rieff (New York, 1963), 173n.

46. I have argued this most fully in *Music and Poetry: The Nineteenth Century and After* (Berkeley and Los Angeles, 1984), 125–70. See also my essay "The Schubert Lied: Romantic Form and Romantic Consciousness," in *Schubert: Critical and Analytical Studies*, ed. Walter Frisch (Lincoln, Neb., 1986), 200–236, which also contains an analysis of Schubert's "Ganymed."

47. On this subject see James Saslow, *Ganymede in the Renaissance: Homosexuality in Art and Society* (New Haven, 1986).

wrote his "Ganymed" around 1774. Goethe's version of the rape story is strongly revisionary: no eagle is involved, and neither is Zeus's desire. What drives this Ganymede into Zeus's arms is his own sexual awakening.

The poem, a monologue by Ganymede, falls into two unequal parts. The first portrays Ganymede's deeply erotic longings to embrace Nature, Beauty, the Earth—all terms gendered feminine in Western culture; the second redirects these longings skyward toward the masculine bosom of the "alliebende Vater" ("all-loving Father").[48] This reorientation does not involve a lapse or sublimation of eroticism; if anything, the reverse is true:

> Es schweben die Wolken
> Abwärts, die Wolken
> Neigen sich der sehnenden Liebe.
> Mir! Mir!
>
> (23–26)

The clouds hover down, the clouds incline themselves to yearning love! To me! To me!

Using a fragmentary, exclamatory rhetoric, the poem matches its rhythmic impetus to the urgency of Ganymede's desire. Much of this urgency stems from the lack of an object, or rather from the way that Nature both veils and reveals the object—we are not yet dealing here with libidinal desire. The poem is deeply object-centered, almost an allegory of what Freud would later call object-finding. Ganymede

48. For text and a translation of the poem, see the Appendix. It is striking that the poem *presumes* the feminine affiliations in its first part, while it explicitly *states* the masculine affiliations of its second part. This difference (which Carolyn Abbate drew to my attention) can be taken to support a reading in which Ganymede concretizes an indefinite mass of desires by assigning them a masculine object.

The reading pursued here, which traces a movement from a feminine to a masculine object, is neatly encapsulated in the climactic image of the clouds' *Schoß*. The German word can mean both lap and womb. Thus, Ganymede is either borne off by masculine clouds that replace the famous eagle or born to Zeus's embrace from the womb of nature. (I take this opportunity to correct my mistranslation of "eurem Schoße" in both *Music and Poetry* and my essay "The Schubert Lied"; the mistake, which I thank Marshall Brown for calling to my attention, does not affect my arguments there.)

repeatedly personifies the natural objects to which he directs his
desire; he turns all perception into a caress as he seeks another body
to join his in a mutual embrace:

> Ach, an deinem Busen
> Lieg ich, schmachte,
> Und deine Blumen, dein Gras
> Drängen sich an mein Herz.
> Du kühlst den brennenden
> Durst meines Busens,
> Lieblicher Morgenwind!

> (11–17)

Ah, I lie on your breast, languish, and your flowers, your grass
press upon my heart. You cool the burning thirst of my breast,
lovely morning wind!

Schubert's setting of the poem (1817), which is as much Wolf's
point of departure as the poem itself, is object-centered in the same
way. Schubert idealizes the process of object-finding in extravagant
terms, at some cost to the eroticism of the text. The effect is clearest
at the close, when Schubert elaborates the phrase "Alliebender
Vater" through three increasingly long and florid melismas.

Wolf's setting recasts Goethe's text as a libidinal idyll. The means
to this end is the *Lust*-trope, which is applied in multiple, overlapping
ways so that no element of the song remains unaffected by it. Wolf
binds together Ganymede's convulsive advances toward fulfillment
with music of undisturbed continuity; moments of textual bliss are
enveloped by the pleasures of texture and sonority but not matched
by musical closures. The song is as subject-centered as the text is
object-centered. Wolf subdues the candid physicality embedded in
Goethe's rhythm and imagery by subduing the physicality of the
music. The song is prevailingly quiet; it avoids sustained climaxes; its
pianistic texture emphasizes the high treble; its tessitura is unde-
manding. The emphasis thus falls on the fluid movement of desire
itself as it slips from object to object, as it hovers, swells, and at every
moment renews itself.

Unlike Wagner's, Wolf's *Lust*-tropes do not focus on specific textual climaxes. Instead, they are diffused throughout the song, as

independent of the text as libidinal desire is of its objects. At certain moments, one trope or another does crystallize into implicit commentary on the text, but never with enough dramatic force to impede the prevailing impression of an endless, self-delighting flow of desire.

The most fundamental of Wolf's *Lust*-tropes is realized at the level of large-scale tonal movement. Cast in ternary form, "Ganymed" is in D major. Both the first and the final sections begin with an extended (and perfectly straightforward) harmonic projection of the augmented triad D–F♯–A♯(B♭). After a brief transition, both sections conclude in the tonic. In the first section, this pattern defers the establishment of key-feeling until the conclusion, and once it emerges, the key-feeling assumes a transitional rather than a closural character, thanks to the absence of root-position triads. Most of the triads in the song, tonic or otherwise, are sixth chords.

The middle section falls into two parts. The first consists of a simple D-major progression; the second is an ambiguous passage that concludes with a sudden tonicization of A♭ major, the key of the tritone (Example 26, mm. 37–39). The establishment of this A♭ is strong enough to polarize it against D, and it is this same A♭ from which, in a startling turn of events, the song makes a direct return to D at the start of the recapitulation (Example 26, mm. 40–42). A♭ and D are, in fact, the only tonalities established in the whole song.

The harmonic processes of Wolf's "Ganymed" thus shuttle between diatonic and whole-tone allegiances. D major forms a lucid and strongly cyclical tonic, but it is a tonic heard continually against the structural projections of a scale that can have no tonic, that can neither accumulate nor release harmonic tension, that encompasses tritonal movement with perfect fluidity. A more complete harmonic realization of libidinal dynamics, of recurrent attachment within a context of pure mobility, would be hard to find.

Cadences also play a major role in Wolf's *Lust*-trope technique—or, rather, their absence does. There are precious few of them to be found, and of these none is a perfect cadence. More important, the primary large-scale process in the song is the gradual dissolution of cadential movement. As the ecstatic union between Ganymede and Zeus draws nearer, the prospect of matching it with a culminating cadence on the model of *Tristan und Isolde* dwindles and disappears. Thus the articulation of harmony in "Ganymed," like the underlying

EXAMPLE 26. Wolf, "Ganymed." At the close of m. 40, the dominant of A♭ that occurs in the parallel location in m. 38 fails to appear. It is replaced by a dominant of D at the start of m. 41. Is it coincidental that the arpeggios in mm. 38 and 40 outline a half-diminished seventh—the basic sonority of the *Tristan* chord?

harmonic conception, exceeds even Isolde's Transfiguration in radicalizing the *Lust*-trope—that is, in taking a rapturous deferral as the trope of fulfilled desire.

The anticadential process unfolds about as follows:[49]

    1. The conclusion of the first section begins with two cadences to the tonic sixth chord (Example 27a). These are sufficient to establish the tonality, but they are also rhythmically and registrally unobtrusive, almost tacit.

    2. The middle section begins on an interrupted cadence and generates no cadences of its own—except to the tritone.

    3. The recapitulation begins with a rhythmic displacement that conjures away the articulation of a seemingly inevitable cadence (Example 26, mm. 41–42). The effect is all the more telling because the recapitulation begins with the first root-position triad in the song.

    4. Later, the recapitulation alters the second of the paired cadences by which the first section establishes the tonic, V_2^4–I^6 becoming the quasi-plagal $iv^{7\sharp}$–I (Example 27b). In late-nineteenth-century practice, the iv_4^6 (later iv)–I cadence rivals the traditional V–I as a source of finality, but Wolf's hybridized $iv^{7\sharp}$ does not convey the same feeling, especially in a piece that articulates its form by deferring a full cadence at each sectional juncture. The displacement of the dominant by the subdominant acts as an enhancement in fluidity.

    5. The vocal line ends over a tonic six-four chord, which some other song might use to herald a full cadence. Not this song. Instead we are given a piano postlude that repeatedly echoes the quasi-plagal move from $iv^{7\sharp}$ to I. The feeling that something is missing (though in no sense missed) is quite specific. The plagal series begins at the point where a full cadence would have paralleled and resolved the interrupted cadence that carries us from the first section to the second. Wolf, who never hesitates to end a song with a transitional

49. This process may, incidentally, be understood as Wolf's principal critique of Schubert's setting, which is virtually an exaltation of the cadence—not only at the close, but even at phrases like "Lieg ich, schmachte."

EXAMPLE 27. Wolf, "Ganymed."

sonority, here coaxes a root-position tonic into the transitional role. To the last measure, his "Ganymed" identifies fulfillment with ecstatic deferral.

What is true of harmonic cadences in the song is equally true of melodic ones. Ganymede's vocal line never comes to rest, and it is at its most ecstatic where it is most restless—notably in the important parallel phrases "Unendliche Schöne" and "Umfangend umfangen," which end on the seventh of a dominant-seventh chord. No vocal phrase in the whole song ends on the first degree of a triad, let alone a tonic triad. In any but the most local sense, there simply are no melodic cadences in this music. Wolf also takes pains to elongate the syllable *Lieb* wherever it occurs, a technique applied to both key terms in the phrase "der sehnenden Liebe." The emphasis is another way of favoring the subject over the object, the movement of desire over the goal of desire. A similar emphasis arises from the tendency of the vocal line to conclude its phrases with a melodic descent, as if to embody a desire that continually folds back on itself, that avoids the climactic intensities of the tenor's highest notes. Only once does the voice rise as high as the G at the top of the staff.

Wolf's harmonic and melodic processes are paralleled by a large-scale rhythmic projection of the movement of desire. Ganymede's vocal line is a model of suppleness and fluidity. Its phrases never begin on the downbeat of a measure, and they end there only once or twice, as if by chance, during the first half of the song. It is continually syncopated but never locked into strong cross-rhythms. Its declamation is perfect, but deliberately smudges points of textual closure. In sum, like libidinal desire, the vocal line responds to fixities and boundaries by sliding past them.

As the song proceeds, the accompaniment undergoes a process of rhythmic loosening, as if the voice were drawing the rest of the music into Ganymede's sphere of all-enveloping desire. The piano part of the first section is largely foursquare, with steady quarter-note motion in the left hand and steady eighth-note motion in the right. The closing measures of the section introduce dotted figures in cross-accents that form a rhythmic transition to the middle section, where the right-hand part is continuously syncopated. The second half of the middle section advances on the fluidity of the first; it introduces sixteenth-note figures that swirl upward in the left hand, the first six measures of them in the irregular pattern ♫♫ ♫♫ ♫ . The recapitulation restores the original eighth-note motion in the right hand, but the left-hand part now becomes a series of unrhythmicized tremolos—accelerations of the sixteenth-note motion heard in the middle section. The tremolos, with their blurring of rhythmic and melodic boundaries, become the ultimate image in the song for the fluidity, the deliquescence, of libidinal desire. This effect is intensified when, after the pivotal phrase "der sehnenden Liebe," the tremolos repeatedly swell to forte and subside to piano or pianissimo. The song ends by expanding on the dotted rhythms that evolved, as we are meant to recall, to effect a transition.

The desire represented by Wolf clearly possesses an immeasurably greater independence from its object than its counterpart in Wagner, but I have not yet commented on the most radical aspect of this independence, its explicit bisexuality. Ganymede's desire turns from a heteroerotic to a homoerotic object, a turn that on a psychoanalytic reading is enhanced rather than diminished by the fact that the new object is an all-loving father. Neither Goethe nor Wolf articulates any difference in quality between Ganymede's desire for nature and his desire for the father; the two desires are equally physical, equally sensual, equally imbued with yearning. Wolf affirms this equivalence, simply and without fuss, by his handling of sectional divisions. Both outer sections of the ternary form trace a movement from recognition to impulse. The first section begins as Ganymede hails springtime as his beloved, and ends with his urgent wish to grasp natural beauty in his arms. The recapitulation begins as Ganymede proclaims that his desire has changed direction, and ends with his even more urgent wish to reach the father's bosom. The musical parallelism between these sections testifies to their libidinal parallelism. As far as desire is concerned, a difference in object is no difference at all.

Some well-placed thematic cross-references arise to confirm this principle. Most notably, the setting of "Mit tausendfacher Liebeswonne" with reference to natural beauty finds an echo in the setting of "der sehnenden Liebe" with reference to the father. We have already remarked on the similar tie between "Unendliche Schöne" and "Umfangen umfangend." Ganymede's desire, however, is inclined not only to disregard the gender of its object, but also to dismantle the gender of its subject. The ease with which Ganymede evades metrical and harmonic boundaries in his vocal line, all the while coursing from one love object to another, would suggest a feminized character to a late-nineteenth-century audience, a personal subject that shuttles undecidably between a masculine and a feminine identity. Gender, in this context, is no longer even a pretext for desire; it is simply a repository for erotic images.

In conclusion, a reflection: It is commonplace to speak of a "hothouse atmosphere" when describing fin-de-siècle eroticism, as if sexuality had condensed into a palpable sultriness around the year 1890. It may well be that this habit is no more than a metaphorical projection of the libidinal split between desire and its object. As free-flowing subjectivity, libidinal desire invites representation by rhetorical figures that deemphasize its material, corporeal dimension without rendering it intangible. Hence desire as water, as humidity, as excess of light or darkness. To put this another way, libidinal desire is detachable from the human body. The traditional identification of the body as the lower part of human nature, a site of shame, dirt, and disease, no longer need carry over to a desire conceived of as libido. Libidinal representations, therefore, open up the unprecedented possibility of idealizing sexuality as the means by which the body transcends itself. What I hope to have shown in this chapter is that the music of the late nineteenth century develops this possibility as intelligibly as any other cultural practice of the age.

6

"AS IF A VOICE WERE IN THEM":

Music, Narrative, and Deconstruction

In his essay "Force and Signification," Jacques Derrida considers the historical antagonism between two principles of understanding, structure and force. By "structure," Derrida means the concept of an organized totality, modeled implicitly on visual/geometric order and characterized by an interdependency of parts. "Force," a deliberately imprecise term, is temporal and dynamic in character and associated with value, beauty, feeling; it is graspable principally as it disrupts structure and compels change. Derrida admits to a certain bias in favor of force, but insists that it is not his purpose to perpetuate the well-established opposition between the terms "through the simple motions of balancing, equilibration, or overturning." On the contrary:

> To counter this simple alternative, to counter the simple choice of one of the terms . . . against the other, we maintain that it is necessary to seek new concepts and new models, an *economy* escaping this system of metaphysical oppositions. . . . If we appear to oppose [force to structure], it is because from within the classical system we wish to make apparent the noncritical privilege naively granted [to the latter] by a certain structuralism. Our discourse irreducibly belongs to the system of metaphysical oppositions. The break with this structure of belonging can be announced only through a *certain* organization, a certain *strategic* arrangement which, within the field

of metaphysical opposition, uses the strengths of the field to turn its own stratagems against it, producing a force of dislocation that spreads itself throughout the entire system, fissuring it in every direction and thoroughly *delimiting* it.[1]

This passage forms one of Derrida's many programmatic efforts to advance the project that he calls deconstruction. The term is widely misconstrued, partly because Derrida regards deconstruction as a practice rather than a principle, an activity that eludes reduction to a formula. As a practice, deconstruction aims at minimizing the authority that may be invested in potentially monolithic structures. Such structures are based on a metaphysical idea/ideal of presence; they incorporate such concepts as true or unitary meaning, absolute or self-evident knowledge, and immediacy of experience or self-apprehension, together with derivatives of these ideas that may at first go unrecognized as such. Deconstruction does *not* seek the obviously impossible (and perhaps even dystopian) goal of doing away with these structures or denying their impact. Instead it employs both rigor and playfulness to affirm the movement of difference, of de-centering, of fecundity within the texts and disciplines of the same. If one can speak of key words in this context, then the key word here is *affirms*. Though deconstruction is in part a practice of vigilance against the repressive effects of structure, its larger purpose is to bring forth an affirmative energy by which both force and structure can invigorate each other.

In "Force and Signification," Derrida is principally concerned with philosophy and literary criticism, disciplines that shade into each other in his text. The strategic arrangement that he celebrates as a force of dislocation, however, is not to be confined to those disciplines, which Derrida himself might call merely "regional." As a structural trope that I will shortly be calling *other-voicedness*, Derrida's strategic dislocation forms one of the major rhetorical and esthetic projects of the West between the late eighteenth and the early twentieth centuries—between, say, the twilight of Enlightenment and the

---

1. Jacques Derrida, *Writing and Difference*, trans. Alan Bass (Chicago, 1978), 19–20. If one substitutes the opposition music criticism/theory for the opposition force/structure in this statement, the results are—to say the least—suggestive.

dawn of psychoanalysis. My purpose in this chapter is to study this trope of dislocation—after filling out its contours a little further—with special reference to its deployment in music.

I

The most explicit nineteenth-century advocate of practical decon-struction, of deconstruction on a daily basis, is Friedrich Nietzsche. Even more than Derrida, Nietzsche professes discomfort with his own "written and painted thoughts" when they threaten "to turn into truths . . . so heart-breakingly decent, so boring." This ossification, he suggests, is unavoidably imposed by a pressure on (and within) language toward uniformity of meaning. "To use the same words," he writes,

> is not a sufficient guarantee of understanding; one [is coerced to] use the same words for the same genus of inward experience; ulti-mately one must have one's experiences in *common*. . . . One must call upon enormous oppositional powers in order to contend against this natural, all-too-natural *progressis in simile*, this continuous progress of man towards similarity, ordinariness, the average.[2]

The lever of contention, as Derrida too would suggest, is language itself. Since it may always be the case that "one of the two [parties] using the same words feels, means, wishes, fears different things with them,"[3] the instabilities of language and in particular its illocutionary forces can be deployed against the deadening effects of sameness. One can speak the words of the same *but in another voice*, a voice that emerges from within language to spread itself throughout the whole system, fissuring it in every direction.

Commenting on Nietzsche's deconstructive strategies, Derrida links them to textual heterogeneity—Nietzsche's stylistic signature—and to Nietzsche's "insinuation" that style is always plural. Nietzsche: "I have many stylistic possibilities—the most multifarious art of style

---

2. Friedrich Nietzsche, *Beyond Good and Evil*, trans. Marianne Cowan (Chicago, 1955), secs. 296, 268.
3. Ibid., sec. 268.

that has ever been at the disposal of one man."[4] Derrida: "[The insinuation] is that if there is going to be style, there can only be more than one."[5] Nietzsche's own favorite metaphor for his other-voicedness is appropriately preverbal, a transposition of voice to movement: it is the dance. "Thinking," he affirms,

> wants to be learned like dancing, *as* a kind of dancing. Who among Germans still knows from experience the delicate shudder that light feet in spiritual matters send into every muscle? . . . One cannot subtract dancing in every form from a noble education—to be able to dance with one's feet, with concepts, with words: for need I still add that one must be able to do it with the pen, too—that one must learn to *write*?[6]

This passage identifies writing as activity rather than expression, as a nimble patterning of words rather than the representation of meaning. And it does so with exemplary other-voicedness, by both affirming and denying that the equation thinking = dancing = writing is metaphorical. Does one think/write *like* dancing or *as* a kind of dancing? If "light feet" in spiritual matters actually make one's body light, which comes first, the dancing body or the figure of lightness? Writing in this choreographed mode explains why Nietzsche, so hostile to language, is hyperbolically proud of his way with words: "The aphorism, the apothegm, in which I am the first among Germans to be master, are the forms of 'eternity': it is my ambition to say in ten sentences what everyone else says in a book—what everyone else does *not* say in a book."[7]

As a structural trope, the stratagem of other-voicedness deploys a technique to produce an effect. The effect is explicit enough in Nietzsche; it can be described in idealized terms as a surge of self-

4. Friedrich Nietzsche, "Why I Write Such Good Books" (*Ecce Homo*), in *"On the Genealogy of Morals" and "Ecce Homo,"* trans. Walter Kaufmann (New York, 1969), sec. 4.

5. Jacques Derrida, *Spurs: Nietzsche's Styles*, trans. Barbara Harlow (Chicago, 1979), 139. I should add that Derrida's concept of "style" in this text is complex, involving notions of defensiveness, gender, inscription, and more.

6. Nietzsche, "The 'Improvers' of Mankind" (*Twilight of the Idols*), in *The Portable Nietzsche*, trans. and ed. Walter Kaufmann (New York, 1954), sec. 7.

7. Nietzsche, "Skirmishes of an Untimely Man" (*Twilight*), sec. 50.

mastery, or in more skeptical terms as an appropriation of power from the discourse that one's other-voicedness dislocates. As to the technique, it is like style in Nietzsche: if there is going to be one, there can only be more than one. This diversity notwithstanding, all techniques of other-voicedness depend on the use of Austinian "misfire" as a constructive principle. "Misfire," as we noted in Chapter 1, is Austin's term for a kind of illocutionary pratfall—or transformation: the slippage of illocutionary force beyond the ostensible or foreseeable purpose of a speech act (for our purposes: an expressive act). Again, as we have seen, *misfire* is an infelicitous term, since, as Derrida shows, what it describes is not a departure from the norm of illocution but the illocutionary norm itself. Other-voiced texts are those that accentuate the always-latent prospect of a misfire, that openly invite a reinterpretation, a revoicing, of prominent expressive acts. Such texts, we might say, mark their illocutions for deconstruction. And such a marked illocution can sometimes serve as the wedge that splits a supposed unity of self, truth, or action into fragments—though the change is not necessarily for the worse.

Two brief specimens of Romantic poetry can illustrate the workings of marked illocution and complete our preliminary survey of other-voicedness. In *The Prelude*, Wordsworth recalls a "spot of time" that befell him in the Alps:

> The torrents shooting from the clear blue sky,
> The rocks that muttered close upon our ears—
> Black drizzling crags that spake by the wayside
> As if a voice were in them—the sick sight
> And giddy prospect of the raving stream,
> The unfettered clouds and region of the heavens,
> Tumult and peace, the darkness and the light,
> Were all like workings of one mind, the features
> Of the same face, blossoms upon one tree,
> Characters of the great apocalypse,
> The types and symbols of eternity,
> Of first, and last, and midst, and without end.

> ([1805], 6.561–72)

From one perspective, the contending natural forces that Wordsworth describes here are reconciled in the structure of eternity, made legible in and through the traditional metaphor of nature as the book of God. Yet a certain strategic arrangement of the metaphors within this passage produces a force of dislocation that makes *one* perspective impossible. The discourse of the sacred, of prophecy and revelation, enters the passage when Wordsworth reinterprets the "muttering" of the rocks in his ears as a speaking voice. This voice then migrates to the plane of writing—of characters, types, and symbols—where the speech of revelation reappears as the narrative of apocalypse. Writing, however—and more especially narrative writing in types and symbols—is the origin and the medium of Wordsworth's text itself. The "great apocalypse" invoked here need not be biblical alone—or at all; the scene/text in the alpine pass may also form a preinscription of its own apocalyptic reconstruction within *The Prelude*. The likelihood of this is supported by Wordsworth's praise, a page earlier, of "usurpations" by the imagination in which "the light of sense / Goes out in flashes that have shewn to us / The invisible world" (6.534–36). A further dislocation comes with the closing line, "Of first, and last, and midst, and without end," which rewrites a moment in Milton's *Paradise Lost* when Adam and Eve enjoin the angels to "extol [God:] / Him first, him last, him midst, and without end" (5.164–65). Wordsworth's version displaces the divine presence, appropriates the divine prerogative, on behalf of a practice of writing that Nietzsche could well endorse: a writing marked by indirection (types and symbols) and self-perpetuation ("Of first, *and* last, *and* midst, *and* without end").

Two years after completing the 1805 *Prelude*, Wordsworth read the poem aloud to its dedicatee, Coleridge, on the evenings of some two weeks. Coleridge had just returned to England from Malta, where he had gone in a futile effort to overcome bad health and serious depression. As he listened, he found himself constantly reminded of the contrast between Wordsworth, "Strong in [him]self, and powerful to give strength," and himself, his "Genius given, and Knowledge won in vain." Nonetheless, his "nobler mind" prompted him to commemorate the readings in a poem, which culminates as follows:

> In silence listening, like a devout child,
> My soul lay passive, by thy various strain
> Driven as in surges now beneath the stars,

> With momentary stars of my own birth,
> Fair constellated foam, still darting off
> Into the darkness; now a tranquil sea,
> Outspread and bright, yet swelling to the moon.

("To William Wordsworth," 95–101)

This passage sets out to pay tribute to Wordsworth's poetic power, most notably by equating Wordsworth's voice with the wind, the traditional *pneuma* of inspiration. The illocutionary force of the passage, however, quickly gives way to other inclinations. Coleridge develops the metaphor that reduces him to passive childhood in terms that appropriate the active manhood supposedly reserved for (usurped by?) Wordsworth. Though "driven" by what he hears, Coleridge also moves under a power of his own, which he identifies as both creative and procreative in the phrase "With momentary stars of my own birth."[8] The movement, moreover, a continuous "darting off," suggests spontaneity, creative/erotic excitement, and perhaps above all, escape. Coleridge admits that this ferment alternates with interludes of tranquillity, but even these incorporate a qualifying movement: "outspread and bright, *yet* swelling to the moon."

Coleridge allows this process of resistance and appropriation to fissure his text in every direction. He elaborates the pictorial content of his metaphor so fully that its "original" purpose—to praise Wordsworth—becomes secondary at best. The metaphor becomes a gesture of mastery; it rivals the beauty of the text it seeks to praise. Not content with this, or perhaps conflicted about it, Coleridge also intrudes a footnote to justify his pictorial emphasis. The note, however, is nothing other than a quotation from Coleridge's own prose: "Every now and then light detachments of [a] white cloud-like foam darted off from [our] vessel's side, each with its own small constellation, over the Sea, and scoured out of sight like a Tartar Troop over a wilderness."[9] The Tartar Troop does in the margins what Coleridge

---

8. The metaphor of birth may be taken to suggest that Coleridge assumes a feminine position of creativity to counter Wordsworth's masculine position. Without denying this suggestion, I would lend greater weight to the traditional metaphor of poetic parthenogenesis, whereby the male poet gives birth to the child of his brain.

9. Samuel Taylor Coleridge, Essay 14 in *The Friend* (1809–10, 1812), ed. Barbara E. Rooke (Princeton, 1969), 2:193.

hesitates to do in the text. In claiming a masculine power to rival Wordsworth's, it also expresses hostility: it declares war.

If we now ask what techniques our specimen texts use to mark their illocutions, a single answer presents itself. Both texts pivot on an act of narration that intrudes where it somehow does not belong. Words-worth rhetorically composes the alpine scene as a chain of immediate presences—a voice, a mind, a face, a blossoming tree—only to re-compose it as a prophetic inscription. (Not to stop there, the images of presence themselves turn out to be appropriated from earlier parts of Wordsworth's own narrative.)[10] Coleridge's distracting footnote suggests that his lyrical imagery has been displaced from a piece of travel writing that itself borrows from a popular eighteenth-century genre, the oriental tale. In both texts, the "other" voice, the voice of affirmative "misfire," is empowered as an effect of narrative.

This common point of technique is no coincidence. The use of intruded or displaced acts of narration is a primary means, perhaps the means *primus inter pares*, for catalyzing other-voicedness. In a pre-liminary way, the reason why is easy to see, though we will shortly be refining our understanding of it. Narrative is a process of continual reinterpretation. Nothing could be more ordinary than for a twist of narrative to alter the meaning, expand the context, redefine the origin of an action. If this interpretive mobility is allowed to impinge on the right expressive act, the result will be an illocutionary flash-point.

II

I would now like to look closely at two instances of other-voicedness in music, one provided by "La malinconia," the finale of Beethoven's String Quartet in B♭, Op. 18, no. 6, and the other by a group of strategically arranged pieces in Schumann's *Carnaval*. Between these two works I will interpolate a third: Freud's essay "The Uncanny." The interpolation is meant partly as a demonstration of the concep-tual "reach" of musical hermeneutics; Freud's illocutions, in my ac-

10. This effect of "narrativization" of apparently nonnarrative figures is wide-spread; for a discussion, see Paul de Man, *Allegories of Reading: Figural Language in Rousseau, Nietzsche, Rilke, and Proust* (New Haven, 1979), 13–19.

count of them, will prove to overlap with Beethoven's and Schumann's. The demonstration, however, should also lend weight to the historical claim advanced in the last chapter, namely that Freud's psychoanalysis is in part a codification of nineteenth-century expressive and discursive practices.

Before we proceed, one last theoretical issue must be faced. There is nothing especially problematical in the claim that a text, or even the musical setting of a text, harbors an intrusive narrative effect; textuality in general presumes (even where it conceals) the possibility of narrative. But what kind of narrative effects, intrusive or otherwise, are possible in a piece of textless instrumental music? The answer to this question cannot simply be framed ad hoc to cover *Carnaval* and "La malinconia"; it clearly depends on the larger question of whether instrumental music presumes narrative possibilities of its own.

It is, of course, commonplace to say that some nineteenth-century instrumental music aspires to the condition of narrative in the sense of telling (encoding, alluding to) a story. In an important series of essays, Anthony Newcomb has taken this idea beyond the commonplace by refining what "telling a story" means in musical terms.[11] Drawing on the work of Paul Ricoeur, Newcomb suggests that following a story and following a work of music entail the same basic activity: the interpretation of a succession of events, possibly quite heterogeneous events, as a meaningful configuration. Such organized successions are historically and culturally bounded. They tend to repeat (vary, transform) a limited number of paradigmatic plots, "standard series of functional events in a prescribed order."[12] What Newcomb succeeds in showing is (1) that paradigmatic plots originating in other discourses can be concretized in textless instrumental music and (2) that the narrative strategies associated with these

---

11. Anthony Newcomb, "Once More 'Between Absolute and Program Music': Schumann's Second Symphony," *19th-Century Music* 7 (1984): 233–50; "Schumann and Late Eighteenth-Century Narrative Strategies," *19th-Century Music* 11 (1987): 164–74; "Narrative Strategies in Nineteenth-Century Instrumental Music," in *Music and Text: Critical Inquiries*, ed. Steven Paul Scher (Cambridge, forthcoming). See also John Daverio, "Schumann's 'Im Legendenton' and Friedrich Schlegel's Arabeske," *19th-Century Music* 11 (1987): 150–63.

12. Newcomb, "Schumann," 165.

plots—techniques of ordering, interpolating, deferring, and so on—can be concretized along with them.

Without challenging the value of this "narratological" approach, we might wish to ask a question that it leaves out of account. To what extent are the musical concretizations of paradigmatic plots and their techniques actually *narrative* in character? For of course not all organized successions constitute a narrative in the ordinary sense of the term, the sense associated with literary storytelling: that is, the recounting of certain significant actions by a representative (or antagonist) of the social world in which the actions assume their significance. The traditional genres of storytelling, for instance—epic, novel, tale, and narrative history—produce typical successions that differ markedly from those produced by lyric poetry. One might say crudely that lyric successions are organized with primary reference to gestures of reflection, expression, and interpretation, whereas narrative successions crystallize primarily around patterns of action and consequence. (*Primary* is a key term here; both kinds of organization occur regularly in both kinds of text.) Or, to invoke a durable concept of Kenneth Burke's, one might say that lyric modes of succession foreground the representation of symbolic action, whereas narrative modes embed symbolic action in a dense matrix of practical, social, and physical actions.[13] Lyric typically foregrounds cyclical, parallel, or graduated patterns; narrative typically foregrounds contingency and causality.[14] Beyond this duality of lyric and narrative, other, messier modes of succession abound in mixed or hybridized texts: Montaigne's *Essays*, Carlyle's *Sartor Resartus*, Whitman's "Song of Myself," Nietzsche's *Ecce Homo*, Woolf's *A Room of One's Own*—the list could go on.

It is arguable that instrumental music leans more towards lyric than towards narrative in its organization of successions; my *Music and Poetry* claimed as much for the nineteenth century.[15] I would like to

13. Kenneth Burke, *The Philosophy of Literary Form: Studies in Symbolic Action*, 2d ed. (Baton Rouge, La., 1967).

14. For a further discussion of the lyric-narrative duality in music, and a treatment of musical narrative not tied (like the present one) to specific narrative effects, see my "Dangerous Liaisons: The Literary Text in Musical Criticism," *19th-Century Music* 13 (1989): 159–67.

15. Lawrence Kramer, *Music and Poetry: The Nineteenth Century and After* (Berkeley and Los Angeles, 1984), 4–23.

take up the thread of that argument here, refining it in terms that may open further the question of music and narrative.

In his book *Allegories of Reading*, Paul de Man suggests that language is literary to the extent that it acknowledges and confronts its own rhetorical (i.e., inescapably figurative) character.[16] If de Man is right, then it should be characteristic of literary narrative to foreground the process of narration—to tell, in effect, two stories: one referential, the other a story about storytelling. Common experience of canonical literary texts, especially those written since the eighteenth (sixteenth?) century, strongly tends to bear out this claim. The result is a certain dissonance between story and metastory. At its weakest, this dissonance simply enacts the familiar distinction between story and discourse, that is, the distinction between what we construct as the story and the textual process of storytelling. But the dissonance is rarely so tame. So many canonical texts thrive on problematized acts of narration that it is almost fair to say that literary narrative is the art of *not* telling a story. The reader must wrest a tale from the text by contending *against* an array of narrative effects that may include limited, biased, or unreliable narrators; multiple narrators who recount or understand events in irreconcilable terms; instabilities and fluctuations in point of view; the narration of events that are imaginary, hypothetical, or indeterminate in relation to the story; patches of exegesis that claim to interpret the narrative, and more.

Broadly speaking, these narrative effects can be sorted into two clusters. The first depends on conflicts among the various fictional persons who are imagined to have a share in producing a given narrative. These narrative agents function in the text as subjects, whether or not they also appear as objects. In principle, at least three distinct types of subject-position may operate within any literary narrative: that of the narrator(s), that of the person(s) whose experience or point of view focusses the narrative, and that of the fictive or projected author, who seeks (not always successfully) to integrate and interpret the others.[17]

16. De Man, *Allegories of Reading*, 3–19.

17. Gerard Genette discusses narrative focusing (which he calls "focalization") in his *Narrative Discourse: A Study in Method* (Ithaca, N.Y., 1980), 185–211; Wayne

This multiplicity of discourse-producing subjects is hard to find in fully composed instrumental music. To recast a well-known suggestion by Edward T. Cone, we do tend to refer musical expressiveness to a presiding authorial subject. Judging from our habits of description, however, we also tend to imagine this subject as autonomous, unencumbered by rivals or collaborators.[18] Texted forms often challenge this attitude; the Lied, for example, often projects a negotiation between independent authorial subjects from the setting and from the text. Most instrumental music, however, seems meant to project a single dominant subject that "surround[s] and include[s]" all others, and in which the authorial, narrating, and focusing activities are merged.[19] Various elements of an instrumental piece may confront this presiding subject with agencies but not with agents, with personifications but not with persons.[20] Characteristic motives, rhythms, or styles may all be highly individualized; so, of course, may instrumental solos. Such elements may even harbor the deconstructive potential to claim or displace an independent subject-position. In their normative role, however, even the most distinctive musical "characters" appear as objects rather than subjects; as products of the musical discourse, not figurative agents for the production of discourse. The subject who supposedly produces the music is not represented directly; in nineteenth-century music, this superiority to representation may act as a sign of the subject's (deep, inner) authenticity.

Following Bakhtin, we might utilize this dominance of a single

---

Booth discusses the authorial subject-position (which he calls the "implied author") in his *The Rhetoric of Fiction* (Chicago, 1961), 71–76.

18. Thus Cone: "[The musical persona is] a projection of [the composer's] musical intelligence, constituting the mind, so to speak, of the composition in question"; "[The orchestral conductor] symbolizes both the composer's actual authority over the musical events and the persona's imaginary control" (Edward T. Cone, *The Composer's Voice* [Berkeley and Los Angeles, 1974], 57, 88; see also 2–40). While I am clearly indebted to Cone's account, my disagreements with it run deep, especially with reference to song (see my *Music and Poetry*, chap. 5, esp. 125–31). I have avoided Cone's term *musical persona* precisely in order to avoid its continuous affirmation of a controlling, all-embracing subject.

19. Cone, *Composer's Voice*, 22.

20. A similar point is made by Fred Everett Maus in "Music as Drama," *Music Theory Spectrum* 10 (1988): 56–73.

subject-position to understand instrumental music on the model of the monologue, in Bakhtin's special sense of the term: a dramatized form of introspection that either represses multiplicity or seeks to "surround and include" it.[21] As a monological form, nondramatic music affiliates itself fundamentally with lyric poetry, which also tends to privilege a single subject-position in which the authorial, narrational, and focusing activities are merged. As Carl Dahlhaus has observed, the assimilation of music to poetry forms the centerpiece of nineteenth-century musical esthetics.[22] It is customary to cite the character piece in this connection, but one might also suggest that large forms like the symphony and string quartet share a common ethos with the extended lyric of English and German Romantic poets, a genre in which the monological unity of the presiding subject is disturbed and—at least pro forma—recovered.[23]

The second cluster of troublesome narrative effects involves clashes and parallels among discrete narrative units. And here, monological or not, instrumental music has found both reason and room to operate. Thus Anthony Newcomb:

> Schumann, like Jean Paul, avoids clear linear narrative through a stress on interruption, embedding, digression, and willful reinterpretation of the apparent function of an event (what one might call functional punning). . . . [He also uses a narrative device that] involves what the Romantic novelists called *Witz*—the faculty by which subtle underlying connections are discovered (or revealed) in a surface of apparent incoherence.[24]

Many of the self-consciously cardinal moments of nineteenth-century music rely on quasi-narrative techniques of interpolation: the interplay of themes, recitative, and *Schreckensfanfare* that begins the finale of Beethoven's Ninth Symphony; the fleeting recollection of the

21. Mikhail Bakhtin, *The Dialogic Imagination*, trans. Caryl Emerson and Michael Holquist (Austin, Tex., 1981), 274–88.

22. Carl Dahlhaus, *19th-Century Music*, trans. J. Bradford Robinson (Berkeley and Los Angeles, 1989), 142–52.

23. The classic account of the extended Romantic lyric is M. H. Abrams, "Structure and Style in the Greater Romantic Lyric," in *From Sensibility to Romanticism: Essays Presented to Frederick A. Pottle*, ed. Frederick W. Hilles and Harold Bloom (New York, 1965), 527–57.

24. Newcomb, "Schumann," 169.

Tristan Prelude in *Die Meistersinger*; the materialization of a brass chorale in the introduction and coda of Brahms's finale for his First Symphony. We may find it suggestive that these moments can all be taken to reveal some unsuspected lack within the monological subject.

The narrative effects we have surveyed here follow an imperative to combine storytelling with the continuous representation of an epistemological gap. This imperative is deeply rooted in Western culture, an offshoot of the Platonic distinction between philosophy and rhetoric. Narrative produced under this dispensation dwells in the disparity between knowledge, certainty, and truth on the one hand and belief, experience, and emotion on the other. This principle, what one might call the law of narrative (laws can be broken), may explain why lyric effects generally retard or collapse narrative and why narrative effects are rarely found in lyric poetry, though all of them are possible there. The lyric treats as continuities the epistemological differences on which narrative depends. It is, indeed, one of two art forms that have historically been both celebrated and attacked for doing just that.

The other of those forms is instrumental music.[25] And from this it would seem to follow that narrative effects in such music constitute a critical or disruptive process rather than a normative one. By assuming or revealing a narrative impetus, a lyrical form begins to deconstruct itself. We would therefore expect to find narrative effects in just those compositions that are the most "literary" in that they most explicitly call attention to their own contingent, historical, rhetorical character. We would expect, also, to find the "fissuring" that results both to problematize oppositions of force and structure and to pry apart the inner unity of the monological subject. In short: instrumental music seeks narrative as a strategy of deconstruction. With that claim in mind, I will now turn to "La malinconia," a piece of musical deconstruction if ever there was one.[26]

25. This was especially true in the nineteenth century. For a brief account on the musical side, see Carl Dahlhaus, *Esthetics of Music*, trans. William Austin (Cambridge, 1982), 24–51.

26. Some cautionary remarks may be helpful at this point. First, my claim that narrative dwells in a certain gap between force and structure, a gap that lyric bridges, does not imply that narrative is "deconstructive" in a way that lyric is not. To

III

The "Malinconia" movement is one of Beethoven's most richly problematical pieces; indeed, it is problematical twice over. The relationship between its "melancholy" Adagio and dancelike Allegretto pushes the conventional looseness and lightness of the Classical finale to a questionable extreme. Even before that question arises, however, the Adagio raises other, perhaps harder questions about the limits of Classical tonality as a musical language. The Adagio is problematical both in relation to the Allegretto and in itself.

The first of these problems appears as a candid provocation. On a superficial hearing, Beethoven seems to have made an esthetic blunder. Having composed a slow introduction of great intensity and originality, he follows it with a main movement that is too lightweight to relieve the earlier intensities and produce a satisfying sense of closure. The contrast, however, is too drastic to be naive, and in case we miss the point Beethoven spells it out in one of his characteristic sublimated cadenzas. The "cadenza" in this case consists of a condensed reminiscence of mm. 1–16 of the Adagio, followed by the signs of an impasse: a fragment of Allegretto, an awkward silence, a fragment of Adagio. (A correlative impasse is marked by the bass of this episode; its framing tones, F and F♯, are, as we will see, in conflict throughout the Adagio.) The Allegretto then resumes its course, only to reach a moment of sudden slackening that nearly

---

articulate an opposition is not necessarily to dislocate it; to reconcile an opposition is not necessarily to negate it. Lyric and narrative, however, can each be employed as a technique to begin a deconstruction of the other—though other techniques are available, too, and a pat matter/antimatter formula should be avoided here. Second, the value of deconstruction, as I see it, is that it keeps discourse circulating and thaws frozen positions. The purpose of a deconstruction, says Derrida, is to *open* a reading (*Of Grammatology*, trans. Gayatri Chakravorty Spivak [Baltimore, 1976], 158). Hence my insistence here, following Derrida, on dislocating rather than reiterating the various oppositions of force and structure. For instance, in saying that Schumann's narrative strategies "keep us wondering where we are in what sort of pattern—in such a way as to stress the process of narrative interpretation," Newcomb ("Schumann," 168) reads these strategies as tropes of reflection or self-consciousness. Historically, this interpretation is unimpeachable. Yet Newcomb's reading itself is also a trope of overturning, a privileging of force against structure. And this is problematical, because his own analyses uncover forces of dislocation that can be confronted only by reading against or across the force/structure polarity.

reduces it to the tempo of the Adagio. This new impasse precipitates a frantic Prestissimo close, as if to settle the issue of the movement simply by jumping from one extreme to the other.

How are we to take all this? One possibility is that the music is meant to dramatize the unstable mood swings common to certain psychological types: Beethoven's, for instance. But if the music is a serious portrait of the manic-depressive personality, it might have done a more convincing job on the manic end than the blithely conventional Allegretto. More credible is the suggestion that the movement is a study in Romantic irony, in which the Allegretto deliberately exposes the uncanny atmosphere of the Adagio (a mood, Beethoven notes, that must be evoked "colla più gran delicatezza") as a mere conjuror's trick. With Romantic irony in mind, we can even link the signature effect of the Adagio, its cyclical use of diminished-seventh chords, to Beethoven's well-known remark that "the startling effects which many ascribe solely to the natural genius of the composer are frequently easily achieved by the right use and application of the chord of the diminished seventh."[27] In other words, illusions of immediacy ("startling effects") and nature ("natural genius") are the results of a practical technique (a matter of "right use and application") that is usually hidden from the listener. The technique is even easy.

From the standpoint of Romantic irony, however, what is really interesting about this movement is not the initial ironic impression, which is fairly blatant, but the way in which the impression is turned back on itself at the close. When the Adagio returns to interrupt the flow of the Allegretto, a second illusion can be said to collapse. This is the illusion of Romantic irony itself: the fantasy that the artist can control his creation from a position of transcendental self-possession.

The repetitions of the Adagio suggest the reality of what was taken for illusion, a reality that assumes the form of obsessional thinking: the haunting return of material that controls, rather than being controlled by, the artist. Drawing on Freud's *Beyond the Pleasure Principle*, Peter Brooks has suggested that repetition of this unforeseeable, often uncanny sort is the basic armature of all narrative.

27. Quoted by Philip Radcliffe, *Beethoven's String Quartets* (New York, 1968), 43.

Such repetition, he writes, "works towards the generation of significance" by binding (controlling, rendering intelligible) "the energy
generated by deviance, extravagance, excess—an energy that belongs
to the textual hero's career and to the reader's expectation." The
binding effect constitutes an "obsessive reminder that we cannot
really move ahead until we have understood the still enigmatic
past."[28] If Brooks is right, then Beethoven has shaped (or, more
properly, misshaped) his quartet finale to produce a primal narrative
effect—and this with the intent of exposing the epistemological rift
between instrumental music as a transparent medium of feeling and
instrumental music as the exercise of a technique. Within "La malinconia" as a whole, the issue of which term to favor, which turn of
irony to prefer, is undecidable. This undecidability shows up strongly
in the closing Prestissimo, which is easy to hear as either exuberant
or trumped up—or as both at once.

Taken by itself, the Adagio raises similar questions even more
acutely. Here the focus is on harmony, and in particular on the idea
of the tonic as a center of orientation around which a coherent
composition revolves. It will be necessary to go into some detail on
this subject, but the basic situation is simple. The key of the Adagio
is B♭ major, but the music avoids even an imperfect cadence on the
tonic triad, proceeds largely without reference to either the tonic or
the dominant for some thirty-two of its forty-four measures, and ends
on a half cadence that starts from the tonic minor—a sort of Picardy
third in reverse. B♭ is certainly the harmony that frames the Adagio,
but it is hard to see in what sense the Adagio is "in" B♭. For that
matter, it is hard to see in what sense the Adagio is in any key at all,
for its various sections are all driven by local processes that are at
bottom indifferent to tonal centering. Even on a Schenkerian reading, the movement forms "a dynamic, indeed a fantastic, statement
of the organizing powers of the tonality of B♭ major-minor."[29]

The broad tonal thrust of the Adagio, then, is to problematize
continuously the relationship between the main body of the music
and its B♭ frame. This structure replicates a fundamental narrative

28. Peter Brooks, *Reading for the Plot: Design and Intention in Narrative* (New
York, 1984), 108, 125.

29. William Mitchell, "Beethoven's *La Malinconia* from the String Quartet,
Opus 18, No. 6: Techniques and Structure," *Music Forum* 3 (1973): 276–77.

effect, the production of an uncertain primary narrative within a more certain secondary (or even marginal) narrative. In Goethe's *The Sufferings of Young Werther*, for example (of which more later), Werther's narrative is strictly speaking a mere construction by Wilhelm, the sympathetic but somewhat slow-witted "editor" of the novel. Beethoven thus once more narrativizes his musical successions in order to render musical succession itself a questionable process.

The Adagio, which is shown in Example 28, follows a concise but highly elaborated design that falls into six sections.

1. *Thematic statement* (mm. 1–12, 17–20). Measures 1–12 consist of three statements of a four-measure theme, the most important feature of which is that it closes with a turn. A fourth statement is deferred by the intrusive appearance of another four-measure passage consisting entirely of

2. *Diminished-seventh chords* (mm. 13–16). These chords appear one to a measure, ornamented by turns and alternating piano and forte. The passage forms a harmonically indefinite elaboration of the turn that ends each statement of the theme.

Between them, these first two sections carry out a process of harmonic entropy. The third thematic statement approaches its concluding turn from a G-major seventh chord. The "natural" (i.e., conventional) way to hear this chord is as the dominant of C minor, the supertonic. Instead, Beethoven interprets the chord as an augmented sixth of B♮, and progresses to a B-minor six-four chord. The "natural" (i.e., conventional) next move is to the dominant of B. Instead, Beethoven goes on to the indeterminate collection of diminished-seventh chords that makes up the piano/forte passage. When the thematic statement resumes at m. 17, the B-minor six-four chord of m. 12 is reconstituted as a B-major seventh chord.[30] There follows a

30. The B^7 appears explicitly in m. 18, but in a sense is already present in the diminished-seventh chord that occupies m. 17. As Richard Kramer ("Ambiguities in *La Malinconia*: What the Sketches Say," in *Beethoven Studies 2*, ed. Alan Tyson [Oxford, 1977], 29–41) points out, the "C in the bass [of m. 17] simply retards the

LA MALINCONIA

Questo pezzo si deve trattare colla più gran delicatezza.

EXAMPLE 28.   Beethoven, String Quartet in B♭, Op. 18, no. 6. Finale.

EXAMPLE 28 (continued)

3. *Fugato* (mm. 21–29). This extended contrapuntal passage begins in E minor, the normal resolution of the preceding B^7. E minor, the tritone of B♭, is completely untenable as a tonal point of reference; the harmonic process of the fugato simply cannot be heard in relation to B♭. That process, in any case, admits only the most sketchy of tonal bearings in its own right. In strict alternation, major and minor triads travel around a circle of fifths in a repeating pattern. And as if starting from the tritone were not enough, the pattern rotates upward, perversely contradicting "the natural tendency of the fifth to descend to its root":[31]

e:	V^7	i	V/V			
b:			V	i	V/V	
f♯:				V	i	V/V etc.

There is—can be—no sense of destination here; one place on this cycle is as good as another. Everything is decentered: even the basic unit of motion embodies a contradiction, as my Roman numerals suggest. Each major chord in the cycle is a dominant; each minor chord cancels a dominant. It is striking, moreover, that the fugato contains not a single non-harmonic dissonance. Its sonority is as purely triadic as that of the piano/forte passage is purely composed of diminished-seventh chords. I will return later to the affinity between these seemingly contrary sections. The fugato finally concludes on a C-major triad that is at once altered to C minor: here is the supertonic of B♭ that was displaced by the B-minor six-four chord at m. 12.[32] What follows, echoing m. 13, is a diminished-seventh chord that introduces a

---

arrival of the root B" (34). Perhaps I should add explicitly that my own analysis is not meant at any point to deny structural continuities of this sort, but only to problematize them.

31. Richard Kramer, "Ambiguities," 30; Joseph Kerman (*The Beethoven Quartets* [New York, 1966], 77) makes the same point.

32. For a complementary account of this chord, see Richard Kramer, "Ambiguities," 30–35.

4. *Reinterpretation (continuation) of 2: The piano/forte alternation (with turns)* (mm. 29–32). Changes of chord and dynamics now fall every half measure instead of every measure, as diminished triads (*p*) alternate with minor sixth chords (*f*) of B♭, C, and D. The essential process here is a melodic ascent by semitones in the upper voice from A to D. This pattern echoes, in inversion, a semitonal bass descent from B♭ to F♯ that, as Joseph Kerman notes in his analysis of this piece, undergirds mm. 1–12.[33] The Dm^6 at m. 32^1 is reconstituted as D^7 at m. 32^2, recalling the Bm–B^7 relationship that links m. 12 to mm. 17–20. The resolution of this dominant seventh leads to a

5. *Reinterpretation (continuation) of 3: The fugato* (mm. 33–36). Beginning with G minor, the upward circle of fifths continues until it arrives at A minor, which is at once reinterpreted as the leading tone of B♭ (m. 35; the B♭ triad is immediately melted down into a diminished-seventh chord). Two points about this passage are especially noteworthy. If the first fugato had picked up where it left off, the G-minor triad of m. 33 would have been G major.[34] The switch to the minor is mystifying, at least at first, though it does prefigure the ultimate switch in the "frame narrative" from B♭ major to B♭ minor. Meanwhile, the B♭ sixth chord that follows the A-minor triad in m. 35 arises as a specific displacement of B major, which, as the dominant of E minor, would have been produced by the fugato cycle at this point. Hence the tonic reenters the Adagio by exactly reversing the semitonal friction that prompted its exit. In the same gesture, the tonic also curtails the process that would have returned the fugato to the tritonal E minor that began it. After this, the cello embarks on a series of turns that map out a

6. *Coda* (mm. 37–42). This is a powerful six-measure crescendo driven by a semitonal ascent in the bass from E to A,

33. Kerman, *Quartets*, 77–78.
34. I.e., the original fugato breaks off after arriving at F minor (m. 28); the next step, were the pattern continued, would have been G major.

echoing the upper-voice ascent from A to D at mm. 29–32. The episode is perhaps the most problematical in the Adagio, and an exemplary instance of marked illocution in music. Measures 40–42 can be taken as a sequence on the model of mm. 37–39, and m. 38 arrives at F^7, so that from one perspective the coda is a prolongation of the home dominant and thus a restoration of the hegemony of the tonic. Expressively, however, what is most forceful about the passage is the melodic ascent of the cello with its turns and, within each three-measure grouping, the increasingly dissonant attacks by which the upper strings respond to each turn. This difference of accent, this interplay of voice and other-voice, reaches a powerful climax in m. 42. Here the first violin reaches the registral apex of the Adagio with a fortissimo attack on gb^3. As Kerman emphasizes in his analysis (77–79), Gb, as F♯ ($\hat{5}$ of B), forms the sore spot in this music; it persistently contradicts the tonic from m. 12 onward.[35] The diminished-seventh chord to which the climactic Gb belongs may "actually" form the upper tones of V^{9b} /B over an implied root, but it sounds like some intractable, unheard-of dissonance that is in some sense the true ending of the Adagio. A related complication emerges from the succession of sonority types in mm. 37–39 and 40–42: minor triad, dominant-seventh chord, diminished-seventh chord. This succession forms a retrograde of the earlier one that leads from the diminished-seventh chords of mm. 13–16 through the dominant-seventh of mm. 17–20 to the E-minor triad that begins the fugato. In this context the coda, with its parallel ascents to climactic diminished sevenths, becomes above all an apotheosis of the diminished-seventh chord as an expressive, or even a structural, sonority.

Looking back over the main body of the Adagio (mm. 13–42), we may be inclined to argue that the primary organizing principle is not harmonic at all but something we might simply call empirical. There may be no genuine key *of* the Adagio, but the key *to* the Adagio is

35. Kerman, *Quartets*, 77–79.

an act of exchange or alternation, an opposition of intensities: of major against minor, minor triad against major seventh chord, B♭/F against B/F♯, the fugato against its reversed form, counterpoint against ornamented block chords, piano against forte, succession against retrograde—ultimately, Adagio against Allegretto. And yet harmonic relationships, all of which entail recognition of B♭ as the tonic, form the very means by which tonal coherence is rendered most questionable in this music. The Adagio may very well take the opposition of intensities as the plot of its primary narrative and consign tonal articulation to the subsidiary position of the frame. The coda, however, makes it impossible to say where the main story ends and the frame resumes. The tonal voice and its empirical other-voice cannot be disentwined. Like any good narrative, the pattern of "La malinconia" is ultimately a bafflement.

We are now in a position to ask whether the narrative effects of "La malinconia" have any specific literary affiliations. The answer may lie in an aspect of the music that I have so far left out of account, namely its intention to express melancholy. Two streams of discourse converge on this topic, one psychological, the other literary. Both are ancient in origin, endowed with new life during the Renaissance, and still active throughout the eighteenth century.[36]

In eighteenth-century medicine, melancholy is preeminently associated with a disordered imagination that can cause physical illness or even death. Melancholy is an impediment to the conduct of life, and incidentally to the conduct of narrative, as witness one of Wordsworth's neurotics:[37]

36. My account of melancholy draws largely on Erwin Panofsky, *The Life and Art of Albrecht Dürer* (1943; rpt. Princeton, 1955), 156–71. Dürer's engraving *Melencolia*, which was widely reproduced throughout Germany, has occasionally been suggested as a source for Beethoven's Adagio.

37. On melancholy and associated disorders in eighteenth-century medicine, see the overview in Alan J. Bewell, "A 'Word Scarce Said': Witchcraft and Hysteria in Wordsworth's Experimental Poetry of 1797–98," *ELH* (*English Literary History*) 53 (1986): 357–90. Eighteenth-century melancholy was also an impediment to musical performance, as C. P. E. Bach observes in his treatise on the art of the keyboard: "In languishing and sad passages, the performer must languish and grow sad. Here, however, the error of a sluggish, dragging performance must be avoided, caused by an excess of affect and melancholy" (C. P. E. Bach, *Essay on the True Art of Playing Keyboard Instruments*, trans. William J. Mitchell [New York, 1949], sec. 13).

> No word to any man he utters,
> A-bed or up, to young or old:
> But ever to himself he utters,
> "Poor Harry Gill is very cold."

("Goody Blake and Harry Gill," 121–24)

As my quotation indicates, melancholy keeps its medical associations in literary discourse, but literature also provides a melancholy of quite another sort. The bridge between the two is an association of melancholy with sensitivity of soul; taking its impetus from Ficino, this idea became almost proverbial. As one Renaissance commentator put it bluntly, "melencolia significa ingegno": melancholy signifies genius. The literary result is the pensive melancholy of the quester after transcendental truth, a figure most familiar from Milton's "Il penseroso." The pensive quester, however, is as removed from the conduct of life as his depressive counterpart. Cloistered in his lonely tower, the *penseroso* figure acts only by thinking.[38]

These two versions of melancholy come together in a narrative effect typical of late-eighteenth- and early-nineteenth-century fiction. At certain moments, a narrator will lose the ability to narrate as the concomitant of a sudden surge in subjective intensity—perhaps depressive, perhaps revelatory, often both. E. T. A. Hoffmann provides a remarkable example in his story "The Doubles." A puppet show "in the customary Italian manner" approaches its close when

> the puppeteer, with a fearfully distorted expression, stuck his head
> into the puppet stage and stared out at the audience with lifeless,
> glazed eyes. Punch on one side and the doctor on the other seemed

38. A brief excerpt:

> . . . Let my lamp at midnight hour
> Be seen in some high lonely tower,
> Where I may oft outwatch the Bear
> With thrice-great Hermes, or unsphere
> The spirit of Plato to unfold
> What worlds, or what vast regions hold
> The immortal mind that hath forsook
> Her mansion in this fleshly nook.
> (85–92)

It is worth noting, apropos of Chapter 4, that medical melancholy is associated especially with women, pensive melancholy with men.

appalled at the sight of the gigantic head; then they recovered . . .
and began a very deep, scholarly argument about the nature of the
head. . . . The doctor said that when Nature had created this
monstrosity she was making use of a figure of speech, a synecdoche,
in which a part is used for the whole. Punch, however, insisted
that the head was an unfortunate fellow whose body got mislaid
because of all his thinking and his crazy thoughts and who, completely lacking any fists, could defend himself from boxes on the
ear and pokes in the nose only by cursing.[39]

The intrusion of the puppeteer both continues the show, deferring
the promised closure, and expands the Italian comedy into a medi-
tation on the rhetoricity of all things. At the same time, the swelled-
up subjectivity signaled by the woeful disembodied head strips the
puppeteer of his ability to carry a narrative forward. In particular he
loses his power to "get the upper hand" over his puppets—the hand
being his chief narrative instrument, as it is (for Hoffmann) the
writer's. Language itself fails this puppet of his puppets. As Punch
observes, in taking over the narrative power that the puppeteer has
lost, the poor fellow can defend himself only by cursing.

In Goethe's *Werther*, Werther's ability to narrate collapses repeatedly, most strikingly when, as often happens, he encounters a story
that parallels his own. Human sympathy then proceeds to merge with
narcissistic brooding; Werther obsessively focuses the other's story
through his own until both stories grind to a halt. At one point he
recounts the narration of a love-crazed peasant. Having made an
attempt at rape, the peasant also attempts to disguise rape as seduction:

At last he also admitted to me, shyly, all the little liberties [his
beloved] had allowed him, and how close she had let him come to
her. He broke off two or three times, repeating the most animated
protestations that he was not saying this to blacken her, as he put
it, that he loved and valued her as before. . . . —And here, my
friend, I strike up my old song again, the one I shall sing eternally:
If I could only place this man before you as he stood before me, as

39. From *Tales of E. T. A. Hoffmann*, ed. and trans. Leonard J. Kent and Elizabeth C. Knight (Chicago, 1969), 248.

he still stands before me! If I could tell you everything properly, so that you should feel how I sympathize with his fate, and must do so. But enough.[40]

Werther, too, breaks off two or three times, each time to proclaim how his feelings paralyze his narrative. And matters are worse than Werther thinks. It is only after he has surrendered the narrator's position for that of the reader that Werther recognizes how completely he has been thwarted: "Now that I read this page over, I see that I have forgotten to tell the end of the story."

As a narrative of melancholy, Beethoven's Adagio can be taken to reenact the subjectively funded collapse of Werther and of Hoffmann's puppeteer. The music narrates in order to fail at narration, to reach the point of narrative rupture at which the subject breaks through, both dislocated and dislocating. I am thinking in particular of the sections most antithetical to tonic (or tonal) orientation, the piano/forte alternation of diminished sevenths and the original fugato. I suggested earlier that these passages, one based on unrelieved dissonance, the other on perfect triads, are only superficially unlike. Both passages are sonorously "pure," both inhibit orientation toward Bb in the highest degree, and both are reiterative rather than progressive—static at the core, surges of motion (registral in the sevenths, harmonic in the triads) that goes nowhere. The two passages, in short, form an uncanny doubling that resonates later when the Adagio returns in the Allegretto. And like Werther in particular, the personal subject of "La malinconia" assigns so much expressive force to these intrusions that they fissure his narrative.

Nor is this effect merely general. The story of the crazed peasant brings Werther to the point of narrative paralysis by revealing the extreme to which Werther's own story tends. When "love" leads Werther's double to attempt a rape and fantasize a seduction, these actions expose the lining of desire and aggressiveness that Werther's idealization of his own love conceals. Overpowering passion, it seems, *must* overpower: if not its object, then—as Werther's suicide attests—its subject will do. Between Beethoven's piano/forte sevenths and the fugato, a similar, if less drastic, play of extremes may

40. Johann Wolfgang von Goethe, *The Sufferings of Young Werther*, trans. Bayard Quincy Morgan (New York, 1957), 102.

hold court. Melancholy finds its most strident expression in a harmonically meaningless texture of diminished chords; the fugato unveils the most radical tendency of such an expression, such a melancholy. Set in virtually mechanical motion by a tritone harmony, the triads of the fugato are as meaningless, as "unnatural," as embedded in technique as any diminished-seventh chord could hope to be. Nature, for the moment, has disappeared.

True to the intermingling of depression and pensiveness, Beethoven's fugato represents both a surrender to melancholy feeling and an effort to master it, both a dislocation of structure and an assent to the force of insight. Something similar even applies to Werther, who attempts to revalue his suffering as a sign of profound inwardness. Similar, too, is Wordsworth's alpine spot of time, which reaches its apex at the very moment when nature disappears into a still-unfolding narrative.

For Beethoven, the capacity of music to break away from nature is a central compositional issue. Perhaps his famous habit (he once called it a bad habit) of immediately writing down his every musical idea represents an effort to stabilize as well as to remember the music in his mind's ear. For if music originates "in the head," then music, like thought, is subject both to the vertigo of epistemological uncertainty and to the sudden eruptions of subjectivity that manifest themselves as impediments to narrative, signs of an inability to proceed meaningfully in time.

IV

Freud's essay "The Uncanny," published in 1919, is an attempt to find a psychoanalytic explanation for the strange blend of familiarity and "creeping dread" so important to nineteenth-century German writers. Characteristically, Freud does not end up with one explanation, but with several: (1) the uncanny occurs when one encounters "something familiar and old-established in the mind that has been estranged" by repression;[41] (2) the uncanny occurs when events conform to infantile forms of thought that have supposedly been surmounted in adulthood; (3) the uncanny occurs whenever something

---

41. Sigmund Freud, "The Uncanny," in Freud, *Studies in Parapsychology*, ed. Philip Rieff (New York, 1963), 47.

reminds one of a compulsion to repeat that operates as a basic principle in the unconscious. Freud's arguments are fascinating, and they have generated a substantial critical literature.[42] For present purposes, however, since my focus is on illocution, I will say no more on this topic. Only one more aspect of "The Uncanny" as a locutionary text is indispensable here, and that is its official illocutionary aura: an attitude of clinical, rigorous, scientific detachment. Freud approaches the question of the uncanny from the outside, stating at the outset:

> The writer of the present contribution, indeed, must himself plead guilty to a special obtuseness in [this] matter, where extreme delicacy of perception would be more in place. It is long since he has experienced or heard of anything which has given him an uncanny impression, and he will be obliged to translate himself into that state of feeling, and to awaken in himself the possibility of it before he proceeds.[43]

The use of the third person sounds a little suspicious (with good reason, as we shall see), but the unusual clumsiness of Freud's prose here certainly measures the effort he makes to assume a detached position.

A similar measure can be taken from Freud's way of introducing his topic. After a preliminary discussion of some esthetic theories, he launches into a close philological examination of the word *uncanny*, involving pages of quotation from dictionaries. This is *Wissenschaft* with a vengeance! Once the philological survey is completed, however, Freud's text is cross-grained, even dominated, by uncanny narratives large and small, most notably by that of E. T. A. Hoffmann's tale "The Sandman," which Freud submits to a searching analysis. Three of the remaining narratives are of special interest. All of them are autobiographical, but unlike similar narratives (and dreams) in Freud's other texts, these are not used analytically. Only one of them is interpreted, and that in the scantiest of terms. Another draws

---

42. My own account is indebted primarily to Neil Hertz's "Freud and the Sandman," in *The End of the Line: Essays on Psychoanalysis and the Sublime* (New York, 1985), 97–121; and Bernard Rubin, "Freud and Hoffmann: 'The Sandman,'" in *Introducing Psychoanalytic Theory*, ed. Sander Gilman (New York, 1982), 205–17.

43. Freud, "The Uncanny," 20.

attention to this interpretive inertia by brushing off its topic as "thoroughly silly" and letting it drop. On the face of it, the stories are just . . . stories. But why, we might ask, is the detached scientific person who occupies the author-position suddenly becoming a raconteur?

A look at the three narratives quickly supplies a first answer. All three contradict Freud's claim about not being subject to uncanny experiences; they reunite him with the uncanny, make him the victim/hero of an uncanny tale like "The Sandman." In the first two cases, this reunion also involves an encounter with the kind of sexual ambivalence that psychoanalysis is intended to master. In story no. 1, Freud finds himself lost in the red-light district of a small Italian town. He tries to hurry away but "involuntarily" keeps coming back to his starting point, where the prostitutes suggestively appear in the windows of the small houses. Story no. 2 is a metastory. "In the midst of the isolation of war-time," writes Freud,

> . . . I read a story about a young married couple, who move into a furnished flat in which there is a curiously shaped table with carvings of crocodiles on it. Towards evening they begin to smell an intolerable and very typical odour that pervades the whole flat; things begin to get in their way and trip them up in the darkness . . . —in short, we are given to understand that the presence of the table causes ghostly crocodiles to haunt the place, or that the wooden monsters come to life in the dark, or something of that sort. It was a thoroughly silly story, but the uncanny feeling it produced was quite remarkable.[44]

It does not take a Freud to put together the key elements here—a young married couple, a swampy miasma, animal movements in the dark, the evasive "something of that sort"—to detect an ambivalent fantasy about unrestrained ("primordial" African or Egyptian) sexuality.

To some extent, Freud's use of these narratives overcomes the ambivalence they imply; he favors them, "involuntarily" returns to the sexual scene, fantasizes himself as a participant or a voyeur rather than as a scientific observer. But more than erotic nostalgia is in-

44. Ibid., 50–51.

volved in Freud's reunion with the uncanny. Story no. 3, which requires full quotation, makes this clear:

> [It] is interesting to observe what the effect is of suddenly and un-expectedly meeting one's own image. E. Mach has related [such an] observation. . . . [He] formed a very unfavourable opinion about [a] supposed stranger who got into [an] omnibus, and thought, "What a shabby-looking school-master that is getting on now." —I can supply a similar experience. I was sitting alone in my *wagon-lit* compartment when a more than usually violent jerk of the train swung back the door of the adjoining washing-cabinet, and an el-derly gentleman in a dressing-gown and travelling cap came in. I assumed that he had been about to leave the washing-cabinet which divides the two compartments, and had taken the wrong direction and come into my compartment by mistake. Jumping up with the intention of putting him right, I at once realized to my dismay that the intruder was nothing but my own reflection in the looking-glass of the open door. I can still recollect that I thor-oughly disliked his appearance.[45]

Perhaps the most striking feature of these twinned narratives is the disagreeableness of the double that confronts their narrators: first a shabby schoolmaster, then an unpleasant-looking old fellow in a cap and bathrobe. In his brief interpretive comment, Freud treats these images as equivalents. By doing likewise, we can both explain their value for him and clarify the antagonism between erotic nostalgia and scientific detachment. In failing at first to recognize their doubles, both Freud and Mach split their egos in excess of the conventional doppelgänger scenario. By also *disliking* their doubles, the two reluc-tant visionaries also reject one half-self in favor of another. Taken as a composite, the rejected half bears the signs of detached intellectual rigor (he is a schoolmaster), of cultural authority (he is an elderly gentleman, a patriarch, in emphatic possession of a private compart-ment), and of propriety (he is properly dressed upon his exit from the bathroom). In other words, the rejected double projects an equation of intellectual rigor with the law that demands deference for old men and the prohibition that keeps the body fully (if shabbily) covered and separates bodily functions from pleasure. Freud's other-voiced

45. Ibid., 54n–56n.

narratives can be taken to rebel against this (implicitly paternal) Law: hence the link of his erotic narratives to license and primitive nature, the brothel and the jungle. Freud's involvement of Ernst Mach in this scenario is especially telling. Mach was the most influential proponent of scientific positivism in Freud's Vienna; for Mach to start seeing doubles makes positivism a shade less than positive.

Still deeper motives become apparent if we look at the elderliness of Freud's double in another light. In most cases, the double or doppelgänger is a "ghastly harbinger of death."[46] The elderly gentleman who intrudes into Freud's compartment after a stroke of violence suggests something similar even before he is (consciously) recognized as a double. When Freud first jumps up from his seat, his impulse is to throw the old man out—to cast out death. When the old man proves to be his double, he masters the dread this elicits in the form of dislike. The dread, as he observes, becomes only "a vestigial trace of that . . . reaction which feels the double to be something uncanny."[47] To deny the Law, then, is also to deny death. Far more than for sexual fantasy, Freud returns to the uncanny in order to *master* it, to appropriate its power in order to go on living.

This reading finds its most striking confirmation in one last othervoiced narrative, this time a displaced one. Apropos, more or less, of nothing, Freud at one point introduces a special version of the uncanny:

> If we come across the number 62 several times in a single day, or if we begin to notice that everything which has a number—addresses, hotel-rooms, compartments [NB] in railway-trains—always has the same one . . . [we] feel this to be 'uncanny,' and unless a man is utterly hardened and proof against the lure of superstition he will be tempted to ascribe a secret meaning to this obstinate recurrence of a number, taking it, perhaps, as an indication of the span of life allotted to him.[48]

This passage wryly acts out a familiar pose: "Doctor, I have this friend . . ."; it is perfectly clear that the man who fears the number sixty-two is Freud himself. But why bring the subject up?

46. Ibid., 40.
47. Ibid., 56n.
48. Ibid., 43.

The answer begins in the 1890s, when Freud, working at white heat to lay the foundations of psychoanalysis, was deeply dependent on the emotional support offered by his friend Wilhelm Fliess.[49] Fliess theorized that human life was governed by something resembling what we call biorhythms. One conclusion he drew from this was that Freud would probably die at the age of fifty-one. In *The Psychopathology of Everyday Life*, first published in 1901, Freud comments indirectly on this prediction:

> I find I have a[n unconscious] tendency to superstition [about numbers], whose origin is still unknown to me myself. I usually come upon speculations about the duration of my own life and the lives of those dear to me; and the fact that my friend in B[erlin] has made the periods of human life the subject of his calculations . . . must have acted as a determinant of this unconscious juggling. I am not now in agreement with one of the premises from which this work of his proceeds; from highly egotistic motives I should be very glad to carry my point against him, and yet I appear to be imitating his calculations in my own way.[50]

In 1907, when the book entered its third edition and its author turned fifty-one in good health, Freud changed the phrase "is still unknown to me myself" to "for long remained unknown to me" and deleted the rest. Freud had indeed carried his point, and capped it by making the whole argument disappear. He cheated death and triumphed over superstition—while still, as his editorial vanishing act shows, remaining susperstitious in his own way.

Unfortunately for Freud, the age of fifty-one was not the last stop on Fliess's schedule; sixty-two came after it. In May 1919, Freud picked up an old mansucript and began to rework it into the essay we know as "The Uncanny." His first public acknowledgment of the essay appears in a letter dated May 12—*six days after his sixty-third birthday*. In a gesture that is uncanny by one of his own definitions, Freud carries his point against Fliess for a second time. Having triumphed over superstition and lived, he returns once more to the

49. On this topic see Peter Gay, *Freud: A Life for Our Time* (New York, 1988), 55–63.

50. Sigmund Freud, *The Psychopathology of Everyday Life*, trans. Alan Tyson (New York, 1965), 250n.

realm of the supernatural in order to act out his mastery over it. As illocution, "The Uncanny" as a whole performs successfully the symbolic action that Freud's narrative of the unrecognized double is forced to curtail: it casts out death.

Freud's other-voicedness in "The Uncanny" is strikingly like Beethoven's in "La malinconia" in its overall effect, although the specific resemblance is less important than the larger recurrence of other-voiced discourse itself. Nonetheless, Beethoven's mutual dislocation of nature and technique is reenacted in Freud's parallel dislocation of superstition and science. Freud's "superstition" is situated (at times explicitly) in the natural world as it appears to a prerational mind; his "science" represents the transformation of that world by the techniques and instruments of rational knowledge. Like Beethoven at the close of the Allegretto, Freud invites—or cannot prevent—the return of irrational (subjective, unconscious, natural) materials upon a discourse, a technique, that is meant to demystify them. In both the music and the essay, what Freud calls "obstinate recurrence" marks an effort to master the nagging persistence of subjective intensities. The result, in both cases, is a vertiginous shuttling between the principle of *melencolia significa ingegno* and its contrary: that *ingegno* is not the signified of *melencolia* but its cure.

V

If instrumental music, like the Freudian text, draws closest to narrative effects when it is at its most heterogeneous, its most self-conscious, its most experimental, does the converse also hold? Do we encounter a culturally instituted defense against the troubling pleasures of dislocation when instrumental music treats its forms as natural or invisibly conventional or spins out a seamless web of linear continuities? Do we encounter a form of the same defense when formalist and organicist modes of understanding insist that music is all syntax and no semantics, that to know a piece is to grasp a formal integrity that transcends culture and history? Is that defense repeated in a new guise when historicist modes of understanding claim that to know a piece is to grasp it as a *reflection* of culture and history, a text in its context? Is to resist dislocation to resist meaning itself? Is there, perhaps, a friction that works against such resistance in at least some music—by Brahms, say—that seems to adhere to it by design? Might one detect a similar resistance even in certain passages of formalist, organicist, and historicist commentary?

These polemical, these rhetorical, questions are, I believe, not merely posed in retrospect by what has waggishly been called a boa-deconstructor, but also, and insistently, posed by the persistence of other-voiced discourse in the recent cultural past. In this light, the deconstructive practice that the present chapter—the present book—describes and enacts forms an effort to reclaim a lost legacy from Romanticism: a legacy, indeed, that has largely not been recognized as lost.

As the literary critic Jerome McGann has argued, the Romantic ideal sometimes called unity of being—"a completeness of idea, completeness of culture, perfection of art"—is typically theorized in fragmentary forms, "brilliant, argumentative, ceaseless, exploratory, incomplete, and not always very clear." Romantic poems take a parallel position; they observe "the realm of the ideal . . . as precarious—liable to vanish or move beyond one's reach at any time"; they "take up transcendent and ideal subjects because these subjects occupy areas of critical uncertainty," and their aim "is to rediscover the ground of stability in these situations."[51] To all of which I would add: yes, but . . .

But consider Schumann's *Carnaval*, which approaches an ideal subject precisely through a kind of fragmentation. The miniatures that make up this collection are either character sketches or dances, that is, personal or social images; the two types come together in the closing piece, "Marche des Davidsbundler contre les Philistins." This appropriately macaronic title signals the expressive force of the collection, which is to affirm the social value of creative idiosyncrasy. (The League of David the Psalmist suggests an aspiration to social authority; that the league assembles in the spirit of carnival suggests the aspiration to debunk or evade social authority.)

---

51. Jerome J. McGann, *The Romantic Ideology: A Critical Investigation* (Chicago, 1983), 47, 48, 72–73. I should add that McGann proposes a hermeneutics that is somewhat, if not perhaps entirely, at odds with the one I propose here. My position has more in common with the one offered by Tilottama Rajan in her *Dark Interpreter: The Discourse of Romanticism* (Ithaca, N.Y., 1980).

My concern here is with just who makes the affirmation. At an early moment, Schumann sets forth a block of pieces (four or five, depending on how you count) that play with the idea of his musical signature. First come Florestan and Eusebius, the impetuous and introspective halves of Schumann's composite persona. The pieces named for these figures duly occur in tandem, but they fail to mesh into a bounded whole. "Eusebius" ends with a tonic (E♭) six-four chord; "Florestan," with a G-minor signature, then begins and ends on an unresolved dominant minor-ninth. Closure, and that only partial, must wait for the next piece, "Coquette," which begins by progressing from the dominant of G through E♭ to its own tonic, B♭. Both "Florestan" and "Eusebius" find a deferred resolution here, "Florestan" in the progression to E♭, which acts as a deceptive cadence (g: V–VI), and "Eusebius" in the B♭ sonority to which its closing E♭$^6_4$ failed to progress. I reluctantly pass over the question of why Schumann's alter egos merge under a feminine sign—a "coquettish" one at that—to focus on questions of identity and plurality.[52] In its harmonic open-endedness, Schumann's double persona proves to be something other than a sign of the self in division. Its complementary halves form a fiction of unity in the midst of a far more fragmentary and fluctuating mode of identity. And lest we think that the flux can be arrested, "Coquette" is immediately doubled in a condensed variant called "Replique," which begins by echoing, then literally repeating, the transitional passage that links "Coquette" to "Eusebius" and "Florestan." The result is a vertiginous trope for the plurality of the personal subject: a double female persona that doubles a double male one. What next?

The answer to that is "Sphinxes," the notation, in double whole notes, of the three pitch cells on which *Carnaval* is based. These famously employ all the letters in Schumann's name that also denominate tones in German usage: S.C.H.A. (E♭–C–B–A) and its anagrams AS.C.H. (A♭–C–B) and A.S.C.H. Now, because Ernestine von Fricken, to whom Schumann was engaged at the time of composition (and who appears in *Carnaval* as "Estrella"), came from the town of Asch, the S.C.H.A./A.S.C.H. anagram suggests a

52. I explore the gender question in "*Carnaval*, Cross-dressing, and the Woman in the Mirror," in Ruth Solie, ed. *Musicology and Difference* (Berkeley, 1993).

further (or more primary?) mobility of identity between masculine and feminine personae, and redoubles the "Eusebius"/"Florestan"– "Coquette"/"Replique" configuration. Yet it is important to note that S.C.H.A. takes pride of place; it is the first sphinx—pointedly a male, not female, sphinx—and it forms "the" signature of the piece by its transcription of the composer's "real" name. Another vertigo here, and one that corresponds quite closely to Friedrich Schlegel's concept of irony as "the clear consciousness of eternal agility, of an infinitely teeming chaos."[53] The sphinxes are never played, and it is commonly assumed they are not meant to be. That assumption, however, rests on an esthetic of unity that *Carnaval* puts into question with great exuberance. Perhaps we should hesitate over this point; perhaps the sphinxes should be played after all, or played sometimes, at the whim of the performer. In any case, to "sign" the piece with sphinxes further emphasizes the eternal play of unity and plurality—that being the topic of the riddle the Theban sphinx posed to Oedipus. Q: "What walks on four legs at morning, two legs at noon, and three legs at evening?" A: "A man."

Schumann's deconstructive play with unity and plurality has parallels in many, indeed most, of the compositions we have studied in this book. Recall Beethoven's two-movement piano sonatas as we saw them in Chapter 2. The sonatas of travesty revalue fragmentation, resistance, and discontinuity as affirmative elements of the ideal. The sonatas of transfiguration repeat and interrogate the same elements at the center of utopian idylls. Op. 90 perhaps comes close to stabilizing the ripple of dislocation—and yet its problematical sonority, the submediant, continues to echo through the closing measures of the rondo. Op. 111 stabilizes nothing and transforms everything. It resolves its longest-standing dissonance (the Dm^7 aggregate) in the midst of a dissonant episode (the *espressivo* passage), which forms an epilogue to a consummatory dissonance (the Eb trills and counterpoint)—all this by way of celebrating C major as the polestar of consonance.

I take these compositions to model a general cultural practice: a practice that resists as well as pursues, challenges as well as embraces,

53. Friedrich Schlegel, "Ideas" (1800), fragment no. 69, trans. Peter Firchow, in *German Aesthetic and Literary Criticism: The Romantic Ironists and Goethe*, ed. Kathleen Wheeler (Cambridge, 1984).

the nineteenth-century ideology of organic unity and subjective wholeness. In aspiring to unity of being, the Romantic subject also aspires to plurality of being, each term forming the necessary and necessarily unstable horizon of the other. Hence, each in its own way, the materials of this chapter. "La malinconia" begins with, then excludes, the major key of the Allegretto; is this a continuity or the refusal of one? The Freud of "The Uncanny" disperses himself into a trio of alter egos—Hoffmann's Nathaniel, Ernst Mach, his own reflection—while a more distanced Freud insists that dispersal is only a (mis)translation of his character. And Schumann's stabilizing division of himself into complementary halves turns out to mask (or is it to empower?) a more radical and affirmative fragmentation. For every S.C.H.A., an A.S.C.H. *and* an AS.C.H; if there is going to be an anagram, there can only be more than one.

Where there is other-voicedness, then—and that is more places than one may think—the critical uncertainty of ideal subject matter becomes, or provokes, a productive agency: productive of meaning, and productive of openness of meaning. As Friedrich Schlegel observes, "Versatility consists not just in a comprehensive system but also in a feeling for the chaos outside that system, like man's feeling for something beyond man."[54] Schlegel's remark slyly exemplifies its own principle; it deconstructs itself with a submerged chiasmus: *system/chaos—something beyond man/man.* The transcendental term, "something beyond man," is made parallel to chaos, otherness; the system is merely human. And yet, of course, only the system makes versatility possible at all; it is the "not just" before the "but also." In short, to promote something I said earlier in this chapter from footnote to text: deconstruction, by which I mean the practical deconstruction exemplified in other-voicedness, keeps discourse circulating and thaws frozen positions. It is a sign of life.

54. Ibid., fragment no. 55.

Appendix: Texts and Translations

Mignonslied (Kennst du das Land)

Kennst du das Land, wo die Zitronen blühn,
Im dunkeln Laub die Gold-Orangen glühn,
Ein sanfter Wind vom blauen Himmel weht,
Die Myrte still und hoch der Lorbeer steht,
Kennst du es wohl? Dahin! Dahin
Möcht ich mit dir, o mein Geliebter, ziehn.

Kennst du das Haus? Auf Säulen ruht sein Dach,
Es glänzt der Saal, es schimmert das Gemach,
Und Marmorbilder stehn und sehn mich an:
Was hat man dir, du armes Kind, getan?
Kennst du es wohl? Dahin! Dahin
Möcht ich mit dir, o mein Beschützer, ziehn.

Kennst du den Berg und seinen Wolkensteg?
Das Maultier sucht im Nebel seinen Weg,
In Höhlen wohnt der Drachen alte Brut,
Es stürzt der Fels und über ihn die Flut;
Kennst du ihn wohl? Dahin! Dahin
Geht unser Weg! O Vater, laß uns ziehn!

—Johann Wolfgang von Goethe

Do you know the land where the lemon-trees bloom,
The golden oranges glow amidst dark leafage,
A gentle wind blows from the blue sky,
The myrtle stands calm, and the laurel tall,
Do you know it, indeed? There! There
I would like to go with you, O my beloved.

You know the house? On columns rests its roof,
Its hall's agleam, its rooms all glitter,
And marble statues stand and look at me:
"Poor child, what have they done to you?"
You know it, indeed? There! There
I would like to go with you, O my protector.

Do you know the mountain and its cloudy path?
The mule seeks its way in the mist,
The ancient race of dragons dwells in caves,
The crag plummets, and over it the flood.
Do you know it, indeed! There! There
Lies our way! O father, let us go!

                                        —L.K.

Ganymed

Wie im Morgenglanze
Du rings mich anglühst,
Frühling, Geliebter!
Mit tausendfacher Liebeswonne
Sich an mein Herz drängt
Deiner ewigen Wärme
Heilig Gefühl,
Unendliche Schöne!

Daß ich dich fassen möcht
In diesem Arm!

Ach, an deinem Busen
Lieg ich, schmachte,
Und deine Blumen, dein Gras
Drängen sich an mein Herz.

Du kühlst den brennenden
Durst meines Busens,
Lieblicher Morgenwind!
Ruft drein die Nachtigall
Liebend nach mir aus dem Nebeltal.

Ich komm, ich komme!
Wohin? Ach, wohin?

Hinauf! Hinauf strebt's.
Es schweben die Wolken
Abwärts, die Wolken
Neigen sich der sehnenden Liebe.
Mir! Mir!
In eurem Schoße
Aufwärts!
Umfangend umfangen!
Aufwärts an deinen Busen,
Alliebender Vater!

—Goethe

How you glow about me in the morning light, Springtime, beloved! With thousandfold bliss of love the holy feeling of your eternal warmth presses upon my heart, infinite Beauty! If I could hold you fast in these arms! Ah, I lie on your breast, languish, and your flowers, your grass press upon my heart. You cool the burning thirst of my breast, lovely morning wind! There the nightingale lovingly calls to me from the misty valley. I come, I come! To where, ah, to where? Upwards! Striving upwards! The clouds hover down, the clouds incline themselves to yearning love! To me! To me! In your lap [womb] upwards! Embracing embraced! Upwards to your breast, all-loving Father!

—L.K.

Textual Sources

Unless otherwise indicated, all poetry is quoted from the follow

Blake, William. *Poetry and Prose.* Edited by David V. Erdmai
mentary by Harold Bloom. Garden City, N.Y., 1965.

Coleridge, Samuel Taylor. *Poems.* Edited by John Beer. Lond

Goethe, Johann Wolfgang von. *Gedichte. Versepen.* Frankfui
1970.

Hölderlin, Friedrich. *Friedrich Hölderlin/Eduard Morike: Selectei*
ited and translated by Christopher Middleton. Chicago, 1!

Keats, John. *Poetical Works.* Edited by H. W. Garrod. Londo

Milton, John. *Paradise Lost.* Edited by Merritt Y. Hughes. New

———. *Paradise Regained, the Minor Poems, and Samson Agonis*
Merritt Y. Hughes. New York, 1937.

Rilke, Rainer Maria. *The Selected Poetry of Rainer Maria Rilke*
translated by Stephen Mitchell. New York, 1980.

Rossetti, Christina. *The Poetical Works.* Edited by William Mic
London, 1904. (A new edition of Rossetti's poems is in p

Rossetti, D. G. *The Pre-Raphaelites and Their Circle.* Edited by (
Chicago, 1968.

Shakespeare, William. *The Complete Works.* Edited by Alf
Baltimore, 1969.

Shelley, Percy Bysshe. *Poetry and Prose*. Edited by Donald H. Reiman and Sharon Powers. New York, 1977.

Wordsworth, William. *The Prelude: 1799, 1805, 1850*. Edited by Jonathan Wordsworth, Stephen Gill, and M. H. Abrams. New York, 1979.

————. *Poetical Works*. Edited by Thomas Hutchinson, revised by Ernest de Selincourt. London, 1979.

Yeats, William Butler. *Collected Poems*. Second edition. London, 1950.

Index

Compositor:	A-R Editions
Text:	11/14 Goudy Old Style
Display:	Goudy Old Style
Printer:	Maple-Vail Book Mfg. Group
Binder:	Maple-Vail Book Mfg. Group